Teaching Parenting the Positive Discipline Way

A Step-by-Step Approach to Starting and Leading Parenting Classes

Lynn Lott, M.A., M.F.T. and Jane Nelsen, Ed.D., M.F.T.

Published by Positive Discipline

ISBN 978-0-9701190-3-2

Dedication

Dedicated to parents past, present and future who contributed their ideas and activities to this manual. A special thanks to the following people who helped put the very first Teaching Parenting Manual together back in 1988: Linda V. Jue and the Stanislaus County Department of Mental Health for their technical assistance; Bob Turk, whose timeless devotion to providing quality parenting programs generated the spark that set this project off to a good start; and Jane Allen, Kate Ortolano, Patti Wilkinson, Sharon Marks, and Sue Ciolino. Another special thanks to the non-profit Positive Discipline Association (www.positivediscipline.org) for organizing the certification and quality assurance for Teaching Parenting the Positive Discipline Way Workshops, and the many certified parent educators that have helped spread Positive Discipline to many countries all over the world.

Table of Contents

The Foundation

In 1990, Lynn Lott and Jane Nelsen joined forces to create the first *Teaching Parenting the Positive Discipline Way* manual. Over the twenty plus years before they collaborated on this manual, they studied, wrote about, and taught Positive Discipline concepts for parents and teachers. This manual represents the house they built on the foundation created by Alfred Adler, Rudolf Dreikurs, other Adlerian colleagues, and their students.

Lott and Nelsen were drawn to the Adler/Dreikurs approach for different reasons.

Lott said of her experience:

In 1969 when my first child was six months old, I picked up a book called *Children: The Challenge* by Rudolf Dreikurs and it changed my life. At that time, there was a group of volunteers leading parenting classes to study the ideas in that book. I took one of these classes, became a volunteer leader, and have been teaching parenting and relationship skills ever since. Though I came to Positive Discipline as a parent, it wasn't long before I was using the ideas in multiple settings, including my private practice as a therapist.

In 1973, I founded an Adlerian organization in northern California. That organization evolved into the Family Education Center where I ran a weekly parent education/family-in-focus program for thirteen years. As parents in the program became more involved and skilled, I created an internship program to teach them how to be parent educators and counselors. The interns learned how to teach experientially, based on what I had learned from John Taylor, so that their parenting groups would be more interesting and effective than the first one I took back in 1969. I created the *Parents Helping Parents Problem Solving Steps* so that new students would have a map to use when they counseled parents using the open forum model introduced by Adler, Dreikurs, Christensen, Walton, Platt and others. The open forum included working with volunteer parents, teachers, and or families in front of an audience. Watching this magical method closely, I could see what these master Adlerians did and turned the magic into steps that others could follow. In the summer of 1987 my students and I created the first *Teaching Parenting* manual for others to use.

Nelsen said the following about her experience with the Adler/Dreikurs ideas:

In 1969, I felt like a failure as a mother. I would be authoritarian until I couldn't stand myself. Then I would be permissive until I couldn't stand my kids. I was a senior in college majoring in Child Development and felt discouraged as I became aware of ideals for children and parents. Unfortunately, the books that explained these ideals did not give much help on how to accomplish them.

In my last semester of college, I enrolled in a class where the instructor, Dr. Hugh Allred, explained that we would not be learning a bunch of theories but only one theory (Adlerian Psychology) which included practical methods to help children learn self-discipline, responsibility, cooperation, and problem-solving skills. I was hopeful about this possibility, but even more gratified to find that the Dreikurs/Adler methods were effective in spite of my "yes, but" attitude.

I became so excited about my own success that I wanted to share these methods with others. I started as a parent study group leader with friends in my neighborhood and then with parents of educationally and emotionally handicapped children (my MA thesis project) and later became the Director of Project ACCEPT (Adlerian Counseling Concepts for Encouraging Parents and Teachers) in the Elk Grove School District. This was a federally funded, Title IV-C project. Our purpose was to show that children would improve their behavior when parents and teachers attended Adlerian parent and teacher study groups to learn more effective ways of working with children in homes and classrooms. The results showing improved behavior were statistically significant at the .001 level, so we were awarded funding for three more years to teach other interested school districts how to adopt this program.

The book we were using in this project went out of print, so I sat down and quickly wrote another one in two months, and self-published it in a format with so many mistakes it would make you laugh today. After several revisions, and 80,000 self-published books were sold, Positive Discipline was picked up by Ballantine Books (now an imprint of Penguin Random House).

Since then many more Positive Discipline books have been written and are now published in more than 20 languages.

Lott and Nelsen Combine Forces

In 1990, Lynn Lott and Jane Nelsen joined forces to revise and expand the manual Lynn and her students put together in 1987. They made the manual more user-friendly, revised the problem solving steps, and added new activities and promotional ideas. Over the next eight years, they updated the manual with many new materials. This 2017 revision (with many thanks to contributors) is an update of the 2008 edition.

This manual has evolved over the years, but the work is still strongly influenced by Adler and Dreikurs and other Adlerian psychologists including John Taylor, Oscar Christianson, Don Dinkmeyer, Gary McKay, Achi Yotam, Pearl Cassel, Mim Pew, Ray Corsini, Edna Nash, Robert Powers, Frank Walton, John Platt, Bill Reidler, Kathy Kvols, Bill Nichols, Jim Bitter, Dan Eckstein, and Barbara Fairfield. For more information about Adler and Dreikurs, go to *www.positivediscipline.com* and read the "About" section a summary of "What is Positive Discipline," and to *www.positivediscipline.org* for information about becoming certified parent and/or teacher educators, and to *www.alfredadler.org* for more information on Adlerian psychology.

Lynn and Jane are learners, teachers, and creators and are willing to make mistakes along the way. They encourage you to be learners and follow Rudolf Dreikurs' profound guidance to "have the courage to be imperfect." Don't wait for perfection before you teach. Teach as you learn and learn as you teach and you will make a huge difference in the world.

Why Teach Parenting the Positive Discipline Way?

Children don't come with a set of directions and effective parenting skills are learned, not inherited. This could also be said of parent educators. You, too, need to learn the skills for teaching parents in ways that are truly helpful—beyond lectures and information. That's what this manual is all about. The manual will show you how to teach parenting experientially— including activities that reach the heart and gut where real change takes place. Most of you will use the materials to teach parenting classes; but with a bit of creativity, you can use the information in many different settings including in on-going classes, in workshops, as counselors or parenting coaches or during in-home visits. The information in *Teaching Parenting the Positive Discipline Way* covers everything from how to get folks together to what to do with them once they show up.

New parent educators will find this manual extremely helpful to give them the confidence, skills, support, and the organization to jump in and start—especially if they also take the two-day training on *Teaching Parenting the Positive Discipline Way* (dates and locations available at *www.positivediscipline.com*). Experienced parent educators will love this manual and the two-day training because the experiential activities and Parents Helping Parents Problem Solving Steps add a whole new dimension to what they are already doing. The training is also now available as a DVD Training or Online Training.

Don't Shoot Yourself in the Foot Before You Get Started

Even with the best materials and training, becoming a parent educator takes a big dose of courage. In response to emails from folks who haven't taught their first parenting class yet and are so discouraged and fearful, Lynn shared the following. We hope it will inspire and motivate you.

I'm reminded of the time I ran the training program for interns at the Family Education Center. The training was set up to get folks out into the community teaching parenting classes and taking the components of Teaching Parenting into their work settings. I had forgotten how much over-preparing some of the students did. The more they prepared, the more frightened and anxious they became and the less effective and more boring they were when they taught. The more classes they took to "get ready" to teach parenting, the less the chance that they'd actually teach a course. What was all that fear about? All that worry about being good enough, smart enough, ready enough, knowing enough, etc., etc., replaced the passion that brought students to the program—the passion to change the world person by person, class by class.

Here's what made the biggest difference and increased self-confidence the most—going out and teaching a class. There was no substitution for sitting with a group of parents and realizing how needy the parents were who came to the classes and how grateful they were to learn theories and techniques that could reverse the negative patterns at home. Many trainers discovered that being a week ahead of the class often was more than enough to be extremely successful. The less they came off like experts and the more they introduced the Parents Helping Parents Problem Solving Steps and experiential activities, the more connected they felt to the participants. Instead of being experts they became excellent facilitators, leaving all those notes at home and simply following the course outline.

I can think of times when I was presenting and fell into the over-preparation trap. It took all the fun, spontaneity and creativity out of teaching parenting. There were times I had so many notes and handouts and overheads to manage that I lost track of the reason I was there in the first place—to help people parent better and enjoy their kids more.

Many of you have discovered the joy of co-facilitating. My favorite way to teach parenting is to work with Jane Nelsen. When we work together, I am able to sit back and watch what is going on, relax, and think about what else might be needed to help parents. If you are fortunate enough to find a co-facilitator you work well with, it can make teaching parenting a lot more fun.

Keep in mind that there is no one correct way to prepare yourself to teach parenting. When I started, we had a book (*Children: The Challenge*) and a model that sent us out to teach after we had attended a parenting class ourselves. There were no experiential activities or course outlines or Parents Helping Parents Problem Solving Steps. There were no study guides or tapes or videos or DVDs or CDs. So many of the props that you have now came out of the experience of simply trusting the process and spreading the word that there was a better way to parent without all that punishment and spoiling. So get yourself a group and take it step-by-step and see what you can add to the world by teaching parenting!

What Makes Teaching Parenting the Positive Discipline Way Unique?

Teaching Parenting the Positive Discipline Way is based on experiential methods that help parents get into the world of children to discover what really works and what doesn't—what children are really thinking, feeling, and deciding based on their parent's parenting methods. In the classes, parents practice their new skills through role-playing and experience encouraging feedback as they learn how difficult it can be to change old habits. The parenting classes invite active student participation rather than passive learning that is less helpful. The classes are fun and easy because participants learn from their personal experiences instead of listening to lectures or watching videos.

Teaching Parenting is also unique because facilitators are taught how to model what they teach. If you want parents to learn how to invite cooperation and empower their children, you start by doing the same with the parents in your classes. As you learn how to invite parents' opinions and encourage them to volunteer to do the jobs needed to run a class, you model positive leadership. You also learn how to be an authoritative (not authoritarian) facilitator who is knowledgeable and kind and firm, thus demonstrating an alternative to controlling and/or wishy-washy parenting. You create opportunities for success so that parents feel empowered and want to continue learning. And you model that mistakes are opportunities to learn and grow so that parents feel understood and know they aren't being judged.

Another unique aspect of this model is that it invites you to trust the process. By following the activities and Parents Helping Parents Problem Solving Steps exactly as they are written, you will be successful no matter what happens. Trusting the process means having faith in people to learn what they are ready to learn—*and trusting that much of the learning takes place as they continue to process their experiences long after they leave the class.* Many facilitators try to control the outcome. For example, they think the role-plays are effective only if they turn out a certain way, where a positive resolution seems obvious. *However, when you trust the process, parents learn just as much, if not more, when it doesn't turn out perfectly.* For this reason, we strongly suggest that in the beginning you use the activities as written. After you feel really comfortable with the components as they are, any changes or improvements you make (not to the PHPPSS) will come from competence, not fear.

It also means having faith in your self as a leader to make mistakes and model imperfection. Another aspect of trusting the process is that following the steps will lead you to success even when you feel inadequate and scared. Many people have decided to skip either the role-plays or the problem solving steps because they didn't feel comfortable doing them. But facilitators who decided to trust the process in spite of their fear and discomfort have experienced the most success.

The Four Components of Teaching Parenting the Positive Discipline Way

The Teaching Parenting model conveys information in a way that makes parents feel safe, welcomed, engaged and involved. And when they go home, they are able to apply what they have learned with success. That happens when parent educators focus on the four components that make up the core of this model. They are:

1. A warm-up

2. Parenting Information: chapter discussion, mini-lecture, or activity

3. Experiential activities

4. The Parents Helping Parents Problem Solving Steps, often referred to as PHP

The bulk of this manual is to help you succeed with each of these components. You'll notice that each component has a corresponding section in the manual where you will find the expanded information. These four components make the model flexible. You can use them whether you are working with one parent or 100. The components work whether your parents are in a counseling office, on the telephone, in a seminar, or coming to a weekly study group. Teaching Parenting the Positive Discipline Way has been used with court ordered parents and parents who volunteer to learn more about being better parents. Parents of children with differences benefit from the model as well as parents of foster children, adopted kids, and gifted children. Teaching Parenting the Positive Discipline Way has been taught throughout the world and in many different cultures. It crosses so-called cultural barriers because people Teaching Parenting the Positive Discipline Way are learning from their own experiences as they process the activities and role-plays in their own words.

Skipping any one of the four components lessens the effectiveness of your parenting instruction. Use them all for the best results, even if it takes you a little longer to learn the components and feel comfortable with them. Practice the components with your friends and family if you need to increase your confidence. In addition to a parenting class, you can use your creativity to put the pieces together for an all-day workshop, a counseling session, or any other format you choose. You will find full sections on each of these components later in this manual.

Notes

Marketing Your Parenting Classes or Workshops

To maximize success and avoid spending time and effort marketing a class only to be disappointed because you have to cancel the class due to low enrollment, *start by approaching groups that are already a group*. PTA's, church groups, parent participation preschools, day care centers, and elementary schools would be some examples. Make a list of possible contacts in your area. Choose several with which you are most likely to have success. The most effective procedure is to get the help of a group (church, PTA, etc.) to set up a one-time introductory workshop (one or two hours) so you can give potential enrollees a sample of what they'll be learning, get them excited and get them signed up. Be sure to have flyers and a sign-up sheet. As a Certified Positive Discipline Parent Educator, you are eligible to join the Positive Discipline Association. (www.positivediscipline.org/Join) As a member you can post your classes which will appear on the following websites: www.positivediscipline.org/parenting-classes and *www.positivediscipline.com/events.*

Consider the advice of others:

When I tried getting classes going the most discouraging efforts were trying to pull folks in one by one. By the time I'd get 5 or 6 signed up, several would change their minds. What worked best for me was finding a group that was already a group (co-op preschools and charter schools) and doing a fabulous demonstration for them that was age appropriate. I like to send folks home with something very concrete they can use and that will work ASAP. I might show them how to set up a little job chart or create a fun morning routine or what to do when their kids are fighting or how to deal with mealtime madness or bedtime hassles. During the discussion and question/answer part of the demonstration, I weave in the philosophical information about different parenting styles and why we use both kind and firm parenting. Then I send around a sign-up sheet letting folks know the dates and times I will be leading the next class. I always take the sign-up sheet home with me after making the mistake of letting a volunteer keep it. She either lost the sheet or decided the parents didn't need a class. She never followed through and I had to watch 25 hot leads slip through my fingers. I also did a lot of classes through our local university in the continuing education department (another way to start with a group that's already a group). I became an adjunct faculty member and offered classes every summer for teachers and during the year for therapists who are always looking for continuing education credits. These classes were advertised by the university in a publication that went to thousands.

During these busy times, more and more parent educators have found it difficult to get parents to commit to a six or seven week class. Joy Sacco has found that the following plan works:
1) Invite people to attend a one hour presentation. (See sample flyer and agenda at www.positivediscipline.com/downloads)
2) Invite people to sign up for a 3-week class called, Positive Discipline I.
3) At the end of the 3-week class, offer a 3-week class called Positive Discipline II. (Joy reports that most parents want more by the end of the first 3-week class, and are happy to sign up for the second one.)

After teaching a parenting class at my children's elementary for a few years, the principal suggested I teach it through Adult Ed or the School District's Adult School. By doing that, the class expanded dramatically. They began by offering 2 classes (8 weeks each) twice a year and now we are teaching 5 classes. The Adult School has a contract with the local women's minimum security facility to provide GED, job readiness, and Positive Discipline for Parenting in Recovery. I kept thinking I'd have to market at some point but word of mouth spreads and now I get calls a lot, many I pass onto the others in the Mentor Group. Other places that I have contracted with to do class series include Montessori Schools, Foster and Kinship Care Programs, and a parenting series as part of Positive Discipline in the Classroom at a school. Consistency works the best. Does a local hospital have a community education program? Women's Crisis and Support? Homeless Shelter Services? Could it be donated the first time? These are all ways I've been able to get and keep classes going.

What works best is to use a personal approach instead of simply relying on flyers, newspaper articles, and/or posters. We can't stress enough that this approach capitalizes on going to where parents already are and telling them about your programs. Finding parents in a group and giving them a sample of what they'll encounter in a parenting class produces results. See the following section on the Introductory Presentation.

The reason we do workshops instead of lectures is that a lot of people are untrained to give lectures. Also lectures (except those by real pros) are often boring. We encourage experiential exercises because we have found that is where real learning takes place. We want people to see ahead of time how the class works and to have a sample of the kinds of experiential activities the class provides.

Here are success stories using these marketing ideas as well as some new ones.

Each time I set up a class I send an email to all of the past participants of my classes — I let them know that they can retake the class for free or share the information with friends who may be interested. This is how I got posted on some mom's chat groups. I have a few parents from every class that are moved enough to spread the word. As it turns out word of mouth has been the most effective source of registrations for me. It also takes time to take root. Occasionally I have posted flyers around the neighborhood as well. I find that parents of preschoolers are very willing to take parenting classes, so posting those flyers at places that they frequent (Little Gym, children's consignment shops and even grocery stores) has had some return. The first few years it was always a concern as to whether I would get enough registrations to make a class "go". Now thanks to word of mouth that worry has lessened. I decided that my minimum class size would be 12-14.

Website

It is a good idea to have a website for your parenting classes. Website creation is becoming more and more accessible. You don't need to have web developer skills. There are many free services like Wix, Weebly, Sqaure-Space, Etc. You can also venture into the world of blogging with Wordpress or Blogger. Here are some examples of parent educator websites:

www.joyfulcourage.com (https://www.squarespace.com)
www.juliettaskoog.com (https://www.weebly.com)
www.debbiezeichnerlcsw.com (https://wordpress.org)

Sample Flyers

To view color examples go to: *www.positivediscipline.com/downloads*

It's better to have a simple flyer with the information than to get stuck because you can't make the perfect flyer! You don't have to spend money on a flyer. Many word processing programs have templates to get you started.

The Introductory Presentation

At the presentation, keep the information simple, practical, applicable, fun, experiential and real. Send folks home with help for situations they deal with everyday and they'll come back for more. A lecture on human growth and development isn't as appealing as what to do when their kids fight in the car or throw tantrums at the supermarket. The following agenda has been effective (see flyer for Introductory Presentation that can be changed to include your info at www.positivediscipline.com/downloads):

Free One Hour Introduction to Positive Discipline

Agenda

00—02 Introduce yourself

02—05 What is Positive Discipline?

There are two kinds of parenting programs. Those that depend on external locus of control (punishment and rewards) that seem to work temporarily; and those (like Positive Discipline) that teach an internal locus of control—to do the right thing when no one is looking. In just a few minutes you will have an opportunity to participate in a demonstration that will illustrate the difference, but first we are going to create Two Lists:

05—10 ACTIVITY: Two Lists (make sure "not listening" is on the list)
　　　　(Prepare flip charts in advance)

10—25 ACTIVITY: Curiosity Questions (Motivational)
　　　　(Prepare laminated asking and telling scripts in advance)

25—26 Why is this hard to do? Because you have buttons, and guess who knows how to push them?

26—30 ACTIVITY: Brain in the Palm of the Hand

30—35 Read Jared's Cool Out Space and talk about the importance of involving children in creating their own Positive Time-Out

35—37 Most parents have a difficult time giving up punishment and/or permissiveness unless they know what else to do. A hallmark of Positive Discipline is the many parenting tools (taught experientially) that help children learn self-discipline, responsibility, cooperation, and the belief that, "I am capable." These skills and beliefs serve a child for the rest of his life, in every relationship.

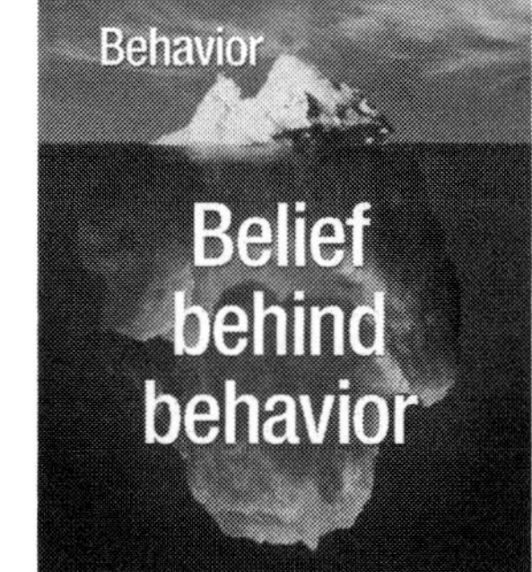

37—40 Positive Discipline Tool Cards.
　　　　(Leave a tool card on each chair before people come. Let them know that they will be learning most of these 52 tools during a Positive Discipline Class or Workshop)

40—45 Display a poster of the Belief Behind the Behavior Iceberg
　　　　(You can draw one on a flip chart)
　　　　Positive Discipline is one of the few parenting programs that deal with the "belief" behind the behavior—the motivating force behind behavior. Most parenting programs deal only with the behavior. The

behavior is unlikely to change unless the belief is dealt with in ways that help a child shift his or her beliefs.
Positive Discipline classes and workshops include many experiential activities that provide parents with tools to accomplish the above, and to increase their joy in parenting.

45 - 60 Q & A. Pass out a flyer of your upcoming workshop. Let them know there are two sign up sheets at the table in the back of the room: one to sign up for your scheduled class, and one to sign up to be on your mailing list to be notified of future classes and workshops. (You might want to have a display of books and tool cards for sale at the back of the room.)

You can follow up with press releases to local papers for publicity. Press releases rarely bring out additional members, but if you are going to continue working in a community, it doesn't hurt to start getting your name in print. Posting flyers has the same effect—name recognition, but rarely more members.

Preparation/Advance Class Planning

As a parenting facilitator, you'll have some planning to do before your class begins. It is important that you take care of these details before the first session of your class.

Find a room to hold the class: In every community there are rooms that can be used for no fee, such as bank community rooms, libraries, etc. However, if you are charging a fee for your class, they may not be available to you. Some parenting classes are held in member's homes. You can rotate homes each week or pick one home that would work well for the meetings. Churches, synagogues, community centers and condo associations often have community rooms to rent for a small fee. If a school is sponsoring your class, they may have a room available. It's fine to delegate the job of finding a room to one of your group members, but create a deadline so that you can notify class participants in plenty of time where to meet.

Determine a fee: Charging for the class helps pay for your time, coffee supplies, handouts, charts, publicity, etc. Offering classes for free is not recommended. People seem to place greater value on things they are willing to pay for. Parenting is one of the most important jobs a person can have and the classes have a great deal of value. Some group leaders believe that parenting classes should be offered free and that leaders should be volunteers. It's your choice as a leader, but keep in mind that the parents attending your classes pay for alcohol, luxury items, getting hair and nails done, etc., so you don't have to feel guilty charging a fee for your service.

Collect fees: It's best to collect fees, or at least a deposit, from each person before the first meeting. This assures that you will arrive to a parenting class that has participants as opposed to an empty room. Even a small deposit guarantees better attendance. If people pay in advance their attendance record and commitment improve greatly.

Childcare: If possible, offer child care, especially for a daytime group. This can be set up with a daycare center or with a private baby-sitting service. Fees for child care could be separate from fees for the program.

Books: You'll want to make sure that group members have books or other materials you're planning to use for the study part of the class. You could purchase them and have them available for group members to pick up before your first class. Most materials needed for parenting classes can be purchased at *www.positivediscipline.com*. You can include the price of materials in the fee you charge for the class or you can charge extra for the materials. If you are working with a lower economic population, you may want to find a person or organization to pay for materials and then donate them to group members.

Job Sharing

When you teach parenting in a group setting, you have many opportunities to model what you are teaching. One of the most important ways to involve all participants in helping with the logistics of a group is to use a job chart. When people have a job to do, the odds are greater that they will show up for their class even when they might otherwise miss. If they have a job and know they are needed, they are less likely to skip a meeting for a good TV show or because they are too tired. It is also a way of modeling job sharing and giving them opportunities to make a contribution and experience the importance of social interest. Now the class is "ours" instead of "yours." The following list of jobs is recommended.

Hospitality: Organize a snack sign-up list, plug in the coffee pot, purchase coffee supplies.

Room Set-Up: Put up chairs, erase boards, take down chairs.

Recorder: Keep a record of the problem solving solutions using forms.

Greeter: Sign people in, collect fees, welcome newcomers.

Bookstore or Lending Library: Obtain books for sale or loan and manage the bookstore/library during the break.

Coordinator: Arrange for volunteers, train them, fill in if someone is absent; make a job chart.

Charts and Posters: Copy sample charts and be responsible for putting them up and taking them down before and after each class. Make large posters of the charts that will be used the following week. Make copies of the "Feeling Faces" chart for each participant.

Facilitator: Present warm-up, lead chapter discussion, facilitate the PHP Problem Solving Steps, and meet regularly with volunteers to ensure continuity.

Other possible jobs may include publicity, day care, etc. No two groups will be the same but the more opportunities there are for group members to help, the more the group becomes everyone's responsibility and not just the leaders. This is also a way to model the cooperation you are trying to teach.

At the first meeting of the group, set up the volunteer jobs for the length of the group. If the group is an ongoing group, it is best to switch jobs at least every 10 weeks so people volunteering don't feel stuck or burdened.

Materials Needed

You'll need several charts and handouts for participants, hospitality supplies, and some additional equipment and materials. You could arrange all of this in advance or you could create a list of what is needed and solicit volunteers from the group to obtain and organize these tasks.

Coffee supplies: to provide hospitality during the break.

Flip chart: to record suggestions from the group during Parents Helping Parents process. It is important for the volunteer and the group to see their ideas written on the flip chart. Charts should be posted in the classroom so everyone can see them and follow them.

Charts:
Parents Helping Parents Problem solving Steps
Feeling Faces
Class Format
Mistaken Goal Chart

Name cards: used so people don't feel embarrassed about forgetting names and new people don't feel out of place.

Notebook with blank "Parents Helping Parents Problem Solving Steps" pages: used to keep track of what the family decides they are going to try for a week. When they come back the following week follow-up by summarizing the problem that was presented and what they were going to try, and asking them how it went.

Attendance Sheet: to keep track of participants.

Group Dynamics Posters: Available in the Resources Section at the end of this manual.

Journals: Suggest that participants start a personal progress journal in a three-hole binder which they bring with them each time since some activities require written exercises. The journal also provides a place to put handouts.

Class Format Charts

It's important to have a format for the class and to provide leadership. The format helps participants know what to expect, how to "behave," and what is expected of them. Have the format schedule posted so everyone can see it. If you don't have a structure, you lose people. Following a structure is also a way of modeling for parents how routine and structure creates a feeling of safety and security. This may make it easier for parents to create structure and routines at home after both seeing and experiencing them.

This manual proposes the following formats that have been tested since 1979. They are popular with parents because they get help with specific problems in the Parents Helping Parents Problem Solving segment at the same time they're learning more generalized skills in the Experiential Topics Section. The first format is best to use in an on-going parenting class where the class is structured around a particular book or set of parenting materials. The other works well for a drop-in parent support group where different people show up each week and where some of the members have been part of the group for a long time and others may be attending for their first time.

Format I

10 minutes Warm-Up or Check-In

30 minutes Parenting Information/Chapter Discussion

25 minutes Experiential Activity

15 minutes Business and Break

35 minutes Parents Helping Parents Problem Solving Steps

5 minutes Appreciations

Format II

10 minutes Warm-Up

35 minutes Parenting Information/Experiential Activity

20 minutes Business and Break

35 minutes Parents Helping Parents Problem Solving Steps

5 minutes Appreciations

Sign-up Sheet and Name Tags

Make sure at some point that you collect a list of names, street addresses or email addresses and phone numbers of participants. One way of helping members stay in touch with each other outside the group is to provide a copy of the sign-up sheet to each group member.

A simple name card can be made by folding a piece of construction paper and setting it on the ground in front of the member with first name printed large enough to be seen across the room. Some groups like to add the birth order of the person along with the children's names and ages and the spouses name and birth order. See the following example:

Home Activity: Create a Family Name Card

Materials:
8 1/2 by 11 (or larger) tag board
Photos of each family member
Colored Marking Pens
Glue

Instructions:

1. Fold the tag board in half so it will stand by itself on the floor (during class, you will place it in front of your feet).

2. Paste a picture of the parent (or parents) on the top of the half of the tag board that will be facing the group. Leave room for descriptive adjectives.

3. Paste pictures of children underneath, in order of their birth. Leave room for their ages and three descriptive adjectives.

4. Use a different colored pen (so that the writing can be seen from across the room) and write at least three adjectives after each picture to describe you and each member of your family.

5. Bring your family name card to each class.

Warm-Ups

(Component No. 1)

Warm ups are experiential activities (usually short) used as a transition to move from a busy hectic day where your brain is filled with a gazillion things to focus on parenting. Warm ups allow skill practice in a humorous, non-threatening environment. They do not include the kind of deeper emotion that is inherent in some activities. The activities in this section provide a few examples. However, many of the activities in the Activities section can also be used as warm-up activities.

Warm-up Questions

A very simple warm-up is to welcome people as they come in and ask if they have anything they'd like to talk about from their week. Invite group members to check-in by sharing success stories, problems, feelings, progress, and more. You could also ask one of the following questions:

- What have you learned since we were last together?

- Name three feelings you've had during the day (week).

- Ask a series of questions and look for a show of hands. Questions might include, "Anybody have preschool age kids? Teens? Anybody yell at their kid this week? Anyone have problems with bedtime, mornings, homework, fighting, backtalk, lack of motivation, manners, etc.?"

- What is something you like to do for fun?

- What is something you have improved upon recently?

- What is something a family member did this week that made you feel good?

Make a Fist

Divide the group into pairs. One person in each pair makes a fist. The partner tries to open it without bloodshed! After 30 seconds ask, "What were your feelings? What did you notice about your own behavior? How many of you asked your partner to open his/her fist? What does this teach you about effective parenting? What about overcoming resistance?" This is a great conversation starter about power struggles as well as an energizing activity to get folks focused and present.

Sources of Strength

Have participants review their sources of strength by thinking of which childhood experiences stimulated feelings of confidence, helped them set goals, give love. Share.

Positive Thoughts about Myself

Have each person fill in the blanks:

a. My _______________ doesn't think I'm special.
b. I'd like to set him/her/them straight and say ___________
c. The thing that is special about me is __________.

Share with a partner.

The Color and Shape of Feelings

Have participants think of a color or shape which best represents how they are feeling now. Ask, "What is one word that best describes the feeling of this color or shape?" Have them share with group or discuss with partner.

I Am My Child

Have participants introduce themselves as one of their children. Tell them to describe themselves as their children might describe themselves.

Goal Commitment

Have each participant fill out the following and ask several to share.
I would like to ___________and I will attempt to accomplish this in my life by doing the following actions ______________________________________which will be done by (frequency and date to be accomplished).

Common Interests

Invite participants to walk around the room and find people who have interests in common with them. Suggest they ask questions, like, "How many children do you have? Do you like the ocean? Are you a fly fisherman? What's your favorite kind of book? Did you have a home delivery?"

After a short time, re-call the participants to the circle and ask for sharing about what they learned.

Positive Influence

Invite participants to think of a person who had a positive influence on them. Ask group members to tell a brief story about who that person was and how they made a positive difference in their lives.

Create Your Own "T" Shirt

Objective: This warm up is best used for a day long workshop as it takes about twenty minutes. It's a great way for group members to meet each other and get to know each other better. It also helps participants become aware of differences and similarities while getting in touch with uniqueness.

Materials: Plain Sheets of 8-1/2" x 11" Paper, Marking Pens, Masking Tape

Comment: Sharing uniqueness is an empowering experience that enhances self-esteem.

Directions:

1. Give each participant a piece of paper. Have them draw a t-shirt shape on it or fold and tear the paper into a t-shirt shape.

2. Ask them to write their name at the top.

3. In the middle write one word that describes them as a person.

4. Write words all over that describe some of their characteristics and special interests.

5. Write one thing about themselves that most people probably don't know anywhere on their shirt.

6. Across the bottom write what they hope to learn from the workshop.

7. Tape their "t-shirt" on their clothes with masking tape and walk around the room. Ask them to talk to at least three other people using the information on their "t-shirts" as the basis of conversation.

Do As I Say

by Ruben Castaneda

Objective: To demonstrate to parents how some children pay more attention to what you do than to what you say.

Directions:

1. Don't tell people the objective. Let them figure it out for themselves.

2. Give the following instructions:
    Place both hands on your knees. Take a deep breath and exhale.
    Make a circle with your index finger and thumb as if signing "okay." Demonstrate.
    Now tell them, "Place your circle on your chin," (while you place your circle on your cheek a few seconds before saying "chin").

3. Notice how many people did what you did rather than what you said? Ask the group to look around the room and see what they notice. (Usually they laugh when they see that some have their circle on the cheek.) Ask, "How many of you heard what I said?" Some will tell you. "How many of you did what I did instead of what I said?"

4. Ask for a discussion of what they learned from this activity. If the point isn't made, ask, "Which is more powerful, what we say or what we do?"

Do Vs. Don't Activity

Adapted from an activity by Kelly Pfeiffer

Objective: Participants will experience what children feel when told "Don't" vs "Do."

Directions:
1. We are going to do an activity to show the importance of telling kids what to do instead of what NOT to do.

2. Give the following commands:

Don't sit down.   Don't look at me.   Don't put your hands by your sides.   Don't stand still.
          Don't close your mouth.   Don't stand up.   Don't open your mouth.

3. Process by asking participants: What are you thinking? What are you feeling? What are you deciding?

4. That was round one. Now I'll make different kinds of requests:

Stand up.   Look at another person.   Raise your hand.   Open your mouth.
          Close your mouth.   Clap your hands.   Sit down.

5. Process by asking participants: What are you thinking? What are you feeling? What are you deciding?

6. Ask participants what they learned from this activity.

Psycho-Geometrics®1

Objective: To give participants another experience with separate realities.

Materials: Flip Chart, marking Pens

Comment: We get along when we respect differences instead of making them right or wrong.

Directions:
1. Draw five shapes on a flip chart: square, circle, triangle, and squiggle (per example below), plus a rectangle.

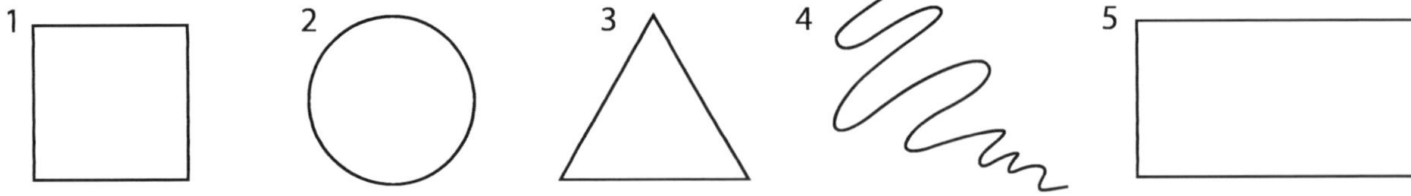

2. Ask participants to rank order of the shapes from their favorite to their least favorite.

3. Ask for a volunteer to share his or her rank order of the shapes and have his or her personality exposed in front of the whole group. (Say this in a joking manner. You will always get plenty of volunteers.)

4. As the volunteer shares his/her order of preference, draw those numbers on the shapes from first favorite to least favorite.

---

1   Susan E. Dellinger, Ph.D. • www.psychogeometrics.com
    "Communicating Beyond Our Differences" (Prentice-Hall/Jade Ink, 1996)

5. Then, using the handout as a guide, say, "This could mean that you ." Proceed to describe a few traits about each shape. For example, "The circle means that you like people. You like working with people and being around people. The squiggle means that you are creative. Creative does not necessarily mean artistic, although it could. It could mean that you like to try new ways of doing things and are open to new possibilities. The triangle means that you are a leader. The triangle symbolizes, "Get to the point" or "What is the bottom line?" The rectangle indicates that you could be in transition or thinking about a change in your life—possibly a new job, children coming or leaving, etc. The square indicates that you like structure and routine. Change is difficult for you. You like the familiar."

6. Ask the person if this was close. You might ask the whole group how close their order fits for them; however, the most important question is "What did you learn from this activity even if it doesn't come close to describing you?" The answers you are looking for are: that people are different with different strengths and references.

7. Here are more traits for each of the shapes that could be used as a handout:

    Square: persevering, perfectionist, patient, resistant to change, loner, complaining

    Triangle: leader, focused, decisive, ambitious, competitive, bottom-line oriented, athletic, self-centered, overloaded, dogmatic, status oriented, political, impatient, driven

    Rectangle: state of transition, exciting, searching, inquisitive, growing, courageous, confused, inconsistent, gullible, unpredictable

    Circle: friendly, nurturing, persuasive, empathetic, generous, stabilizing, reflective, gossipy, self blaming, indecisive, lazy, manipulative

    Squiggle: creative, conceptual, futuristic, intuitive, expressive, motivating, witty, sensuous, disorganized, impractical, illogical, eccentric, naïve

Getting to Know You

Materials:

Marking Pens
Flip Chart Paper for each group
A Flip Chart Poster with the questions listed in No. 2

Objective:

1. To help participants start the bonding process.

2. To learn more about participants, how they work with children, where they come from and how many children they have.

3. To learn about workshop expectations of participants.

Directions:

1. Have people form groups of 6 to 8 and choose a volunteer recorder for their group.

2. Have them respond to the following questions:

    1) How many children they have

2) The age range of their children
3) How many boys and how many girls
4) How many states they represent
5) Who traveled the greatest distance to attend the workshop
6) How they work with children
7) What they hope to gain from the workshop.

Variation by Lisa Larsen

Objective: To provide an icebreaker (warm-up) activity that helps people begin to know each other, bond a little, and feel more comfortable working as a group.

Materials: Loud timer, prepared questions (see No. 3 below)

Directions:
1. Ask participants to form two lines of chairs in even rows and to sit facing each other knee to knee.

2. If you have an "odd" person, ask that person to be the timer. If you have even numbers, you can be the timer.

3. Ask several questions. Allow 30 to 40 seconds for responses. When the timer goes off yell, "Rotate!" (Be sure that only one row rotates.)

4. Make up your own questions or use any of the following:

What is your birth order and what decision did you make in that position? What is your favorite thing to do, and why?

When and why did you decide what you want to be when you grew up? In what capacity do you work with children, and why?

Share your most encouraging moment in your work. Share your most discouraging moment in your work. Share your favorite joke.

Share your most embarrassing moment as a child (or as an adult) Share your greatest asset as a teacher or a parent (or just as a person).

Share the one thing you most want to improve in your classroom or home. If you had one year to live what would you chose to do?

Comment: We have seen CEOs laughing with their employees that they have worked with for years. All have agreed that it helps facilitate closeness even among old colleagues.

Piaget Demonstrations: What Does Your Child Under the Age of Four Really "Know" About "No?"

Children under the age of four do not understand "no" in the way most parents think they do. (And a full understanding of "no" doesn't occur magically when the child turns four. It is a developmental process.) "No" is an abstract concept that is in direct opposition to the developmental need of young children to explore their world and to develop their sense of autonomy and initiative.

Oh, your child may "know" you don't want her to do something. She may even know she will get an angry reaction from you if she does it. However, she cannot understand why in the way adults think she can. Why else would a child look at you before doing what she "knows" she shouldn't do, grin, and do it anyway? 'Knowing' things as a toddler and preschooler means something far different than 'knowing' things as an adult. Her version of 'knowing' lacks the brain development and maturity necessary for self-control and judgment. They do not understand cause and effect (an excellent reason not to try to lecture and argue a young child into doing what you want). In fact, "higher order" thinking like understanding consequences and ethics may not develop until children are as old as ten.

The stages of child development and age appropriateness do not mean children should be allowed to do anything they want. It does explain why all methods to gain cooperation should be kind and firm at the same time instead of controlling and/or punitive. This is a time of life when your child's personality is being formed, and you want your child to make decisions about him or herself that say, "I am capable. I can try, make mistakes, and learn. I am loved." If you are tempted to help your child learn by guilt, shame, or punishment, you will be creating discouraging beliefs that are difficult to reverse in adulthood.

Piaget Demonstrations

The following Piaget demonstrations illustrate intellectual development, and help parents understand why children can't understand some concepts (such as 'no') as soon as adults think they can.

1. Take two balls of clay that are the same size. Ask a three-year-old if they are the same. Make adjustments by taking clay from one ball and adding it to the other until the child agrees that they are the same size. Then, right in front of her, smash one ball of clay. Then ask her if they are still the same. She will say, "No," and will tell you which one she thinks is bigger. A five-year-old will tell you they are the same and can tell you why.

2. Find two glasses that are the same size, one glass that is taller and thinner, and one glass that is shorter and fatter. Fill the two glasses that are the same size with water until a three-year-old agrees they are the same. Then, right in front of her, pour the water from one of these glasses into the short, fat glass, and the other one into the tall, thin glass. Then ask her if they are still the same. Again, she will say, "No," and will tell you which glass she thinks contains the most water. A six-year-old (sometimes a five-year old) will tell you they contain the same amount and can tell you why.

When we understand that perceiving, interpreting, and comprehending an event are so markedly different for young children, our expectations as adults alter. The meaning children attach to their experiences does not match the meaning adults attach to the same experiences.

Notes

Parenting Information
(Component No. 2)

Most parents who come to classes, workshops, groups, or counseling have been using parenting methods based on the conventional wisdom. The focus may have been on control, punishment, rewards, micro-managing, over-protecting, and or enabling. In order to help parents improve their parenting, they need to become familiar with the philosophy and ideas of Positive Discipline. The bulk of this manual is made up of activities that can be used with parents of all age groups in many different settings.

We recommend getting information from Positive Discipline parenting books, DVDs, CDs, podcasts, and other materials by checking out: *www.positivediscipline.com*. If you happen to be an interesting lecturer (few and far between), you could offer information through mini-lectures, but most parents resist lectures just like their children do. For this reason, we recommend using experiential activities or chapter discussions (see tips below) for the information section of the class.

If you are conducting a parenting class where people sign up for a series and you are assigning readings to group members, the parenting information time of your class would be the time for chapter discussions. (With non-readers, use CDs and DVDs).

Using Outlines for Parenting Classes

Many of you will want to use a book study format for your parenting class. A book study group usually is a closed group that meets for a pre-determined number of sessions. Participants have assigned chapters to read and discuss at the group meeting. We include a number of outlines for this type of parenting class to save you endless hours planning curriculum (see class outlines in next section). If you prefer to use a book for which there is no outline, follow the Class Format and use the activities in this manual.

Give participants the outline the first night of the parenting class so that they know what to expect and can be prepared even if they miss a class. Notice the outlines tell what the class topic for the week will be, what experiential activities will be done in class, what chapters need to be read before the class, and what practice participants can work on after the class. This same kind of outline can be used if the parenting information part of the class consists of CDs, podcasts, DVDs, or other educational materials instead of books. Using the outline is a way of sharing responsibility with participants instead of the teacher having all the control.

Some parenting leaders want an outline for the group that is more detailed. Jane Nelsen shared the following about one of her parenting classes. Her experience of over-preparing is not unlike that of many new parenting class teachers. When she felt more comfortable, she enjoyed her work more and the parents got more involved.

"Recently I decided to teach my first parenting class in 30 years. I fell into the trap of over-preparing. I spent weeks preparing an outline of what I would do to the minute. I got so flustered trying to follow my outline that I did a terrible job of facilitating the class (well, that is what it felt like to me). After the second class I had a huge AHA! We have a very simple outline in the Teaching Parenting Manual called the Four Components.

Warm-up (15 minutes)

Parenting information from a book or activity (30 minutes)

(You can find more outlines and other resources at: *www.positivediscipline.com/downloads)*

Experiential Activity (30 minutes) sometimes we would do two shorter ones.

Parents Helping Parents Problem solving Steps (PHPPSS) (30 minutes)

6 Week Positive Discipline Parenting Class Outline

Participant Materials: *Positive Discipline Book, Workbook, and Tool Cards*

Week	Topic	Activities from Teaching Parenting Manual	Read Chapter	Weekly Practice
1	• What Do You Want? • Curiosity Questions • Hugs for Connection • Positive Discipline Tool Cards	• Two Lists • Asking vs. Telling • Hugs • Parents Helping Parents Problem Solving Steps	1 & 2	• Remember what you want for your children. • Go a whole day (or more) of asking not telling. • Try a hug. • Choose a PD Tool Card for inspiration.
2	• What is Positive Discipline? • Kind and Firm • 4 R's of Punishment • Five Criteria & PD NO NOs • Understanding the Brain • Positive Time Out	• Competent Giant • Kind AND Firm • Brain in the Palm of the Hand • Piaget Demo • Positive Time Out • PHPPSS	3 & 4	• Practice being kind AND firm. • Treat your children the way you would like to be treated. • Create a positive time-out area WITH your child.
3	• Not so Perfect Parenting • Birth Order and Sibling Rivalry • Belief Behind the Behavior • Not your Job to Make your Children Happy	• Four R's of Recovery from Mistakes • Mistaken Goal Chart Introduction • Fighting & the 3 Bs • PHPPSS	5 & 6	• Practice using the Mistaken Goal Chart. • Avoid taking sides when children fight—treat them the same.
4	• Why Children Misbehave • Natural and Logical Consequences • Solutions • Family Meetings • Routine Charts	• Mr./Mrs. Punishment • Family Meetings • Routine Charts • PHPPSS	7, 8, 9	• Be aware of how you might contribute to misbehavior. • Start family meetings. • Create a routine chart WITH your child.
5	• Not Perfect Review • Connection before Correction • Encouragement vs. Praise • Wheel of Choice	• Thermometer Demo • Encouragement vs. Praise • Wheel of Choice • Don't Back Talk Back • PHPPSS	10, 11, 12	• Remember to make a Connection before Correction. • Create a wheel of choice with your child. • Model what you want from your children.
6	• What is My Part? • Lifestyle Priorities • Mistakes as Opportunities to Learn • Empowering vs. Enabling	• Top Card • Empowering vs. Discouraging • PHPPSS • Ball of Yarn		• Notice your part in conflicts. • Use empowering statements • Practice mistakes as opportunities to learn.

Class and Workshop Outlines

You will find outlines for 7-week classes for several Positive Discipline books at www.positivediscipline.com/downloads

Many new Positive Discipline Parent Educators have found it very helpful to use the Positive Discipline Workbook to go along with the original Positive Discipline book for their first classes (https://www.positivediscipline.com/products/positive-discipline-workbook-printed-version) along with the Positive Discipline Workbook Facilitator's Guide (https://www.positivediscipline.com/products/positive-discipline-workbook-facilitators-guide-e-book-download-pdf-file). The Guide includes a 2 1/2 hour outline for each of the six lessons illustrated in the Workbook, complete activities for each week (with page references to the workbook) and 27 Positive Discipline posters. It also includes a one page agenda that can be copied for participants that includes topics, activities, reading assignments, and practice ideas for each week.

Solving the Mystery of Parenting Your Teens

For parenting teens classes, facilitators and parents appreciate the Solving the Mystery of Parenting your Teen curriculum by Lynn Lott and Kimberly Gonsalves, which includes a Facilitators Guide and Participants Handout Guide available at https://www.positivediscipline.com/catalog/download-products

Hints

The purpose of these agendas are to give you suggestions. The ideas proposed here are not written in stone, and can be changed to reflect your personality and style. We experience the most satisfaction and success when we have a well prepared agenda and then relax and follow the needs of the participants. In other words, "be present." If someone asks a question, you may want to skip to an activity that is scheduled for later because it has come up now. This is what makes a workshop so much fun.

You may have other favorite activities that you want to use. Be prepared, and then trust your heart and your wisdom. Let your ego take a vacation (we all struggle with this), and remember the important work is to share a philosophy, principles, and parenting tools that can change the lives of others the way it has yours.

The purpose of experiential teaching is so that the learning comes from the participants not from you— and to be enjoyable. Trust the process—and know that it isn't your job to "make" everyone learn, but to be a source that invites learning from those who are ready.

A one-day workshop in Positive Discipline is a great introduction for parents who may find it difficult to commit to a seven or eight week class. However, whether they know it or not, parents need on-going support to make the paradigm shift necessary to implement Positive Discipline on an ongoing basis—and to continuously learn from mistakes. Be sure to have dates set up for ongoing four to eight week classes.

One-day Positive Discipline Workshop Agenda

9:00 – 9:15
   Your story: (how you became interested in Positive Discipline and what it has done for you and your family).

9:15 – 9:40
   Activity: Two Lists

9:25 – 9:40
   Activity: Curiosity Questions Motivation.

9:40 – 10:00
   Activity: Discipline: What Have You Tried?

10:00 – 10: 15
   Activity: Parenting Styles: What is Yours?

10:15 – 10: 35:
   Activity: Mistaken Goals Introduction

10:35 – 10:45 **Break**

10:45 – 10:50
   Questions, Comments, or Sharing (Let people know that if they have a question re: something that is coming up, you'll wait till then to answer. Comments can be an "aha," Sharing can be an example of something they have tried.)

10:50 - 11:10
   Activity: I Love You And The Answer Is No

11:10 - 11:30
   Activity: I Need A Hug

11:30 - 11:35
   Hug stories by Steven Foster.

11:35 - 11:45
   Connection before Correction. Podcast clip of Marianne McGinnis telling her Pee on Toilet Seat Story. (Listen to podcast on *www.positivediscipline.com/positive-discipline-podcast* to become familiar with this story)

11:45 - Noon
   Segment on why is it so hard?

   Buttons—reptilian brain "When your buttons are pushed you go into your reptilian brain and reptile eat their young."

   Activity: Brain in the Palm of Your Hand

   Follow-up with following discussion:
   Most popular discipline method—Time out
   Where did we ever get the crazy idea that to get children to do better, first we have to make them feel worse?

Children do better when they feel better

Let people know that after the break you will discuss the most popular discipline method used today—
Time-Out

Noon – 1:00

Lunch Break (Just before break, talk about the importance of on-going support during 4 week or 8 week classes, and let people know you have sign-up sheets at the back of the room.) If you provide a box lunch, 45 minutes is enough and you will have more time for "catch-up."

1:00 – 1:10

Questions, comments, sharing

1:10 – 1:20

Activity: Positive Time-Out

1:20 – 1:30

Demonstration: Piaget Two Glasses Of Water. (Why even positive time-out is hardly ever appropriate for children under the age of 3 ½ to 4) See attached article on Piaget Demonstrations and "What Does Your Child under Three Really 'Know' about 'No'?"

1:30 – 1:35

Young children: supervision, supervision, supervision, distraction, redirection.

1:35 – 1:40

Activity: Do As I Say

1:40 – 1:45

Demonstration: Hitting: show them what to do, not what NOT to do. Ask for a volunteer to be a 2-year-old. Instruct this "toddler" to hit you. Be ready to grab his or her hand, lead it to your cheek and teach him or her to stroke your cheek while saying, "Touch nicely." Repeat.

1:45 – 1:50

Follow up after positive time-out (Sometimes PTO is enough to change behavior. At other times follow-up may be advisable through curiosity questions.)

1:50 – 2:10

Activity: Curiosity Questions (all or just the Expanded Version)

2:10 – 2:15

Definition of educare: to draw forth. Adults usually try to "stuff in" and then wonder why it goes in one ear and out the other.

    Help children develop the belief, "I am capable." Don't do anything for children that they can do for themselves

2:15 – 2:30

Activity: Routine Charts

2:30 – 2:45 Break

2:45 – 2:50

Questions, comments, sharing

2:50 – 3:15
Activity: Mr. Punishment, Logical Consequence, Reward, Focus On Solutions (It is really fun to have all the props for this activity.)

3:15 – 3:30
Activity: Decide What You Will Do And Follow Through

3:30 - 3:45
9 Steps for Effective Family Meetings
Handout at the end of this activity

3:45 - 4:15
Parents Helping Parents Program-Solving Steps (with volunteer who wants to present a "real" problem.

4:15 - 4:30
Sharing of what people got out of the workshop.

4:30 - 4:45
Sign-up for six- or seven week class and passing out certificates of completion.

Be sure to let people know that there are many more activities they can do for deep learning, and explain the parents helping parents problem solving steps that is done in each 2 ½ hour class.

Extra (in case you have time) **Activity: Encouragement Vs. Praise**

Improving Chapter Discussions

As you read through this information on improving chapter discussions, you will see small versions of the Group Dynamic Posters. Larger versions can be found at the end of this manual. The chapter discussion portion of a parenting group is an important time to help participants understand and clarify what they have read and what it means to them. It is a time they can speak their feelings and hear what other participants think. It's important for group leaders to promote lively discussion and help participants stay on task rather than provide answers. When using a parenting book, let the book become the expert rather than the group leader or co-leaders. It is the responsibility of group members to read the chapters, be prepared to discuss the questions, and cooperate with the leaders by staying "on task." If no one in the group knows the answer to a question, a group leader can ask, "Could someone find the spot in our text that answers that question and let us know next week?"

As a group leader, you want to be encouraging to the parents in your classes. When they start using the Positive Discipline approach, warn them that the changes may appear to backfire at first. That's because children are used to getting certain responses from their parents. They know how adults are going to react and are disappointed when they don't live up to their expectations, even when the reaction is negative. It is similar to what happens if you put money in a coke machine that doesn't work. When you don't get your expected can of soda, you kick and pound on the machine to try and make it do what it is supposed to do. Children will do

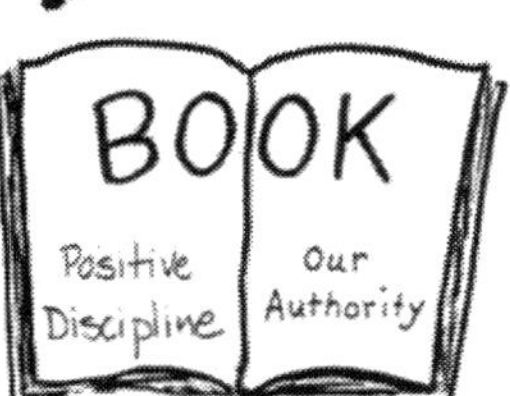

the same. When parents begin to change their responses, kids will probably exaggerate their misbehavior (get worse) in their effort to get their parents to respond as they are supposed to. When parents continue being kind and firm, their children will learn that misbehavior does not achieve the responses they are expecting and will be motivated to change their behavior.

Here's another way to explain what happens when parents use kind and firm Positive Discipline methods. The line above the Usual Parenting Approach illustrates that when misbehavior is met with punishment, the behavior stops immediately but soon begins again and again, and again.

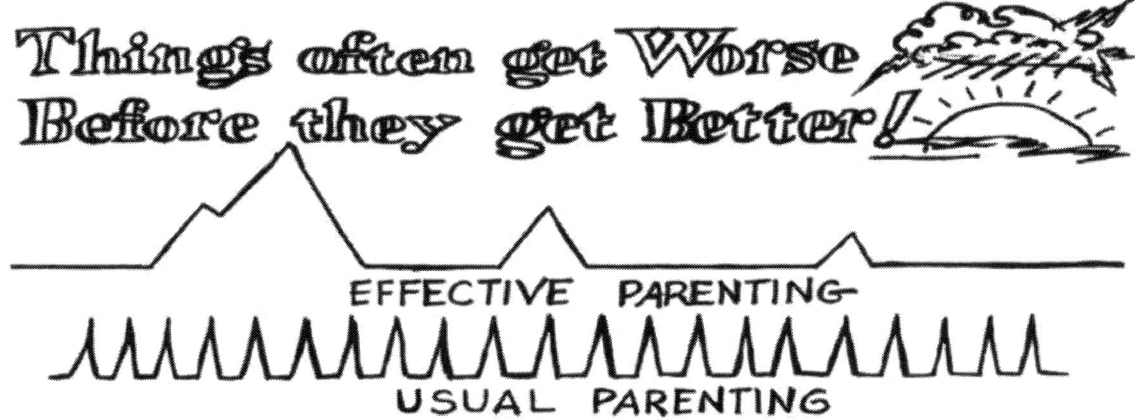

The second peak in the line above the Effective Parenting Approach illustrates how misbehavior might get worse when new skills are used. You will notice, however, that there is a leveling off before the child misbehaves again. The next two peaks show that misbehavior gets less intense with longer leveling off periods, when the Effective Parenting approach is used consistently.

To keep chapter discussions lively, we suggest using any of the following methods:

1. Copy the following statements, cut them into strips, and put them in a basket. Ask each participant to pull out one question and take turns reading and discussing it.

   I AGREE WITH THIS

   I DON'T AGREE WITH THIS

   I DON'T UNDERSTAND THIS I FOUND THIS PROFOUND

   I NOTICED THIS ABOUT MY FAMILY SINCE I READ ABOUT I DO THIS SINCE I READ

   I TRIED THIS

   I LEARNED THIS

   I WISH MY PARENTS HAD KNOWN ABOUT THIS

2. Underline important points in the book. Ask participants to turn to a page with underlining and have one participant read it. Discuss. Be careful when asking people to read out loud, as many people can't read and might be embarrassed to be put on the spot.

3. Some leaders have books set out on a table and wait for people to ask if they're available for sale. Other leaders let participants know that if they would like to do more reading, the books on the table are supplements to the Positive Discipline ideas and are available for sale.

4. Assign a chapter and ask participants to write down their questions and a statement of the most important thing they learned. A good way to start the discussion is to ask people to share their most important thing they learned before asking their questions.

5. Suggest that participants look for the following while reading assigned chapters and be prepared to share their answers with other group members:

   a) The most important thing I learned or relearned was:

   b) I need more help understanding how I could apply the following concept:

   c) I'm not sure I agree with the following and would like to get feedback from other members of the group:

   d) Following is an example of how I applied something I learned from this chapter:

6. Improve your facilitation skills by following the guidelines below and using the group dynamic charts found in the Resource Section at the end of this manual.

Facilitation Skills

Class Facilitation Skills

The following facilitation skills are very simple, yet they prevent many problems.

1. Set up ground rules about respect on the first night that you can refer to throughout the class. Show and discuss the group dynamic posters described (found at the end of this manual), before a monopolizer, debator, or quiet person is identified. This can help prevent problems that can drive other people away. (See group dynamics posters in the Resources Section for explanation.)

2. Stay on schedule.

3. Make sure that all participants get to have a share of the time.

4. Interrupt if necessary! It's important to know that it is okay to interrupt if someone is going on too long or is off the subject. You can say something like, "Excuse me. I'm sorry to interrupt, but I'm wondering if you would be willing to save that problem and volunteer during the Parents Helping Parents Problem Solving Steps," or, "Excuse me. I'm sorry to interrupt. Could you summarize quickly so we'll have time for everyone?" Or, "Would you be willing to write that question on a sticky note for our "Questions Parking Lot" flip chart, and we'll cover it during the Q and A time." Or, "The answer to that will be covered in an activity we are doing next week." Or, "That will be covered later, and we won't be able to cover everything if we don't stick to our schedule."

5. Tell people it's okay to pass.

6. Invite participants to let themselves be learners instead of experts.

7. Let parents decide what fits for them. There is no one right way to parent.

8. Deal with actual issues and not "what ifs."

9. It is not your job to become an expert. It is your job to learn how to help the participants in your classes and workshops discover how much expertise they already have and how many skill skills they can learn to be 'experts' with their own children."

10. It can be discouraging to participants if the facilitator acts like an expert. On the other hand, it is encouraging for them to see the facilitator make mistakes. Model that they don't have to be perfect when they teach.

11. Emphasize, "trusting the process," and, "having the courage to be imperfect" when you facilitate activities. Trusting the process means that the activities can work in spite of you, not because of you. Embracing your imperfection is a great model for everyone.

12. Jane jokes with participants that she almost feels sorry for so many of the people in her earlier workshops and classes because she didn't know as much as she knows now. But hundreds of people from those early classes and workshops now share how much it changed their lives. So, don't rob all those people you could help but don't because you are waiting to be more of an expert. Follow the admonition of Dreikurs and just go teach.

13. The reason we ask participants to share what they learned from an activity instead of lecturing is that they learn so much more form each other and from the wisdom that is reached when they do the activities.

14. Timing is a tricky facilitation skill. We need to sense when everyone is still engaged in the sharing, and when it has gone on so long that people are getting bored.

15. Share mini lectures ONLY if some important point has not been brought out during the processing of activities. Do not repeat what participants have already said. This makes your job much easier. Do the activity and trust the process. An example from a DVD trainer: *They felt that it was nice to hear other's experiencing the same challenges with their children along with the same hopes and dreams. They shared that fearing other's challenges validated their own feelings and experiences. They felt like they could have used more time to openly discuss and share their experiences.* Exactly—the reason it is so effective when the teaching and the learning come from the group as much as possible.

16. It is okay if you have the activity in your hands and refer to it. (You probably won't with more practice, but it is okay.) In fact, sometimes it helps confirm that you are not meant to be an "expert."

Facilitation Skill Tips

Every tool is based on foundational principles.

If you try to use any *Positive Discipline* tool as a technique, without understanding the principle, it may sound false and manipulative in a negative way.

A principle can be used in many ways. For example, when you use the principles of math there are many ways to get to 4: 2+2, 3+1, 8-4, etc. When a Positive Discipline tool is based on one or more Adlerian principles, and you add your heart and wisdom, the tool can be used in many different ways. For example, when you base Curiosity Questions on some basic principles (such as connection before correction, understanding the belief behind the behavior, kindness and firmness) and then add your heart and wisdom, your Curiosity Questions will fit the situation and be encouraging and empowering. If you use Curiosity Questions as a "script" they will sound false and manipulative in a negative way.

Is Positive Discipline Manipulative?

A participant in one of our workshops commented that she thought a *Positive Discipline* tool sounded manipulative. Of course, all *Positive Discipline* tools are manipulative. Don't we all want our children to develop the Characteristics and Life Skills we hope for them? Perhaps the word "guidance" sounds better, but it is still manipulative.

The key is what the "manipulation" looks like. Is it respectful and empowering—or disrespectful and discouraging? Positive Discipline tools are all designed to be empowering and encouraging, based on the basic Adlerian principle of treating everyone with dignity and respect.

Participant Sharing After an Activity

The reason we ask for sharing about what participants learned from an activity instead of lecturing (telling them what they should have learned), is that they learn so much more from each other and from the wisdom that is reached when they participate in the activities—even as observers.

Timing is a tricky facilitation skill. We need to sense when everyone is still engaged in the sharing, and when it has gone on so long that people are getting bored. Awareness of the need for this skill is the first step.

Offer mini lectures ONLY if some important point has not been brought out. Do not repeat what participants have already said. Allowing the learning to come from the group makes your job much easier. Do the activity and trust the process.

Having the Activity in your Hands

It is okay if you always have the activity in your hands. (You probably won't with more practice, but it is okay.) In fact, sometimes it helps confirm that you are not meant to be an "expert." It is also part of "trusting the process." The activities usually work in spite of us, not because of us.

Role-Playing

Remember to suggest that the volunteer role-playing the child, "be the child", but to also "be in his or her body." By that we mean to role-play what they are feeling like doing, as the child, **in response to what they are experiencing now**, rather than to keep responding the way the child behaves **in response to what parents and teachers usually do**.

Exaggerating during Role-playing

1. It brings more fun into the learning.

2. It is not easy to get into role-playing anger when you are not angry—when you are not in a flipped lid state. It is easier if you exaggerate.

3. It can be helpful if you demonstrate so they can watch you exaggerate.

Why only 60 seconds or so for a role-play

1. Letting people know you are looking for a 60 second role-play script discourages including too many details when describing a situation—no explanations, causes, etc.

2. Keep reminding the volunteer to stick to the last time the challenge happened: "Who said and did what? Then what happened?"

3. 60 seconds is usually plenty of time for participants to get the "feelings" that are going on. Of course you can use your judgment about allowing a role-play to go a little longer.

Mistaken Goal Chart

Many people are not used to being aware of their feelings and share what they "think" instead of what they "feel." For example many parents and teachers say they feel irritated and annoyed, when they really feel threatened, defeated, hurt, or disappointed. They may not realize that they think it is more "acceptable" to say "irritated and annoyed". Some parents and teachers say they feel hopeless and helpless when they feel challenged or defeated. What they really mean is that they feel "hopeless and helpless to win the power struggle." Others don't like to admit that they feel hurt. Hurt feelings are often covered up with anger or hopelessness.

Don't tell people they feel different from what they say. Just make note of it in your mind. Whatever goal is guessed, say, "This gives us a working hypotheses. Let's see what comes out in the role-play." Then, during another class, you might teach an activity to help participants learn to be more aware of their deeper feelings.

THTPPS/PHPPSS

I (Jane) share with participants that I had problems in the beginning when doing the THTPSS/PHPPSS. It was hard to stick to the steps. But I was told to "trust the process" —or I would be fired. (I wasn't really told I would be fired, but I like to joke with people to make my point.) Then I tell them that these steps have been very carefully designed by Lynn Lott (and used for over 30 years) to follow the Adlerian model for helping people learn what they need to learn and are ready to learn. It does not work if we talk about more information or give more advice. There is an Adlerian philosophical reason for sticking to the steps. It is called Holism. This means that any small part (and we don't mean id, ego, and super ego) represents the whole. In other words, if we find ways to be encouraging for a small part of a challenge, that encouragement will generate to the whole. On the other hand, if we analyze and look for "causes" the small part becomes too big and discouraging.

One way to keep participants more fully engaged in the PHPPSS is to ask participants to take turns reading the steps—one at a time. Then, as the facilitator, follow the step that has been read. Participation is increased even more by asking for at least one other person to "interrupt us" if anyone "gets off the steps" by talking, or asking more questions or giving advice, other than making suggestions for what could be tried, during the brainstorming for solutions step.

Directing participants to direct their advice to the volunteer writing on the flip chart, not to the volunteer.

Recently, I (Jane) volunteered to be the person who needed help with one of my grandchildren. I learned from experience how uncomfortable it feels when people didn't realize how vulnerable I felt for sharing my challenge when they wanted to "discuss causes and give their opinions." I also felt extremely uncomfortable when people looked at me when they were giving the suggestions, instead of looking at the flip chart and the person who was writing down the suggestions. I felt bombarded with advice—some of it that I didn't like and wouldn't choose. This is why it is so important to protect the volunteer by making sure all advice is directed to the scribe.

Interrupting

Recently, while coaching a group doing the PHPPSS, the volunteer wanted to give more information. The facilitator kept interrupting and saying, "No. Just stick to what happened to provide a script for a 60 second scene to role-play." She kept trying to give more information, and the facilitator kept interrupting and telling her she couldn't. When the PHPPSS process was done, she laughed and told everyone how much it helped her that she had to stick to the steps, and that the process helped her so much.

This is why we keep saying, "trust the process" and why it is so important to stick to the steps and to be very firm about it. Tell your participants that Jane Nelsen and Lynn Lott have spies watching to make sure you stick to the steps. (Just joking.)

Role-playing during PHPPSS/THTPSS

Be careful about facilitating role-plays too much. A lot of information comes out when the role-players are spontaneous instead of trying to stick too much to the script. Recently a volunteer was role-playing a teacher who was having problems with a child who was being defiant no matter what the volunteer (as the teacher) tried. As the volunteer role-played the teacher, the feeling that came up for her was such frustration that she spontaneously said, "You little stinker."

The "real" teacher burst out laughing and said, "That is exactly how I felt." She may not have even admitted to herself what she was feeling and thinking while describing the scene. This is why it is important to get a good description of what happened, and start the role-play out that way; and then allow for spontaneity as people get into the role. This can allow for rich information that can be very helpful to the volunteer and everyone. To add to this example, the brainstorming for solutions produced some good ideas that the "real" teacher tried that worked well in the second role-play.

When the Second Role-play doesn't seem to Work

It is important to remember that the PHPPSS is not just for the volunteer. It is for everyone. Often observers learn more than the volunteer because they can be more objective. They often see themselves and their situation in the volunteer, and learn some ideas/tools to try in their challenges.

Do not try another role-play with the good intention of wanting to make sure the volunteer gets help. We learn as much from what "doesn't seem to work" as we do from what does seem to work. The most important part of the PHPPSS/THTPSS is that the volunteer and everyone else feel encouraged and supported.

The Mischief Shuffle

By Lynn Lott

The mischief shuffle consists of the things you think and do that get in the way of your long-term parenting goals. This shuffle not only keeps you from being on your child's side but keeps you from taking care of yourself with dignity and respect. Some of the most common characteristics of this dance help you justify short-term parenting techniques such as control or permissiveness:

1. A need to "fix" everything that goes wrong, rather than allowing teens to grow by "fixing" their own mistakes. This attitude distracts you from being on your own side and growing by fixing your own mistakes.

2. A fear of what others might think which makes "looking good" more important than "finding out what's best" for your children and for yourself. You cannot be on your own side when you are busy trying to please mythical "others."

3. A need to protect children from all pain, which also protects them from learning and growing into capable adults by learning they can survive the pain and learn from it. Being on your own side means facing some of your own pain, forgiving yourself and continuing to grow.

4. A fear of anger, which means giving up, giving in, or doing whatever it takes to avoid the wrath of your children. This teaches teenagers that anger is bad and should be avoided or that it can be used to manipulate others instead of showing that anger is a valid feeling and can be handled appropriately. Being on your own side will make your children angry at times, especially when you say "no" when you believe it's right for you. They will survive and will learn from your model that it is okay to be on their own side.

5. A belief that you are selfish if you aren't self-sacrificing, which means that you are never allowed to enjoy yourself. Being on your own side means finding your own balance between doing things for yourself and doing things for your children.

How to deal with difficult participants

In spite of your best efforts, you may still have some challenging participants in your classes. One parenting educator wrote the following:

> The one obstacle I ran into was that the mother of three children ages 8, 5, and 3, kept doubting that this style of parenting is possible with older children. She interrupted what I was saying a few times with comments like, "I hope you're not planning on having more than one child," or "Just call me in six years when your daughter is 8." I kept trying to ask her what she wanted to get out of the group, but she seemed focused on trying to convince others that this type of parenting isn't possible.
>
> I wonder if others have encountered this type of situation, and what is the best way to handle it? I know that I would have difficulty listening to suggestions from others who have never raised a toddler, so I understand her position, but would still like to help her move beyond the attitude that "this isn't possible."

Several of her colleagues responded. Here's what one of them had to say.

> I have certainly encountered similar situations. Here's what I've come to understand. This parent is very discouraged, maybe even hurt/traumatized or ready to give up (looks a little like a mistaken goal chart doesn't it?). Her 'glasses' (the ones through which she views the world — through her beliefs) are on in a way in which she can not see other possibilities. She must be allowed to take very tiny steps. The material therefore must be 'sliced thin enough' for her to accept and digest. I find experiential exercises very helpful with that — but they must be chosen carefully as to not push but to invite. I find it very helpful in these situations to ask myself, "How do I feel? What could her mistaken belief about belonging be? What would be useful/helpful to her?" This is very effective at raising my own compassion – which is helpful to all.
>
> Also, I find it is helpful to introduce the material with a disclaimer, one that indicates that I don't want them to adopt these beliefs because I said so, and that I find that if they are willing to play with these ideas and explore them, they will find success that will work for their family. I often ask parents to embrace their skepticism that it is worthwhile and helpful — these ideas are radical and questioning them is healthy. (The experiential activities resolve this issue as the class goes on.) In taking these approaches I've had some class members who originally were the biggest skeptics become the biggest enthusiasts.

Another colleague wrote:

> Oh my gosh, this happens almost every time I give a workshop on Positive Discipline — I try to honor where they're at, and not push anything on them — basically model the Positive Discipline principles yourself. Sometimes I can get into a discussion with them and say something like, 'I know this technique seems like it may not work — it's so different then what many of us are used to,' acknowledging their doubt vs. challenging it. Sometimes I'll say something like, 'The technique is so unusual, and I can see why you might not trust it — I wouldn't either if it were being offered to me in this type of format. I could try to assure you that it does work with children of all ages, because I've seen it work — but, really, that would be pushing this on you, and I don't want to do that.' That way, I haven't challenged them, but I've also managed to address their doubt in a way that doesn't come off as a threat (I hope).
>
> Sometimes, at the beginning of a workshop, I'll say something like, 'Don't believe me when I say this will work — but, think about trying just one of the suggestions, and see how it might change things.' However it happens, I just try to trust the process, understand that I can't reach everyone at every workshop, and model Positive Discipline behavior as I present by not pushing a particular agenda on anyone. If I can even help someone reflect on what/how they're interacting with children, I've done a great job. Progress, not perfection...

Another colleague asked:

Have you tried using the Class Dynamics Posters at the end of the Teaching Parenting Manual. I have found it very helpful to present these posters during the first class—especially since I can confess my own process. When I present the monopolizer poster, I admit that I have a tendency to be a monopolizer and follow the suggestions given with the presentation of this poster. When I present the 'Oh that won't work' poster, I share that I was a 'what if, yes but,' type of learner and didn't know how the professor put up with my negativity. However, I kept trying things and was surprised that they worked. When they didn't, I later found out pieces of the puzzle that were missing from my efforts. I also love the 'don't throw out the baby with the bathwater' poster to point out that this isn't the only way and that everything doesn't work for every child all the time.

Jane responded with:

I developed these posters because the negative people were driving me crazy when I let myself get hooked. Now I realize that these people are really a gift because all the other group members seem to want to defend the concepts and prove them wrong. I'm not saying I encourage that. I agree with what others say, that it is important to be respectful, understanding, and encouraging. It is just what happens.

I like to present these posters before negative people and monopolizers are identified. I have seen so many negative people later become huge advocates. One woman in one of my classes later admitted that she kept coming because she thought it was a Communist Plot (a long time ago when that was popular) and that she felt obligated to keep an eye on us. She later became a group facilitator because of how much the concepts improved her relationship with her children (and her husband).

Here's another response:

I was a Juvenile Probation Officer for 30 years and taught parenting classes for the parents of those children for ten years and believe me, we got a lot of nonbelievers and 'this will never work' participants. First, I always told them to be assured that my goal was not to take anything away that they might be doing, but only to add to their resources. I also invited them to take from class only what made sense to them. I explained that I too was sure these things wouldn't work when I started trying them with my own children. I did them knowing it was just too easy to really make it different and OH MY GOSH, it DID work....I told them, it was like a miracle! As my own learning grew and I became more Positive Discipline-d, I thought, I'll try this with the kids I supervise at work. WOW, more miracles. Finally, my working partner and I began teaching at the court. I have never done more rewarding or impacting work because it empowered parents to be the change agent for their families. I can assure you, the principles of Positive Discipline can and do make a difference not just for kids but it helps parents be the kind of parent they want or hope to be. I assured those difficult parents that they didn't have to do anything different and thanked them for their comments saying I suspected they were voicing what others might be thinking and that open dialogue always made better classes. Giving them permission to do what they were already doing often ended their challenging behavior and made it OK for everyone to be respectfully direct.

Group Dynamics Posters

As has been recommended by many parent educators, present these posters (found at the end of this manual) at the first group meeting to prevent situations that can be frustrating to groups and cause them to fall apart. You might want to make copies of the pictures or blow them up and post them around your room.

The Same Boat: The universal reaction of parents and teachers who attend parent study groups is "What a relief to know I'm not the only one who is experiencing frustration!" It is comforting to know that others are in the same boat.

The Monopolizer

The Monopolizer: To group members say, "I am sure you have had the experience of being in a group with a monopolizer. This can be deadly for everyone else in the group." Then suggest the following:

1. Count to five before speaking. This gives others a chance for a turn.

2. Limit your comments to those you think will be interesting to others as well as to yourself.

3. Make your comments short and to the point. Most monopolizers repeat themselves and summarize several times.

4. Make sure you are staying on the subject being discussed.

5. Be aware of other group members who may not be as assertive as you are. Help them get into the conversation.

The Quiet Member

The Quiet Member: There are many reasons why an individual may be a quiet member of the group. Perhaps the person can't get a word in edgewise because of monopolizers, and doesn't feel comfortable interrupting. Some people prefer to remain silent because that is their learning style. Others don't speak up because they are afraid of saying something "stupid." Encourage group members to interrupt if need be by saying, "Excuse me, may I interrupt for a minute?" Remind them that there are no "stupid" questions, and that someone asking a question is usually asking something several other people were wondering about but uncomfortable bringing up. Group leaders can also help a quiet person by asking, "Mary, did you have something you wanted to say?" On the other hand don't embarrass those who prefer to remain quiet by calling on them if they prefer not to speak.

The Debater

The Debater: Anticipating that something won't work is often a good excuse to avoid trying, due to lack of knowledge and understanding about the basic attitudes and concepts. It is not necessary to accept all the concepts. Recommend that the debater use what he likes and reserve judgment on the rest until he learns more. Remind the debater that it would be very surprising if he could not find some good ideas that will enhance his understanding and relationships with children even if he does not accept everything.

Yes, but . . .: There is usually a "yes, but," member. Group leaders can suggest that though it is difficult to imagine how these new ideas can help, often by trying them out at home the results can be like mini-miracles. Ask the yes-but person to try something out for one week and then bring up the concerns during the warm-up at the next group meeting.

Another way to encourage the yes- butters is to suggest they choose only those suggestions they are willing to try. They don't have to buy the whole package to achieve benefits. This goes along with the next poster.

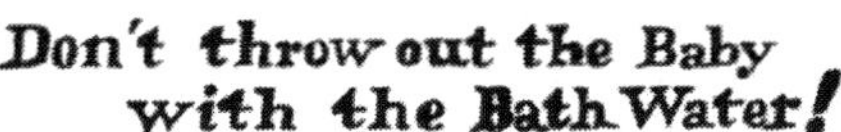

The purpose of an Adlerian parent or teacher study group is to understand and practice the Positive Discipline concepts, not to completely change everything at once.

This does not mean it is the only way. Rather, it is one very effective way to work with children. If time

is spent discussing other theories there will not be time to cover the Positive Discipline theory for full understanding and practical application.

If Only My Spouse Would...

If Only my Spouse Would…: Some people become so enthused with these principles that they want to convert others immediately. For example, a wife might come home from a study group and say to her husband, "This is the way we are going to do it from now on." A spouse may be inspired to try some of these techniques after having the opportunity to observe the effectiveness of your example, but is sure to resist pressure to change. Of course it is nice if both adults are working together on the same approach, but not necessary. Children are so clever that they can switch their behavior according to the approach of the adult with whom they are interacting. It will not hurt them to experience different approaches from different adults.

Notes

Handouts

As we mentioned, handouts can supplement learning or serve as a replacement to a book to teach parenting ideas. Many of the activities in the Activities Section include suggested handouts. Following are some sample handouts that Positive Discipline Associates have used when teaching parenting. If you use handouts that someone else has put together, make sure you give them credit for the information, but do put your name and contact information on a handout as a way of promoting future groups and contacts.

Do not overwhelm group members with so many handouts that they stop reading the text you are using for the class. If you aren't using a parenting book, then handouts can be a great help. Any of these handouts might also be appropriate to pass around when you are giving an introductory presentation. Make sure you put your contact information somewhere on the handout so folks can get back to you.

More handouts can be found at: https://www.positivediscipline.com/downloads

Positive Discipline Feeling Faces

Positive Discipline Tools

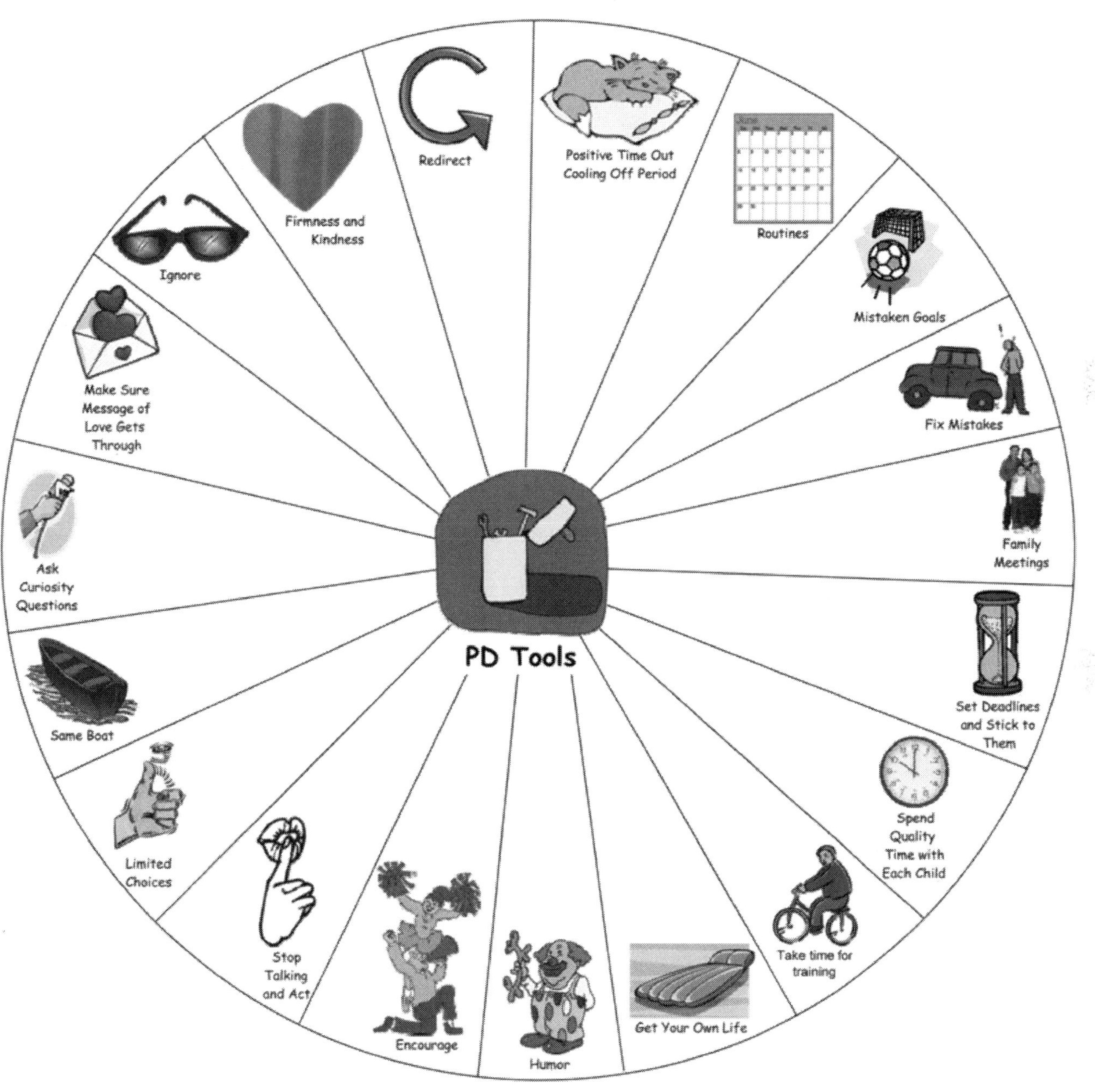

Based on Positive Discipline principles
by Jane Nelsen, Ed.D.
www.positivediscipline.com

Molly Henry
Certified Positive Discipline Associate
Abintra Montessori School

Wheel of Choice

Anger Wheel of Choice

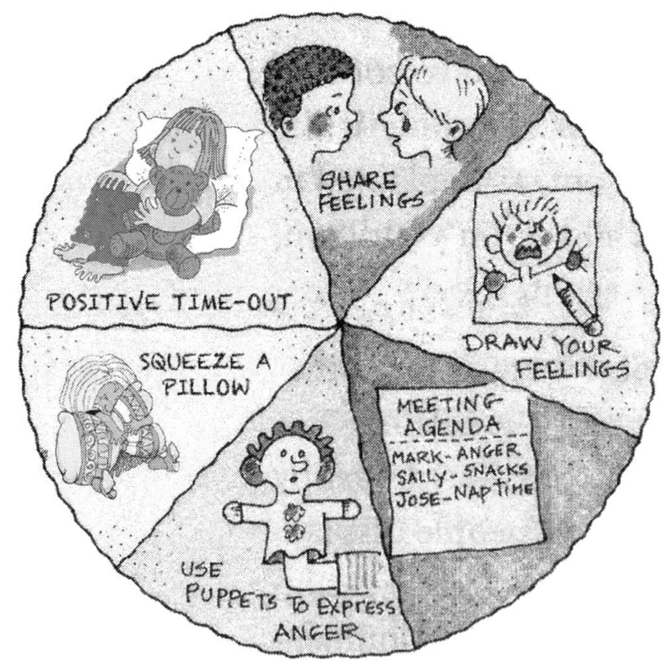

Developing Capable Young People

Seven Strategies for Developing Capable Young People

From the book Raising Self-Reliant Children in a Self-Indulgent World by
H. Stephen Glenn and Jane Nelsen, *www.positivediscipline.com*

Recognize that the rate and intensity with which knowledge, technology, and lifestyle are changing have created conditions in which resiliency and personal resources are critical to effective living and learning. Encourage the development of seven resources of highly resilient and capable people:

1. Strong perceptions of personal capabilities. "I am capable of facing problems and challenges and gaining strength and wisdom through experience."

2. Strong perceptions of significance. "My life has meaning and purpose, and I contribute in unique and meaningful ways."

3. Strong perceptions of personal influence over life. "I can influence what I do in life and am accountable for my actions and choices."

4. Strong intrapersonal skills. The ability to manage personal emotions through self-assessment, self-control, and self-discipline.

5. Strong interpersonal skills. The ability to communicate, cooperate, negotiate, share, empathize, listen, and work effectively with people.

6. Strong systemic skills. The ability to respond to the limits and consequences of everyday life with responsibility, adaptability, flexibility, and integrity.

7. Strong judgmental skills. The ability to make decisions based on moral and ethical principles, wisdom, and understanding.

Provide opportunities in homes and classrooms for children to develop the significant seven. Strategies such as family/class meetings, mentoring, and firmness with dignity and respect can provide opportunities for children to develop all of these resources.

Create and use rituals, traditions, and service projects as opportunities for growth and empowerment for children.

Increase the use of dialogue (a meaningful exchange of ideas and perceptions) as the essential process for encouraging closeness, trust, and learning: "What are your thoughts about that?"

Avoid "Did you? Can you? Will you? Won't you? Is everything okay?" etc. Instead use "What? How? When? In what way____?" etc.

Build closeness and trust, and convey respect by avoiding the Five Barriers and using the Five Builders instead:

Barrier #1: Assuming: Acting on limiting assumptions about what a person can or can't do, say, think, etc. "I didn't tell you because you always get upset." "You always think _____." "You're too young to try that!" etc.

Builder #1: Checking: Giving people a clean slate: "How do you want to deal with this?" "What are your thoughts about_____?" "What will you need to have ready for_____?" etc.

Barrier #2: Rescuing/Explaining: Problem solving for a person: "_____ is what is happening." "_____ is why it is happening." "_____ is how to deal with it." "Do it this way." etc.

Builder #2: Exploring: Problem solving with a person by letting them try something and then asking: "What did you experience in that situation?" "Why is that significant?" "How might you apply what you have learned in the future?" etc.

Barrier #3: Directing: Telling people what to do: "Pick up your shoes." "Put that away." "Don't forget your lunch." "Be sure and _____." Etc.

Builder #3: Inviting: Asking for participation/assistance: "I would appreciate any help you could give me in straightening up the room." "How do you plan to _____?" "What will you need to do in order to _____?" etc.

Barrier #4: Expecting: (too much too soon) Using potential as a standard and discounting people for not being there already: "I was expecting this room to be spotless." "You should know that already." "I appreciate _____ but you forgot _____." etc.

Builder #4: Celebrating: Focusing on effort progress and/or what was gained by trying: "I appreciate the effort you have made to clean up this room." "What did you learn from trying to do that?" "What progress do you see yourself making?" etc.

Barrier #5: Adultisms: Using stereotypes when dealing with people: "Teenagers are like that." "You know better than that! Surely you realize!" "You are too young to appreciate that." "Grow up!" "Why are you so childish." etc.

Builder #5: Respect: Allowing for people's uniqueness and individuality: "What is your perception of _____?" or "Let me check out what you think." "How do you see this issue?" etc.

Improve your relationships 100% by avoiding the ***Five Barriers***. Where can you get that kind of return for doing less? Replace the ***Barriers*** with the Builders and double the positive impact of your contributions!

Pampering Creates Weakness in Children

Jane Nelsen

You may have heard about the little boy who felt sorry for the butterfly struggling to emerge from its chrysalis. He decided to help so he could save the butterfly from the struggle. So he peeled the chrysalis open for the butterfly. The little boy was so excited to watch the butterfly spread its wings and fly off into the sky. Then he was horrified as he watched the butterfly drift to the ground and die because it did not have the muscle strength to keep flying.

Like the little boy, parents too often (in the name of love) want to protect their children from struggle. They don't realize that their children need to struggle, to deal with disappointment, to solve their own problems so they can develop their emotional muscles and the skills necessary for the bigger struggles they will encounter throughout their lives.

Children need to develop the belief that, "I am capable," to be successful in life. Children don't develop this belief by hearing their parents tell them they are capable. They need many experiences to practice their capability. Too many parents are robbing their children of these opportunities—all in the name of love.

I'm sure none of you do this, but did you know that some of your neighbors are dressing their two to six-year old children in the morning? And why do you think they do this? Everyone knows--because it saves time and because the children look better. Their clothes match.

The questions your neighbors need to ask themselves are, "Which is more important: expediency and looking good for the neighbors or that my children learn to feel capable and competent?" Your neighbors need to realize that when they dress their children, they are robbing them of the opportunity to develop skills and perceptions of capability.

The first thing these parents could do is create a badge for their children to wear that says, "I dressed myself this morning." Then they can take time for training to make sure their children know how to dress themselves (and realize that sometimes they don't care if their shoes are on the wrong feet or their shirt is inside out). Next, it would be helpful to get these children involved in the creation of morning routine charts. Then let the charts be the boss instead of the parent having to coax and nag. It is much more effective to ask, "What is next on your morning routine chart?" than to nag over and over, "Hurry up and get dressed. We'll be late." Of course, it always helps to get up a few minutes earlier in the morning—after training children how to set their own alarm clocks so they can avoid the nagging game.

You will hear me say over and over again—consider the long-term effects of what you are doing. Always consider what your children may be feeling, thinking, learning, and deciding. Are they deciding, "Love means getting others to take care of me," or, "I am capable. I can take care of myself and enjoy cooperating with others."

Raising Self-Reliant Teenagers in a Self-Indulgent World

By Mike Brock, CPDA

Comment: *If you want to extend your influence over your teen, you need to reduce your control. Only by reducing your controlling behavior can you improve your relationship with your teen, and the only way to extend your influence is to work on your relationship.*

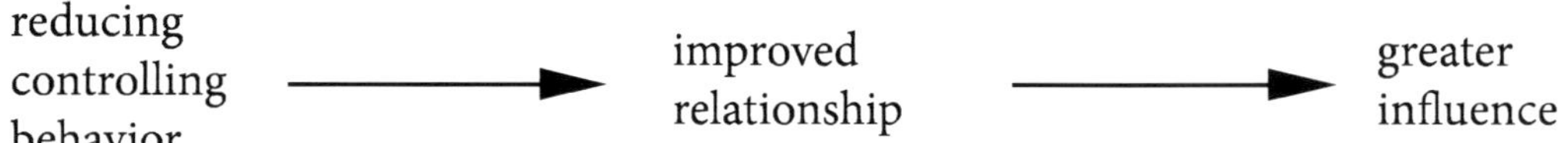

Fifteen Keys to Raising Self-Reliant Teenagers in a Self-Indulgent World:

1. Avoid the giving and taking back of "stuff"
2. Provide a consequential environment
3. Listen and ask—the two best relationship builders
4. Remember what it was like when you were a teen
5. 5. Honor that "Keep Out" sign on the bedroom door
6. Accept the fact that your kids already know what you want them to do
7. Avoid making success in school a measure of your love
8. Practice problem solving and "solutioning" rather than making demands
9. Have the courage to "drop the rope"
10. Provide opportunities for the learning of self-discipline through teaching wants vs. needs
11. Know that sometimes it pays to give in
12. Note how you treat your friends and use that as a benchmark for how to treat your teens
13. Worried about drugs and alcohol (and who isn't?)—don't forget the basics about relationship
14. Enjoy your teen—don't neglect laughter and play
15. Be that role model your kids need

The Question: "If you were given the opportunity to ask your parents one question and were guaranteed an honest answer, what would you ask them?"

Resources:

Unhappy Teenagers, William Glaser, M.D.
Positive Discipline for Teenagers, Jane Nelsen and Lynn Lott
Raising Self-Reliant Children in a Self-Indulgent World, Steve Glenn and Jane Nelsen
7 Strategies for Developing Capable Students, Mike Brock and Steve Glenn
Positive Discipline in the Christian Home, Jane Nelsen, Cheryl Erwin, Mike Brock, and Mary Hughes

The Basics of Dealing with Sibling Rivalry and Conflict

By Jody McVittie, CPDA

1. **Some sibling conflict is normal and healthy.**

2. **Sibling conflict can teach valuable life skills.**

   Examples: Cooperation, learning conflict skills (problem solving, walking away, cooling off, standing up for yourself), more than one point of view is valid, finding solutions that work for more than one person, fixing mistakes (owning a mistake, apologizing, working together for a solution). Just being physical is important too.

3. **Parents can make sibling conflict a LOT worse. Instead, develop the skills to minimize competition. Avoid comparing siblings.**
   Avoid rewards but don't forget to celebrate each child's achievements in a way that is appropriate for them. (There is a fine line between rewards and celebration. The question to ask is why am I doing this? Is it to get them to "keep it up?" Then it is a reward. Is it a -perhaps quieter- acknowledgment and celebration of achievement? That is a celebration.)
   Use encouragement instead of praise.
   Avoid labeling one as the bully, one as the victim (you never know exactly what happened).
   If you have to intervene in conflict treat all parties the SAME.

4. **Sibling conflict is more about you (the parent) than you think.**
   Kids don't understand that love is not finite.
   Your negative reaction can be better than what else is happening. Learn to stay out of fights.
   Even though they have mistaken beliefs about how to get there, each child wants belonging and significance.
   Spend special time with each child.

5. **Teach children basic safety standards/skills. Teach them:**
   Stop means stop (when they say this to each other).
   When to walk away
   When to ask for problem solving help (Remember that helping is not rescuing.)

6. **Develop the skills to use the sibling conflict to empower children with important life long skills.**
   Support kids by teaching them: problem solving skills, how to listen, how to walk away, why people act the way they do, how to ask for and give meaningful apologies (but not before they are ready), etc.

7. **Parents can learn to take care of themselves so sibling conflict is no longer a problem.**
   Understand the issues and learn skills to maximize the benefit, minimize the ruckus.
   People do better when they feel better - even parents. Take care of yourself!

Resources:
Positive Discipline by Jane Nelsen
Teaching Parenting the Positive Discipline Way by Lynn Lott and Jane Nelsen
Siblings without Rivalry by Adele Faber and Elaine Mazlish
The Tale of the Second Mother by Ed Janoe and Barbara Janoe

Positive Discipline Tools for Young Children

By Cheryl Erwin, CPDA

1. Be firm and kind

2. Decide what you will do.

3. Distraction and redirection (tell children what they can do)

4. Follow through (remember to be kind and firm!)

5. Positive time out

6. Create routines (get children involved)

7. Check perceptions

8. Take time for training

9. "What" and "how" questions (with an attitude of curiosity)

10. Offer limited choices

11. Use ten words or less

12. Active/reflective listening

13. Invite cooperation (classroom job chart)

14. Create a game

15. Do it with them

16. Ask for help

17. Take care of yourself

18. Hugs, hugs, hugs!

The Language of Firmness

Based upon Positive Discipline for Preschoolers, Chapter 9
By Jane Nelsen, Cheryl Erwin, and Roslyn Duffy

As parents we often have a good grasp of how to show kindness. Sometimes, however the language of firmness is a little more difficult for us. We try to be patient until our communication elicits fear or open rebellion. When a child wants to do something other than what you are asking or what is expected, the following "tools" may be helpful:

- **State Clear Expectations**…"As soon as you finish____, then you may____"
- **Respond with a question**…"Would you like to do this yourself, or do you want/need my help?"
- **State a given (i.e. a rule or condition)**… "This is bath time."
- **Check the child's knowledge or understanding**… "What needs to happen before you can_____?"
- **Invite cooperation**… "I need you help…can you figure out the most helpful thing you could do right now?"
- **Limited choices**… "Would you rather set the table or feed the dog?""Would you like to get dressed now or take your clothes to school in a bag?"
- **Say what you want**… "I want you to stay with me while we shop."
- **Negotiate an agreement**… "If I let you ___, when will you___?
- **Follow through**…."Time to ___ , now." Or "What was our agreement?" – then wait for their response. Don't argue, just calmly repeat the main word "now" or point to your watch. (A word of caution on this one: if you might get so busy you run the risk of forgetting to follow-through, don't choose this option!)

Dealing with the Spanking Question

by Fritz Mumm a parent educator living in Reno, Nevada.

My experience is that, deep down inside, the spankers in my class want to know it is okay not to spank and what tools they can use instead.

I have found that dealing with this issue in the first hour of the first session gets it out of the way for the rest of the class. Normally in the first few minutes of class, after the introduction exercise, I tell people that I believe society equips us with five parenting tools: Expecting, Correcting, Directing, Threatening, and Spanking. For emphasis, you can start with your hand closed and open one finger for each of the five and after you hand is open, slap (or clap) your other hand for emphasis.

I then ask them how many of them wake up in the morning saying to themselves, "I hope my kid does something I can spank him for?" I may get a few smiles, but nobody says yes. Then I say something like, "Of course you don't. Most parents look at spanking as being a last resort."

Then I ask, "How many of you would be willing to try one other thing before spanking if I show it to you?" They all raise their hands. "What about two. What if I show you two things that you could try before spanking, would you try them?" They agree. I then tell them that I look forward to seeing how many things we all learn over the weeks of the class that we can try before we need to resort to spanking. In the last class where we made a list as the last exercise of the class, we counted 42 things that could be considered before spanking (and for that matter before the other four tools listed above). Another thing you can do is keep a running list of things to do before spanking and add to the list at the end of each session. This list is a "New Tools in My Box" list and a reinforcement of what they know. It is also a reference during the Parents Helping Parents Problem Solving Steps.

Sometimes I ask them if they can let it go for the duration of the class. I then promise that, if they read the book and participate in the exercises and still feel that spanking is a tool they want to use, I will take them to lunch to discuss it with them. I have yet to buy that lunch and don't think that anyone who reads the book and participates in the exercises will hold on to spanking as a desirable parenting tool.

Temperament and Development,[1] Why Do They DO That?

Compiled from Positive Discipline the First Three Years and Positive Discipline for Preschoolers
by Jane Nelsen, Cheryl Erwin, and Roslyn Duffy

1. A child's behavior is the result of

    • individual temperament
    • emotional, physical, and cognitive development
    • what he or she has decided about how to find belonging and worth

2. Temperament is inborn and appears to remain constant throughout our lifespan. (See Chess and Thomas' "Know Your Child")

3. Behavior is a dance between temperament, development, and what your child believes about himself, you, and the world around you.

Temperament:

1. Activity Level

   High activity - Low activity

2. Rhythmicity (predictability of physical functions)

   Predictable - Unpredictable

3. Initial Response (reaction to something new)

   Approach - Withdrawal

4. Adaptability (ability to adjust to change over time)

   Adapts quickly - Adapts slowly

5. Sensory Threshold (sensitivity to sensory stimulation)
   Very sensitive - Less sensitive

6. Quality of Mood

   Optimistic - Pessimistic

1

7. Intensity of Reactions (response to events)

Intense reactions - Mild reactions

8. Distractibility (willingness of a child to be distracted)

Highly focused ---Easily distracted

9. Persistence and Attention Span (ability to stay focused on an activity for a length of time)

Persistent/long attention span ------Gives up/short span

Parents have temperaments, too; "goodness of fit" refers to how well a parent's temperament matches his or her child's.

Effective parenting means planning for the child you actually have!

***

In the early years, a child's behavior has more to do with development than with "misbehavior"; children are young and unskilled, and need discipline that teaches, rather than punishment.

***

No matter how old your child is, it is important to know your child!!

Experiential Activities
(Component No. 3)

Experiential Activities

Why teach experientially? Many people misread this word and think we are talking about experimental. There is nothing experimental about experiential teaching, as we've made it part of our groups and classes for over thirty years. Have you ever taken a class where you fell asleep through the lecture? Spent all your time doodling? Thought you were the only one not getting it? Wished you'd stayed home? Or been so overwhelmed you had no idea how to use what you learned? These are a few reasons we recommend teaching experientially.

Positive Discipline is taught primarily by creating an environment where parents and teachers can learn by doing—where the class participants have an opportunity to see, feel and think about their world in a new way. Most people remember what they do better than what they hear or see because it reaches people on a feeling rather than an intellectual level. Also, once participants get over their initial resistance and fear, it's more fun to participate, share, role-play, and talk with others than to sit passively and listen. Finally, it's easier to go home and try new things if they seem simple and doable. By practicing in a safe space, it gives people confidence to try out a new behavior with the real situation.

Experiential learning is encouraging, gives people a sense of being part of the group and a way to learn from their peers, and it provides a way for parents to learn from a non-expert. To maximize learning, be sure to ask parents what they thought, felt and decided in the role they were playing while doing the activity. This self-reflection helps parents learn from the inside out. In many cases, they are role-playing a child, so they have more opportunities to get into the child's world.

Facilitating experiential exercises takes practice. That does not mean that you have to have practice to begin (you have to start somewhere!) but that you will notice significant changes as you gain experience. There are some things to pay attention to.

It may be tempting as the teacher to want to tell your group either what they will learn or what they have learned. Summarizing is fine, but it's better to let information come from participants as they answer your questions and discuss their experience.

Asking participants what they are feeling, thinking and deciding brings out different participants' perceptions and interpretations. It lays the ground for new beliefs (and new behaviors). It also teaches participants to notice their internal process so that they can use it to understand themselves and their relationships. This kind of self-reflection is a rarely taught life skill that is incredibly useful to parents and teachers.

Even though some of the concepts and principles we teach seem clear to you, they can be quite foreign to many of the participants in your classes. By teaching experientially, participants get a chance to feel rather than think, thus tapping into basic human emotion and understanding.

When an Activity Doesn't Work

One of the things that new facilitators are worried about is what might happen when the activity doesn't go right. What they really mean is the activity did not turn out the way it did last time, or the way the facilitator wanted the activity to turn out. It can be a pretty unsettling experience, but it happens, and especially at the beginning it can happen frequently.

Here are some things that may be helpful to remember. Trust the process. As long as you are not trying to over teach, the process works very well. You cannot always see it working the way you think it should…but trust the process. The participant's response is an honest expression of where they are. It may not be where you are, but you can learn a lot from it. Sometimes the participants who volunteer for the exercise don't get it, but the rest of the group does. Other times, the volunteer doesn't seem to get it, but information is "cooking" and may produce some aha's over time. It can be just as valuable to learn from what doesn't work as from what does work.

Honor that and allow the group to share. What doesn't work can give you valuable information about what to teach the next time (through other experiential activities).

As you practice you will find that you become more agile and no longer expect the activities to turn out a certain way. You will get better at using the participants' response, WHATEVER it is, to support and enhance the teaching point.

Though there are many ways to teach experientially, the primary tool is the collection of activities provided in this manual. Until you are ready to create your own experiential activities it's helpful to use the activities that have been created for you exactly as they are written.

You'll notice the activities each have an objective and comment. These serve as a guide for the leader and as a way of limiting the activities, which could otherwise become too unwieldy. You may wish to write the objective on the flip chart when you begin, though some facilitators prefer to allow the objective to unfold.

Some activities have two versions. The first is intended to be used for a 20-minute segment available in a parenting class, while the second expands the topic to 35 minutes for a drop-in parenting program schedule. Depending on how much time you leave for discussion and input, the activity can be expanded or shortened. Keep directions simple for participants and remember to process thoughts and feelings and decisions.

If you wish to create your own activities, we suggest you follow the "Presenter's Checklist" on the next page. Use the checklist to make sure that your activity will truly be experiential.

Experiential Activity Worksheet

Activity Title:

Objective:

Materials:

Comment:

Directions:

1.

2.

3.

4.

Presenter's Checklist

To guarantee that you will be teaching experientially, make sure you can answer yes to most of the questions on the list below.

1. Is the presentation simple?

2. Is it entertaining and fun (or powerful, such as The Jungle)?

3. Are the directions clear?

4. Does the activity teach the point you want to make?

5. Will it fit within your time limit?

6. Is there room for involvement?

7. Would a handout or visual aid help?

8. Did you give permission to participants to make mistakes, exaggerate, and have fun?

9. Is it okay not to participate?

10. Do you need to demonstrate first?

11. Did you allow for processing at the end of the activity?

12. Do participants have enough information to succeed?

Experiential Learning Techniques

There are many techniques that help parents learn experientially. Several are listed below.

Role-play:

Role-play is a universal language. To set up a role-play, take any specific problem situation described by a participant, pick people to pretend to be the various participants in the situation and give them a few guidelines as to how those people would behave. Then set the stage and let them go for it, giving role-players permission to exaggerate, have fun, and make mistakes while doing their best to get into that person's thoughts feelings, and actions. Go all the way through the scene without stopping for corrections. Then process by asking every role-player how they felt what they were thinking, and what they were deciding in that role. If corrections are needed the scene can be replayed. After a role-play, ask group members watching what they learned. A role-play closely simulates the real world and usually teaches more than theorizing about behavior.

Guided Imagery:

People relax, perhaps close their eyes, and visualize a scene that is being read to them.

Journaling:

Participants write out answers to questions and are informed in advance if this information will be shared or kept private.

Dyads, Triads, etc.:

Members are divided into pairs, threes, or fours to practice or discuss information or do activities together.

Simulated Situations:

Situations that simulate life but don't really happen teach a lot on a feeling level. For instance two people can push on each other's palms to experience the thoughts and feelings of a power struggle and then discuss places where this happens in real life.

Scripted Skits:

Leaders write out the lines for participants and they read them out loud (see the activity Empowering vs. Discouraging for an example.)

Art, Movement, Dance:

Drawing, painting, moving, dancing, any of the expressive arts are tools for experiential learning.

The rest of this section includes experiential activities to use with your groups. Notice in the course outlines there are suggestions of which activity to use for each topic. They are simply suggestions. As you read the activities, you may find some that you prefer to use. There are other manuals with experiential activities that can be purchased at the Positive Discipline website.

Anger and the 3 A's: Acknowledge, Allow, Acceptable Solutions

Adapted from *Facilitator's Guide for Positive Discipline for Single Parents*
by Jane Nelsen and Cheryl Erwin

Objective:

To help parents/teachers know how to deal with children's anger in ways that help children accept their anger as a legitimate feeling; and to help children find acceptable ways to express their anger.

Materials:

Cue cards with the following lists (below): "Should/Shouldn't" and "Acknowledge, Allow, Acceptable Solutions"- 6 of each

Should/Shouldn't List

You don't really feel that way.

You know that isn't a nice way to feel.

Well what did you do?

You should love your (brother, sister, friend, parent).

Don't let me hear you talk that way.

You can just go to your room until you can talk nice.

Acknowledge, Allow, Acceptable Solutions List

Acknowledge anger:

Sounds like you are really angry.

Allow anger:

Everyone has a right to feelings.

I don't blame you. I have felt angry many times.

Acceptable solutions:

Would you like to punch a pillow?

Would you like to scream at the stuffed bear?

Would you like to jump up and down on the porch?

Comment:

Many people do not know what they feel because they were not allowed to express their feelings as children. You cut off a large percentage of your intelligence when you suppress your feelings because much of your behavior is based on feelings that you aren't even aware of. When you acknowledge your feelings, allow them with dignity and respect, and find acceptable ways to express them, you have more self-acceptance and more control over your actions.

Directions:

1. Have participants stand in a circle.

2. Ask for a volunteer "child" who will stand in the center of the circle.

3. Pass out a "Should/Shouldn't" list to six volunteer participants. Tell the participants that when you say "Begin", the "child," who is upset, is to say: "I am so angry I could hit Mike!" Then the participants with the "Should/Shouldn't" lists will take turns reacting to the child, using the statements on the list. (Remind them to exaggerate for emphasis.)

4. Process with the "child" what he or she is feeling, thinking and deciding after hearing these reactions from the "adults." Then, process the same with the adults.

5. Next, pass out the "Acknowledge, Allow, Acceptable Solutions" list to six other volunteer participants.

6. Have the same "child" repeat the "I am so angry…" statement. The participants with the "Acknowledge, Allow…" list will take turns reacting to the "child" with statements on the list.

7. Process with the "child" what he or she is feeling, thinking and deciding. Then, process the same with the adults.

8. Ask the entire group what they learned from this activity.

Anger: Taking Care of Yourself

Adapted by Jody McVittie, Terry Chadsey, Melanie Miller

Objective:

Recognizing how we feel impacts how we respond. We do better (as a parent or teacher)when we feel better.

Materials:

Sticky notes (2 per participant)

Flip chart

Markers

Time: 10-15 minutes.

Comment:

Taking care of ourselves is more than a "should," it is an essential if we are to do our best with young people. We do better (parenting, teaching) when we feel better. It is also important to model self care skills so the young people and our lives can learn them.

Directions:

1. Give each participant 2 sticky notes and ask them to write one thing that makes them angry on each note Sometimes giving examples that are humorous or very common breaks the ice (people who blink their lights at me when I am going the speed limit, my mother in law inviting herself to visit when I have other plans).

2. On the flip chart draw a large flask (an almost circle with a neck). It looks vaguely like a time bomb. It should be big enough to "hold" about 2/3rds of the post it notes.

3. When they are done invite them to walk up to the flip chart and put the note "in" the "pot" you have drawn (by sticking it on the paper) and share what makes you angry with the group as they read it out loud. Give permission for a participant to merely come up and place it in the pot without speaking by saying "If you are not comfortable sharing what makes you angry, that is ok, just walk up here silently and put it in the pot, but remember that knowing that you are angry about what ever it is might help someone else recognize that it makes them angry too."

4. Ask the question, "If this (pointing to the flip chart full of sticky notes) is what your day looks like and your child does something really annoying, what kind of reaction are you likely to give them?" (Participants usually recognize that the child gets a reaction out of proportion to the incident.)

5. Ask the question, "Do you do your best job as a parent when you feel good, or when you have had a day like this?"

6. Ask the question, "What kind of things do you do to take care of yourself?" You will get responses like: exercise, talk to friends, walk pets, listen to music, read, pray, take a hot bath etc. Each time you get a response, take one of the sticky notes off of the flip chart, write the response where that sticky note was. Gradually instead of a container (on the flip chart) filled with sticky notes, you have a container filled with suggestions of how to take care of yourself. The sticky notes are stuck at the margin of the flip chart. (All on top of each other makes a good visual.)

7. Talk about Steven Covey's demonstration of the rocks in the jar. If you take a jar of rocks…all kinds of rocks, big and little and dump them out you will have a pile of rocks. If you then put in all the small rocks, then the medium rocks and then try to get the big rocks in, what happens. (The big rocks don't fit.) Ask, "Is taking care of yourself a big rock or a little rock?" "What does that mean for planning your day?" You can stop here…as people "shift the rocks" inside themselves or go on:

8. Offer a short time for comments about what participants learned. If it doesn't come up, it may be appropriate to ask how children learn to take care of themselves. (Just like they learn other things, by modeling).

9. Acknowledge that we are all different, and different things help us feel better. This list is not the answer. It is a starting point. Encourage the group to go home and make a list of just 10 things that THEY like to do to "empty their pot."

Other ideas:

Sometimes this story (true) is useful for humor value …and for making the issue more personal. It can be inserted after step 4 or at the end.

One of the parents that I taught liked this exercise so much she decided to try it at home. She had 3 children under the age of 4 and felt like her husband did not understand why she was so short when he came home and she had no more patience. She put a drawing like this (refer to pot) on the side of her refrigerator one day. Every time she felt angry or really irritated during the day (as any normal human being would with three small children) she put up a post it note. When her husband came home she silently led him to the refrigerator. He gained a new understanding and was able to support her by giving her some "time off" as soon as he came home.

Anger: Using It, Not Losing It

Objective:
To learn anger management

Materials:
Flip chart
Marking pens

Comment:
Anger is simply an emotional response to a grievance. By learning to manage your anger, you have control over it instead of it having control over you. Then you can act rather than re-act. The first step in managing your anger is to acknowledging the fact that you are having a legitimate feeling. Too often when you are angry, you're told you shouldn't feel that way. This activity shows you how destructive that can be.

Directions

1. Ask the group: "What messages were you given as a child when you got angry? List responses on the flip chart. (For example: "You shouldn't get angry." "Don't raise your voice;" "Getting angry takes too much energy." "It's okay to feel angry, it's what you DO with it that really counts;" "You always have to get YOUR way, don't you.""I can always tell when you're angry – you look like a pot getting ready to boil."

2. Pair with a partner: have the first person say: "I'm angry" The second person responds with one of the messages from the flip chart.

3. Process by asking how each person felt and what he or she was thinking. Ask, "What were you deciding, (about feeling angry or about yourself, or the person who gave you the response)? Talk about how different it is to be shut down than to be expressive and accepted.

4. Now ask participants to think about a real life situation that they are angry about and would be comfortable talking about. Each partner will take turns playing both A and B. A's job is to accept that it is okay to be angry and to express it, and B's job is to listen and reflect back without fixing.

5. The first time around, "A" says, "I feel angry." "B" reflects back exactly what "A" has said, "You feel angry."

6. Then "A" says, "I feel angry because" and fills in the rest. ___________."
    "B" reflects back "You feel angry because" and reflects back what "A" said. Notice how tempting it is to either want to fix the problem or start analyzing what the problem really is. ___________."

7.	This time "A" says, "I feel angry because _______," and fills in the blank, and then adds, "and I wish ________," and fills in the blank.

8.	"B" reflects back, "You feel angry because __________ and you wish ____."

Note: It is important that the person listening repeat exactly what his or her partner says, substituting "you" or "I".

9.	Have partners switch roles and repeat steps 5 through 8.

10.	Process by asking how each person felt and what he or she was thinking.

Comment:

It is important to be able to know what you feel without expecting anyone else to feel the same way. It is equally important to say what you wish would happen without expecting anyone to give you your wishes.

11.	Invite the group to discuss what might have helped them deal with their angry feelings in a more useful way. Add the following to the list:

- Take responsibility for your part of a problem
- Apologize.
- Poor Timing
- Ask for what you want
- Go into your heart and see things differently

12.	Ask, "What did you learn from this activity, and what will could you do differently now with your children (or yourself) when they (or you) get angry?"

Animal Kingdom

Objective:

To help parents understand and appreciate differences

To encourage parents to focus on the assets of each child

Materials:

Four flip chart sheets prepared in advance, one for each animal at the top: (see example below)

Eight colored marking pens

Pictures of a lion, an eagle, a turtle, and a chameleon (or stuffed animals of each)

Why we want to be a Chameleon		
Why we didn't choose to be a		
Lion	**Turtle**	**Eagle**

Comment:

This activity can be a fun warm-up for participants to brainstorm, have fun, and experience some bonding in small groups.

Directions

1. Before participants arrive, post the prepared flip charts in four different areas of the room (using masking tape).

2. Ask participants:
   - "How many of you know people who think there is always a right or a wrong answer, or only one way to see things?"
   - "How many of you sometimes get frustrated because others don't think the same way you do?"
   - "How many of you sometimes wish your child had a different personality?"

3. Show your pictures (or stuffed animals) of a lion, an eagle, a turtle, and a chameleon; or just point to the names of the animals on the chart paper. Ask participants, "If you could be one of these animals for one day, which one would you like to be?"

4. Have participants move to the chart in the room that represents their chosen animal. If there are too many people at one chart, and not enough at another, ask for volunteers to change to the group that needs more people.

5. Ask for their attention and use one of the charts to explain what they will be doing. Tell them that each group will list all the characteristics they like about their chosen animal under "Why we want to be (their animal). Under "Why we didn't choose," have them list all the reasons why they don't want to be that animal. Invite them to exaggerate and have fun.

6. Allow about 3 to 5 minutes to brainstorm and write down their ideas.

7. When the time is up, ask them all to tape their charts next to each other on one wall. One at a time, have each group come to the wall. Ask for one volunteer from their group to read all the reasons why they want to be their animal. Then ask for another volunteer from their group to go to the other charts and read all the reasons why the other three groups did not want to be their animal.

8. Invite participants to share what they learned from this activity. If any of the following do not come up, ask, "Did you notice __________?:
   - What some see as faults, others see as assets.
   - Everyone has some assets and some liabilities.
   - We can choose to focus on the positives or the negatives.
   - Different personalities bring different strengths to a team. We need all kinds.
   - What would the world be like if we were all the same?

Example of the Chameleons' Choices

Why we want to be a Chameleon		
Can change – flexible, adaptable Hide easily to watch things Cute Harmless		
Why we didn't choose to be a		
Lion	Eagle	Turtle
Loud Females do all the work Meat eaters Lazy Power hungry Want to be King	Lonely Unapproachable Live in rocky places Look bald Push their babies out	They hide Avoid things Slow Have to carry their house every-where Bite

Example of the Turtles' Choices

Why we want to be a Turtle		
Always have our house with us Safe inside our shell; sturdy Can live on land or water; can lay in sun Old and wise We are gentle; don't hurt or bother anyone; trusting, relaxed Patient - slow and steady Lay eggs and go		
Why we didn't choose to be a		
Lion	Eagle	Chameleon
Fierce, gruesome, violent destructive; ruthless Arrogant "Kings" Lazy Predatory Loud Cunning Hunted	Power hungry Loners	Moody, volatile Phony - unreliable Inconsistent Not very strong Sneaky Unpredictable

Example of the Eagles' Choices

<table>
<tr><td colspan="3">Why we want to be a Eagle

Observe; have keen eyes
Can fly & soar - great view from up here
We have freedom & strength & long lives
Control our own destiny
Protected, beautiful, faithful, aware
Respected by Indians Intelligent
Symbol of great country, independent
Masters of our lives</td></tr>
<tr><td colspan="3" align="center">Why we didn't choose to be a</td></tr>
<tr><td>Lion

Dangerous
Live in hot, dry, arid places
Aggressive
Lazy
Loud
Macho</td><td>Chameleon

Too changeable
Run from problems
Blend in too much</td><td>Turtle

Slow, weak
Have a hard, heavy shell to carry around
They hide
Bottom of totem pole
Not attractive</td></tr>
</table>

Example of the Lions' Choices

<table>
<tr><td colspan="3">Why we want to be a Lion

King of the jungle
Playful, especially with our children
Proud, passionate, strong
Nice warm environment
Independent, respected
Sociable, passionate
Good looking; great hair
People respond to the roar</td></tr>
<tr><td colspan="3" align="center">Why we didn't choose to be a</td></tr>
<tr><td>Chameleon

Too small, insignificant
Always blending in
No courage</td><td>Eagle

Lonely life
Who wants to fly???
Bald and beady eyed</td><td>Turtle

Underfoot
Shy
Slow</td></tr>
</table>

Baby Makes Three

Objective:

To gain awareness of the impact of a new baby and to practice effective ways of supporting the couple relationship as well as the new family relationship

Materials:

None

Comment:

The arrival of another family member affects everyone in the family. Without preservation of the couple relationship, a child's arrival can create big problems for all.

Directions

1. Divide the group into groups of 3-5. Ask group members to choose a role. A group of 3 could represent a single parent, a child, and a new baby. It could also represent two parents and a new baby. A group of 5 could represent 2 parents, 2 children and a new baby, etc. Once everyone is part of a group and has chosen a role, ask all of the "new babies" to leave their group and form a separate group.

2. While you are giving instructions to the "baby" group, have the other group members get to know each other by sharing something very special about themselves—perhaps something they wouldn't usually tell.

3. While the small groups are getting to know each other, take the "baby" group aside and give each baby a specific role assignment: to have a handicap, to be needy, demanding, helpless, cute, or other baby stuff.

4. Have the "babies" join their families and act out their assigned roles. Do this for a short time and then ask everyone to stop.

5. Discuss:

   What happened?
   How did it feel?
   What happened to the couple relationship?
   How were the babies treated based on their assigned roles?
   How did adding a new baby affect the children who were already members of the family?

6. Have the participants list as many ways as they can that would help the couple maintain a good relationship with the addition of a new baby. List suggestions of how to help the existing children deal with the arrival of a new baby.

Bad Habits

Objective:
To learn how parents feed bad habits instead of starving them

Materials:
"Chart of Bad Habits" (below)
Flip chart
Marking pens

Comment:
Habits serve a child's unconscious purpose (one of the mistaken goals). The more fuss we make the worse they get.

Directions

SHORT VERSION:

1. Display the "Chart of Bad Habits." Ask the group if they have anything to add to the list.

Chart of Bad Habits:	
Nose picking	Interrupting
Giggling	Yelling from another room
Nail biting	Masturbation in public
Crotch grabbing	Sniffling
Clearing throat	

2. Instruct the group to pair off. One person is the parent and one is the child who will have the "bad" habit. Have the partners role-play how they usually react to their children while they are performing their "bad" habits.

3. Process by asking how the participants were feeling and what they were thinking and deciding.

4. Have the group brainstorm alternative methods for dealing with bad habits. For example: ignore, share how they feel, give a signal. You will find additional suggestions in the Goal Chart, tab, under "Alternatives."

5. Have the partners role-play again using suggestions.

6. Process as above.

EXPANDED VERSION:

In addition to the above:

7. Discuss: Did they have any bad habits when they were children?

    What were they?

    What helped?

    Were there things that worked?

    What are their issues around their children's bad habits?

    For example: do they feel their children are being defiant? Do they embarrass their parents?

    Do they take their children's behavior personally?

8. Have the partners demonstrate mutually respectful ways of dealing with the bad habits by role-playing for the whole group.

9. Process by asking the group what they were thinking, feeling, and deciding.

Ball of Yarn – A Closing Activity

Objective:

To give participants an opportunity to reflect on what they have learned and to share it with others

Materials:

A large ball of yarn (It usually takes two skeins of yarn rolled into a ball if you have more than 20 people)

Comment:

This activity usually serves as an excellent summary of the workshop and helps people remember all the wonderful things they have learned.

Directions

1. Ask everyone to move their chairs into a tight circle.

2. Hold the ball of yarn in your hands while explaining, "Now is the time for every one to reflect back on the last two days (seven weeks, or whatever amount of time the group has been working together). Think about your experiences. Think about what you have learned. If you had to choose one favorite thing you learned what would it be?

3. Now take a few moments to think about what you will do differently because of your experience in this workshop. What is the first small step you will take? What are your long-term goals?"

4. Allow a few minutes for reflection before saying, "We are now going to create a web of connection that will remind us of the power we have together to be a positive influence in the lives of children. We will toss or roll this ball of yarn across and around the circle."

5. When it comes to you, share what you have learned, or what you plan to do, or anything you feel in your heart. Then hang onto a piece of the yarn before rolling or tossing it to someone across the circle. (It is better to roll or toss across instead of passing it next to you in order to create a web.)

6. Start by sharing what the workshop has meant to you before tossing it to someone across the circle. When everyone has had a turn, tug softly on the web to remind yourselves of the inter-connectedness of the group members. At the end, either roll up the ball of yarn or invite participants to break off a piece of the web to keep with them as a reminder of their work together.

Notes

The Balloon Activity

Objective:
To help parents understand the trauma of children hearing their parents fight

Materials:
6 balloons
List of Characteristics and Life Skills from the Two Lists Activity

Comment:
Most parents are not aware of what their children are thinking, feeling, and deciding when they fight.

Directions

1. Ask for 6 people to be parents and 3 people to be children.

2. Give one balloon to half of the parents and have them blow up their balloons (any size they want) and tie a knot. (The other 3 balloons are to use in Part Two if these get popped). Then have them pair up with a "parent" who doesn't have a balloon.

3. Ask the children to sit on the floor in a place where they are very visible to the observers (preferably in the center where the action can take place around them). The children don't necessarily belong to specific parents. They just represent how children feel when parents fight.

4. Tell the parents that the balloon represents a challenge and they are now going to **fight** over it **(not have fun with it)**. (Emphasize that this activity doesn't work if they think the balloons are for fun, instead of representing a challenge.) The parents who don't have a balloon will try to take it away from the ones who have one, and maybe even try to pop it. The ones who have a balloon will try to keep it. **Both will be angry.** Again say to the parents without balloons, "You believe it is your job to have a fight to get and/or pop the balloons. Go."

5. **FACILITATORS NOTE:** Caution the group that this activity can get extremely rowdy and ask for help so people don't injure themselves, others, or the environment.

6. After one minute or less, stop the activity. Ask the group to sit down for processing.

7. **Process with the observers first.** Ask what they noticed or learned from watching this activity. (It is likely that the first thing participants will want to discuss is what was going on for the children. If they don't, ask, "What did you notice about the children?")

8. After the observers talk about what they noticed or learned, process with the children what they were thinking feeling and deciding. Did they learn any of the Characteristics and Life Skills from the Two Lists? What did they learn about relationships?

9. Then process the thinking, feelings, and decisions of the adults.

Part Two

10. Ask "partners" to again stand in the middle of the room, and the children again to sit on the floor where observers can see them. Again give a balloon to the same people that had them before and ask them to blow it up (if theirs was popped).

11. Let them know that the balloon represents a challenge in their relationship and ask them to use a Positive Discipline tool to work together for a plan to solve the challenge, such as a family (couple) meeting, or focusing on solutions.

12. Process with the children what they were thinking, feeling, and deciding. Did they learn any of the Characteristics and Life Skills from the Two Lists? What did they learn about relationships?

13. After processing with the parents what they were thinking, feeling, and deciding; ask what Positive Discipline tool they used (or could use) for solving a challenge: perhaps a family (couple) meeting, or focusing on solutions, or listening to each other.

14. Invite the whole group what they learned from this activity.

Birth Order

Objective:

To understand the influence of birth order on the early decisions children make and how this might influence their behavior.

Materials:

Flip chart paper
Marking pens

Comment:

Each family member has a unique position in which he or she is both influenced by and influences others in his or her family.

Directions

1. Ask participants, "How many of you were oldest, middle, youngest, or only children in your family of origin?"

2. Have participants divide into groups according to their birth order position. Comment on any birth order characteristics which were apparent as they moved into groups. For example, youngest may be playful and may ask for special service, oldest may get right down to business, middles may socialize, only children may act like oldest or youngest.

3. Give each group a piece of flip chart paper and ask them to brainstorm the characteristics they have in common while someone from their group records their list.

4. Ask them to create a motto that could represent their group.

5. After allowing 5 minutes or so for them to brainstorm, ask the group to reconvene and post their flip chart paper on a wall next to each other. Invite someone from each group to read their list.

6. Discuss: What did you learn?

   How does this relate to your own family constellation?

   What have you learned about your children?

   How can you use this information to encourage your child?

7. If it seems appropriate, share typical mottoes for birth order positions that might be different from the ones they created.

    Oldest: "I was the first and first I'll stay."

    Second: "I'll try harder."

    Middle: "Life is unfair."

    Youngest: "I'm entitled."

    Only: "I'm special."

Brain in the Palm of the Hand

"The Brain in the Palm of the Hand" is the work of Daniel J. Siegel, M.D., first published in his book, *Parenting from the Inside Out* (2003) and more recently published in *The Whole-Brain Child* (2011). Dr. Siegel is not associated or affiliated with, and does not endorse or sponsor the Positive Discipline Association and its activities.

Objective:

To demonstrate a useful visual to help parents and kids understand what happens in the brain when we " lose it."

Materials:

None

Facilitators Note:

You can watch Daniel Siegel demonstrate using a hand as a model for the brain by going to:
https://www.positivediscipline.com/videos

Directions

1. Introduce the brain in the palm of your hand by asking everyone to hold up their hands in an open position. Ask them to follow along with what you do.

2. Point to the area of your palm to your wrist, and explain that this area represents the brain stem, which is responsible for the fight, flight, or freeze response.

3. Fold your thumb across your palm. Your thumb represents your limbic system which is where you process emotions and store memories. It is also where you have your "safety radar" (the amygdala).

4. Then fold your fingers over your thumb (so you now have a fist). This represents the cortex. The prefrontal cortex (point to the front of your fist where your fingertips touch the palm of your hand) is where "rational thinking" and "emotional control" takes place.

5. What happens when our buttons get pushed and we "lose it"? We flip our lids (let your hand open, keeping the thumb in place...fingers up).

6. Now our prefrontal cortex is not functioning. In this state we cannot think or behave rationally.

7. Because of "mirror neurons" (one reason why modeling is the best teacher), when you flip your lid, your child will flip right back. (Hold up both of your hands in the flipped lid position facing each other.) If your child flips his or her lid first, you are likely to flip your lid right back. (Two flipped lids facing each other.)

8. Is this a good time to try problem solving? Why not? (Let the group respond and expect to hear: "Can't be rational; can't hear each other; can't control emotions; no connection; etc.")

9. Why do parents try to solve a problem when they or their children are in a "flipped lid" state? Let the group respond. (Afraid they aren't doing their job; afraid they are letting the child get away with something, reacting from fear, etc.)

10. What can you do to regain access to your prefrontal cortex? (gently close hand again) Take a few ideas from the group. (Take an adult time-out, breath, count to 10, take a walk, take a bath, read a book, etc.) You can decide if you want to take time to have a volunteer record these ideas on a flip chart.

11. Follow with the activity on Positive Time-Out.

12. It is important to point out that if children can't understand this demonstration, they are not old enough even for Positive Time-Out. However, it might help parents remember to take some positive time-out—providing good modeling for children.

Comment:

After the demonstration, let parents know they can share this with their children who are old enough to understand (around five or six and older), to increase their understanding of how their brains work. Parents can then follow-up by helping their children create self-soothing methods such as Positive Time-Out, using the Wheel of Choice, and putting problems on the Family Meeting Agenda. (If you haven't already, you will learn all of these tools through future activities.)

Children Do Better When They Feel Better

Objective:

To help parents understand respectful ways to help children feel better instead of being permissive, rescuing, fixing, and over-protecting.

Materials:

Four sheets of flip chart paper labeled as follows:

1) Conventional methods for helping children feel better

2) Possible long term-results of conventional methods for helping children feel better

3) Positive Discipline methods for helping children feel better

4) Possible long-term results when adults use Positive Discipline methods to help children feel better.

Comment:

Where did we ever get the crazy idea that in order to get children to do better, first we have to make them feel worse? The truth is that children do better when they feel better. In this activity we will explore the latter statement in more depth.

Directions

1. Ask for a volunteer to record on the first piece of flip chart paper while participants brainstorm answers to the following question, "What are the conventional methods to help children feel better?"

2. One group came up with the following, which should not be shown to your group. However, if your group doesn't come up with some of these, you could say, "What about __________?"

> **Conventional thinking about helping children feel better**
>
> Rewards such as candy, toys, or whatever they want
> Praise, "I'm so proud of you."
> Patronizing/pacifying, denying feelings, "You'll feel better," or, "You are okay."
> Rescuing or fixing. Not allowing them to experience feeling upset or disappointed.
> Giving in to their demands
> Making them happy at all times
> Over-protecting them so they never suffer

3. As participants look at the list, ask, "Will these methods help children feel better?" (Obviously they do, but some participants may start to get the idea that it may be only a short-term "feel better.")

4. Display the second flip chart and ask participants to brainstorm the possible long-term results of these "conventional" methods to help children feel better. After they have come up with a few ideas, probe deeper by asking, "Try getting into the child's world and make some guesses about what he or she might be deciding about him or herself, about the world, and what he or she needs to do to find belonging and significance in the world."

5. One group came up with the following, which should not be shown to your group. However, if your group doesn't come up with some of these, you could say, "What about ___________?"

Long-term results of conventional methods for helping children feel better

Children:
- feel inadequate (don't learn how to do for self)
- learn dependence on things and people
- become materialistic
- feel entitled
- believe love means getting others to take care of them and give in to all their demands
  develop manipulation skills to get their way

---

6. Display the third flip chart and ask for brainstorming about Positive Discipline methods that help children feel better. If this is a group new to Positive Discipline, you may need to make a list of what you know after allowing them some time to see what they can come up with. Or, you could show them the following list that was brainstormed by some graduates of a Positive Discipline workshop.

Positive Discipline methods for helping children feel better

- Validating their feelings
- Listening to them
- Helping them discover their own resources.
- Giving choices and responsibility
- Empowering them by having faith in them
- Allowing them to develop their "disappointment muscles" so they can feel capable.
- Giving unconditional love
- Proving opportunities to help and contribute
- Providing experiences where they can feel capable
- Teaching that mistakes are wonderful opportunities to learn

---

7. Ask participants if they think these methods will help children feel better. (Point out that most of them will help children feel better immediately, such as validating their feelings and listening to them, but some, such as allowing them to experience their feelings may not feel good temporarily. But what are the long-term results?)

8. Display the fourth flip chart paper and invite brainstorming on the possible long-term results when adults use Positive Discipline methods to help children feel better. Again, ask them to get into the child's world and make guesses about what he or she might be thinking, feeling, and deciding. The same group came up with the following, which should not be shown to your group. Again, if your group doesn't come up with some of these, you could say, "What about __________?"

> **Possible long-term results when adults use Positive Discipline methods to help children feel better.**
>
> Children feel capable, confident, worthy, open to possibilities, curious, have faith in themselves, believe they can learn from mistakes and can handle disappointment, make healthy decisions about how to experience belonging and significance.

9. Ask participants to discuss what they learned from this activity—what insights did they have? The group mentioned above came up with the following:

> **The things that help children feel better also help adults feel better.**
>
> Children treat us the way we train them to treat us.
>
> Sometimes doing what works long-term isn't easy. It is easier just to give a child what she wants in the moment or to rescue her so she won't have to suffer (unless you remember that she may develop a sense of capability when she learns she can handle it).
>
> The conventional methods to help children feel better actually create weakness in them.

Comment:

Another important way to help children feel better is by understanding how the brain works, and that positive-time out allows children (and adults) time to calm down so they can stop accessing their midbrains (fight or flight) and access their rational brains. Sometimes this is enough to change behavior. Sometimes follow up, in the form of brainstorming for solutions, may be required.

EXPANDED VERSION:

10. Set up role-plays from the brainstormed lists. First role-play would include a volunteer to play a child who is upset about something (perhaps not having a toy he or she wants) and an adult to play a parent doing one of the "conventional ways" to help children feel better. Tell the "child" to just notice what he or she is thinking, feeling, and deciding about him or herself and what they will do in the future.

11. Process what each role-player is thinking, feeling, and deciding.

12. You might want to end with the article called "Pampering Creates Weakness in Children) in the Handouts section.

Notes

Competent Giant

Adapted from an activity by John Taylor (inspired by Virginia Satir)
Person to Person, available at www.add-plus.com

Objective:

To help parents understand the long- term effects of punishment, scolding, or any form of humiliation to a child.

Materials:

Characteristics and Life Skills and Challenges Lists from the Two Lists Activity
Sturdy chairs for everyone

Comment:

Be aware of what works. Sometimes punishment stops the behavior for the moment. However, in the long-term the child may be feeling discouraged, resentment, revengeful, or inadequate — leading to more misbehavior in the future.

Directions

1. Ask participants to find a partner and decide who will be "A" and who will be "C."(A for adult and C for child.) After a few seconds, ask people who don't have a partner to raise their hands. Help people with raised hands find each other. If one person is left over, he or she can be your partner.

2. Share the following: As I give you instructions, please know that you can change them for your comfort. I will be asking you to take turns standing on chairs and kneeling on the floor. If this is uncomfortable for you, it is okay to take turns sitting on a chair while the other stands.

3. I want all the A's (adults) to stand on chairs. or on the floor. All the C's (children) will kneel down in front of the adults (or sit on a chair in front of them)."

4. Continue giving instructions by asking A's to think of a behavior that really pushes their buttons and then to pretend that C's just did that behavior. A's are then to scold C's while shaking their finger. (You can joke with them and say you know they have never done anything like this, but they can pretend they are role-playing a neighbor.) Point out that it is important to have fun and to exaggerate, because this speeds up time.

5. Model what you want them to do by asking for a volunteer who will be your child. (This is a good time to instruct them not to get up on a chair without asking their partner to assist for safety.) Ask your volunteer to assist you to stand on the chair, and then to kneel in front of you as the child.

6. Model by doing and saying something like the following: "I can't believe you would hit your little brother. How could you do such a thing? I'm so disappointed in you. Do you want me to hit you and show you what

this feels like? When will you ever learn? Why can't you be like your brother? You just go to your room and think about what you did." Then ask your "child" to help you down.

7. Now ask C's help A's get up on their chairs so A's can scold C's.

8. After about 60 seconds, ask C's to help A's step down from chairs so they can switch roles to experience both positions. Allow another 60 seconds for role-playing before asking the new "children" to help the new "adults" down.

9. Process by asking them to share what they were thinking, feeling, and deciding in each position—starting with when they were "children." Point out that, just like children, they may not be consciously aware of what they were deciding as the child, but if they think about what they want to do (withdraw, rebel, get even, give up, be good to get love, not listen, etc.), that is their decision.

10. Jokingly ask, "How many of you, while looking up at those nostrils, were thinking, 'This person is so helpful. I appreciate this feedback so much. I can hardly wait to bring all my problems to this very encouraging person?'"

11. Point to the Characteristics and Life Skills list and ask, "In the role of children, how many of you were learning any of these while being scolded?" (Probably none, but you may get a few who think scolding worked for them without realizing it "worked" because of fear or because they became approval seekers.)

12. Point to the Challenges list and ask how many of them felt motivated to engage in some of these behaviors because of the scolding. (Probably many of them.)

13. Then process what they were thinking, feeling, and deciding while playing the adults. After they share, ask, "How many of you, when you were standing on those chairs acting so controlling, felt totally out of control?" Point out that many of us act more controlling when we feel out of control.

14. "How many of you have noticed that when you hear someone else treat a child like this it sounds so terrible, but when you are doing it, it is because the child darn well deserves it?"

15. **Powerful final part:** Have them take turns doing the following while sitting face to face: The "child" will tell the "adult" what he or she wished the adult would say to him or her about the behavior he or she was scolded for—what would help him or her feel connected and encouraged. Then the adult will tell the child what he or she wanted to hear.

16. Switch so both have a turn.

17. Process by asking participants what they learned from this activity. (No need to ask the "children" to look at the Two Lists again because the sharing is usually so powerful.)

Facilitators Note:

You might also want to follow this activity with Curiosity Questions (Conversational) and to use the problem that invited the scolding as an opportunity to ask curiosity questions.

Communication Tools

Objective:
To understand that improving your relationship with your children is even more important than solving "the problem."

Materials:
None

Comment:
Parents complain that kids won't talk to them and that they don't communicate. This activity is guaranteed to provide you with skills to create good communication with your children.

Directions

1. Ask participants to pick a partner: one to role-play a parent and one to role-play a teenager (or child of any age).

2. Instruct the child to start telling the parent something the parent has strong opinions about, such as, "I don't want to do my homework." "I don't want to go to church." "I want to go to parties." "School is irrelevant." Instruct the parents to say anything they want without their lips separating, such as, "Uhmm" in different intonations. When the child runs out of things to say, the parents say, "It was really nice talking with you." Allow one minute for participants to complete the activity.

3. Invite sharing about how the participants felt in each role, what they were thinking, and deciding.

> **Comment:**
> A big problem with children (especially teens) is that they like to have the last word. Unfortunately, so do their parents.

4. Now have the parents and children get into an argument about something like doing the chores when the parents want them to, what they are wearing, how they are spending their money, telephone use, etc. Instruct the parents that when the argument gets going, to stop and let the child have the last word.

5. Ask, "How difficult was it for you to stop? How many of you still have smoke coming out of your ears because you let your kids have the last word? Even though you didn't get your way, did you invite your kids (especially teenagers) to want to communicate with you again?"

Notes

Communicating Ineffectively: Direct, Indirect, Non-verbal, and Double Messages

Objective:

To create awareness of what happens when you are communicating ineffectively.

Materials:

None

Comment:

You are communicating all the time. Sometimes you are not aware that you are communicating in ways that are ineffective.

Directions

1. Ask for two volunteers. Take one aside and ask him or her to nonverbally show the second volunteer that he or she is angry, disappointed, wanting something, or hurt. Ask the second volunteer to simply notice what is happening for him or her.

2. Process by asking how each volunteer felt and what he or she was thinking and deciding.

3. Discuss:

    Did you experience this kind of nonverbal communication from adults when you were a child? Would anyone like to share an example? How did you feel?

    In what ways do you do this with your kids? How do you think they feel?

    Does your partner or children know what you want or do they have to guess?

    Are you a good mind reader?

4. Ask for two volunteers to repeat steps 1 and 2 using words and being as indirect as possible. "Do you really want to wear that today?" "That isn't what I had in mind." "It would be so nice to come home to a clean house."

5. Ask for two volunteers to repeat steps 1 and 2 giving double messages, i.e., your words say you're not angry, but your actions say you are. Fold your arms, purse your lips, and say in an angry tone of voice, "I'm not angry," or tell your child he has done a good job cleaning his room while you are remaking his bed.

6. Now have volunteers take turns giving a direct communication to each other. For example. "I'm angry.""I feel hurt.""I'm scared you might get hurt.""Anything you would be willing to do to help would be greatly appreciated."

7. Discuss, "What did you learn from this activity? What kind of communication patterns were operating in your family of origin? How would you like it to be different in your present family?"

Continuum of Change

Kate Ortolano and Laurie Stolmaker

Objective:
To recognize change as a process involving awareness and skill development.

Materials:
Flip chart
Marking pens

Comment:
Once you recognize change as a process, you can become encouraging and compassionate with yourselves and others during the process.

Directions

1. Make four vertical lines on a flip chart with no labels (for each column leave some space at the top).

2. Invite participants to remember when they could watch other kids riding their bikes and were imagining-how wonderful it would be to ride. What were they feeling or thinking? Record in the first column.

3. Next invite them to imagine getting on the bike and trying to ride the first (and second) time. Write feelings and thoughts in the second column.

4. Fill the third column with feelings and thoughts about the time after they could ride, sort of, but it was still challenging around corners and hills.

5. Fill the fourth column with the feelings and thoughts of being really skilled at riding the bike.

6. THEN over each column fill in with the appropriate title: (1) unconsciously unskilled, (2) consciously unskilled, (3) consciously skilled, (4) unconsciously skilled.

7. Draw an arrow from the right to the left above the continuum as you explain that sometimes we move backward. Ask "What feelings might come up when you or others move in this direction?"Write comments above the arrow in the chart.

8. Ask the group what they are learning about themselves and others. What insights are they having?

> **Comment:**
>
> Remind participants that once we learn to ride a bike, the skill is mastered. However, when we are using skills that involve people, our emotional buttons may get pushed and the skill may be lost temporarily.

9. This is a great exercise near the end of parenting class for two reasons:

a) You can point out to participants that it is normal to have feelings of being consciously unskilled— and occasionally consciously skilled. That is where they "could" be after 6 or 7 weeks of parenting class.

b) It is really important to imagine what will happen to your neighbors when you, in your enthusiasm, go share what you have learned. They may be unconsciously unskilled; and you start telling them about all these new things. Where do they go? (Move your finger from the feeling column of unconsciously unskilled to consciously unskilled.) Is this person going to like the shift? Is it going to make him or her eager to welcome you and your information? If the neighbors have a negative reaction—which for the above reason they might have—don't let that shake your confidence.

Curiosity Questions (Motivational)

Objective:

To demonstrate how a challenge (such as not listening) from the Challenges List can be used to teach valuable social and life skills.

To help children feel respected and capable to figure things out for themselves.

Materials:

Challenges and Characteristics and Life Skills from Two Lists Activity

Asking and Telling statements (below for parents or teachers of different aged children) that can be printed and laminated in advance

Wind up chattering teeth (if you can find them)

Facilitators Note:

For "Conversational" curiosity questions" see the activity called "Curiosity Questions (Conversational)".

Directions

1. Give a mini lecture, something like the following: How many of you have ever complained that your children don't listen, or heard other parents voice this complaint? (Wait for show of hands.) What do parents really mean when they say their children don't listen? (Someone will probably say, "They don't obey." If not, you can.) What I've noticed is that many parents don't model good listening. Instead, they talk. They tell children what happened, what caused it to happen, and what they should do about it. They look something like this. (Show your wound up chattering teeth.) We are now going to do an activity to illustrate the results of talking/telling, and then what to do instead.

2. Ask for one volunteer to be a child.

3. Ask for nine volunteers (or fewer if you want to use fewer statements, or have some volunteers take more than one statement) to be parents or teachers to stand in a line.

4. Give each parent/teacher a laminated strip that has a "telling" statement.

5. Ask the volunteer parents/teachers to prepare by reading the statements to themselves, and to memorize as best they can, so their statements sound more real than "reading" (but they can read if they need to).

6. Let the volunteer "child" know that he or she will walk down the line and listen to what the parents/teachers have to say. He or she is not to say anything in response to the adults—just to notice what he or she is thinking, feeling, and deciding (about what to do). In other words, the "child" will stand in front of the first parent/teacher in the line, listen to the statement, notice what he or she is thinking, feeling, and deciding, and then go to the next "parent/teacher."

7. After the "child" has listened to all of the "Telling" statements, process with the child by asking, "What were you thinking, feeling, and deciding when hearing the statements from these parents/teachers?"

8. Take the child to the list of Characteristics and Life Skills and ask if there is anything on that list that he or she is learning. (Usually none of them)

9. Take the child to the Challenges list and ask if he or she is feeling inspired to do any of these. (Usually a few of them)

10. Now collect all of the "telling" statements and pass out the "asking" statements while saying, "You have now attended a Positive Discipline Parenting class and have learned some new skills." (Another way to do this is to have the "telling" statements on one side of the laminated strip, and the "asking" statements on the other side—maybe in different colors, so you can ask them to turn their strips over because they have now attended a PD Class.)

11. Again, ask the volunteer parents/teachers to prepare by reading the statements to themselves, and to memorize as best they can, so their statements sound more real than "reading" (but that they can read if they need to).

12. Now ask the "child" to walk down the line again, stopping in front of each parent/teacher to listen to what they have to say. Again, he or she is not to respond, but to notice what he or she is thinking, feeling, and deciding (about what to do) when listening to each statement.

13. Again, process with the child by asking, "What were you thinking, feeling, and deciding when hearing these statements"?)

14. Take the child to the list of Characteristics and Life Skills and ask if there is anything on that list that he or she is learning. (Usually most of them)

15. Process with the "parents/teachers" by asking what they were thinking, feeling, and deciding during both rounds.

Comment:
Point out the physiology of asking vs. telling as follows: "Notice what happens in your body when you are given a command (telling). Your body may stiffen and the message that goes to your brain is resist. Notice what happens to the body when you are respectfully asked a question. Your body relaxes and the message that goes to your brain is, search for an answer. During the process of searching you are feeling respected, capable, and are more likely to cooperate."

Facilitator Note:
The advantage of doing the activity with one line is that the parents/teachers get to experience being both the ineffective parent/teacher and then the effective parent/teacher. However, an alternative is to have two lines (one for Asking and one for Telling), with the same number of adults in each line, because it can be effective and fun to watch the body language of the "child" who walks back and forth between the Asking and Telling adults.

Facilitator Note:
This activity is called Curiosity Questions Motivational because it doesn't require a conversation. The questions are usually enough to motivated cooperation. For questions that invite conversation see the activity called "Curiosity Questions (Conversational)".

Parents of children 3 to 12 (Telling)

1. **Go brush your teeth or you'll have a mouth full of cavities.**

2. **Don't forget your coat.**

3. **Go to bed now!**

4. **Do your homework.**

5. **Stop fighting with your brother.**

6. **Put your dishes in the dishwasher.**

7. **Hurry up and get dressed or you'll miss the bus.**

8. **Stop whining. You are driving me crazy.**

9. **Pick up your toys or I'll give them to children who don't have any.**

Parents of children 3 to 12 (Asking Statements)

1. **What do you need to do so your teeth will feel squeaky clean?**

2. **What will you wear so you will be warm outside?**

3. **What is next on your bedtime routine chart?**

4. **What is your plan for doing your homework?**

5. **How can you and your brother solve this problem?**

6. **What did we decide, at our family meeting, to do with our dishes when we have finished eating?**

7. **What is your plan for catching the bus on time?**

8. **What words can you use so I can hear you?**

9. **What is your responsibility when you are finished playing with your toys?**

Parents of Teens (Telling)

1. **Go take a shower.**

2. **Don't forget your uniform.**

3. **Do your homework.**

4. **Get off the phone!**

5. **Stop fighting with your brother.**

6. **Pick up your clothes and put them in the hamper.**

7. **Hurry up and get dressed or you'll miss your ride.**

8. **Stop yelling!**

Parents of Teens (Asking)

1. **What do your friends say when you are sweaty and smelly?**

2. **Have you checked your game preparation list?**

3. **What are your plans for getting your homework done?**

4. **What was our agreement about when phones would be in the parking basket?**

5. **What can you and your brother do to solve this problem?**

6. **What will happen to your laundry that isn't in the hamper?**

7. **How will you get to school if you miss your ride?**

8. **What could we do to solve this problem respectfully?**

For Early Childhood Teachers (Laurie Prusso) Telling

1. **It's time to pick up your toys.**

2. **It's nap time. Go get your mat.**

3. **It is not okay to hit our friends.**

4. **It's cold outside. Don't forget your coats.**

5. **Don't forget to wash your hands.**

6. **Put your dirty dishes in the bucket.**

7. **Please stop whining.**

8. **You need to wait your turn.**

For Early Childhood Teachers (Laurie Prusso) Asking

1.　**What do we do during clean-up time?**

2.　**What do you need to do to be ready for nap time?**

3.　**How do we treat our friends?**

4.　**What do you need to take so you will be warm outside?**

5.　**Where do your dishes go after you are finished eating?**

6.　**What do you do with your hands after you go potty?**

7.　**How can you talk so I can understand what you want?**

8.　**What would help you wait for your turn—a timer or counting to 10?**

Elementary Teachers (Telling)

1. **How many times have I told you to remember your homework?**

2. **Don't forget to take your coat for recess. It's cold outside.**

3. **If you don't get your work done in class, you will stay in during recess and get it done.**

4. **Why can't you sit quietly like Sally?**

5. **Stop complaining.**

6. **Who started this?**

7. **Put your papers away, books back on the shelf, and clean up the classroom before you leave.**

8. **You just got a red card. Go to the principal's**

Elementary Teachers (Asking)

1. **What is your plan to help you remember your homework?**

2. **What will you wear if you want to be warm outside at recess?**

3. **What do you need to do to get your work done before recess?**

4. **How do we demonstrate that we are ready for the next lesson?**

5. **How can you share your concern so others want to hear you?**

6. **How much time do you two need to work this out?**

7. **What does everyone need to do to clean up the classroom before we leave?**

8. **Would you like to put this problem on the class meeting agenda, or would you like to see if you can find a solution on the wheel of choice?**

Middle/High School Teachers (Telling)

1. **You know you should have your books and homework ready before you come to class.**

2. **If you don't do your homework again, you will have to serve a 30-minute detention.**

3. **Put your papers away, books back on the shelf and clean up before you leave the classroom.**

4. **Stop asking so many questions when you could find answers for yourself.**

5. **Get to class. You are going to be late. Hurry up.**

6. **Stop talking to your neighbor**

7. **Don't wait until the last minute to do your report or you will get a lower grade.**

8. **Stay in your seat and quit bothering others.**

Middle/High School Teachers (Asking)

1. **What would help you remember to bring what you need to be prepared for class?**

2. **What is your plan for getting your homework done and turned in on time?**

3. **What needs to be done so your desk and the classroom is clean and tidy before you leave?**

4. **What could you do to find this information?**

5. **What are your ideas for getting to class on time?**

6. **When is the best time to discuss ideas or ask each other questions?**

7. **What is your plan for finishing your assignment on time?**

8. **When you need to leave your seat, how** can you make sure you are respectful to others?

Curiosity Questions (Conversational)

Objective:

To help parents learn to "draw forth" instead of "stuffing in."

To help children feel respected and capable to figure things out for themselves.

Materials:

Characteristics and Life Skills from Two Lists Activity

Handout of Sample Conversational Curiosity Questions (below)

Two examples of Conversational Curiosity Question stories in action

Comment:

Education comes from the Latin root educaré which means "to draw forth." Many parents try to "stuff in" and then wonder why it goes in one ear and out the other.

Directions

1. Pass out the handout of Sample Conversational Curiosity Questions. (Let them know that when they role-play asking curiosity questions, their questions should be from their hearts and wisdom. They can use the Chart of Sample Curiosity Questions for ideas, but they should not be used as a script. Their questions should be relevant to the topic.)

2. Ask all participants to think of a challenge they are experiencing with a child (didn't feed the dog, hit brother, didn't do homework, brought the car home without much gas left, bike left in the rain, didn't do chores, told a lie, etc.).

3. Invite them to pair up and decide who will be the child and who will be the parent. Let them know they will do two rounds so they can switch roles to experience being both the parent and the child. The one playing the parent will tell the one playing the child what challenge is.

4. The one role-playing the parent is to practice asking curiosity questions, starting with, "I notice______________," (The behavior) and then to ask curiosity questions about it.

5. After each curiosity question, they are to listen carefully to what the child says and be really curious about the child's world as they ask more curiosity questions.

6. Allow about 2 to 4 minutes for the first round. (You'll be able to notice when they look like they are finished.)

7. Process by asking the kids to share what they were thinking, feeling, and deciding during this process. Then ask them to look at the Characteristics and Life Skills list and share what is on the list that they were learning.

8. Process with the parents about what they were thinking, feeling and deciding.

9. Ask them to switch roles and repeat Nos. 4 and 5 above, and you can repeat Nos. 7 and 8.

10. Ask for two volunteers to read the two examples of curiosity questions to provide examples of not using the sample questions as a script.

11. Invite sharing about what they learned from this activity.

Comment:

Parents have an ingrained habit of "telling" instead of "asking." You might want to jokingly challenge them just to notice how often they "tell" for two weeks, and to put money in a jar every time they do. At the end of two weeks they will have enough money for the vacation of their dreams.

At the same time they are noticing themselves "telling" they could think about how they could ask, so they will be ready in the future.

---

　　　　　　　　　　　　　　　　　　　　　　www.positivediscipline.com

Sample Conversational Curiosity Questions (not to be used as a script).

Unless obvious, start with, "I notice _______________." (Whatever the challenge)

What happened?

Then what happened?

What were you trying to accomplish?

How do you feel about what happened?

What do you think caused it to happen?

What did you learn from this experience?

What ideas do you have to fix what happened?

What solutions will help you experience a different outcome in the future?

Example No. 1 of Curiosity Questions

One of my (Jane Nelsen) favorite examples is the time my daughter shared with me her intention to get drunk at a party.

I gulped and said, "Tell me more. Why are you thinking of doing that?"

She said, "Lots of kids do it and it looks like they are having fun."

I stifled my temptation to lecture and asked, "What do your friends say about you now that you don't drink?"

She thought about this and said, "They tell me how much they admire me."

I continued, "What do you think they'll think or say after you get drunk?"

Again, I could watch her think (one of the clues that the child believes you are really curious and not judgmental) before she said, "They'll probably be disappointed in me."

I followed with, "How do you think you'll feel about yourself?"

I could tell this question made her think a little more. She paused and said, "I'll probably feel like a loser." This was soon followed by, "I don't think I will."

If I hadn't known about curiosity questions, I would have been tempted to impose a punitive consequence, such as grounding her. Chances are that this would have inspired her to get sneaky instead of trusting that she could discuss things with me. The biggest loss would have been that she would not have had the opportunity to explore for herself the consequences of her choices and what she really wanted in her life.

Example No. 2 of Curiosity Questions

When he was 16-years-old, my son hated school. I engaged in classic power struggles every morning trying to get him out of bed and off to school on time. Then I remembered Curiosity Questions:

Me: Why don't you want to go to school?

Son: It is stupid?

Me: I can see why you would think that. And, I no longer want to have power struggles with you about going. You are now old enough to drop out if you want to get a job and pay rent here until you are 18. Before you decide, I have a few questions?

Son: (Glare.)

Me. Have you thought about what will happen if you don't get a high school education?

Son: Lot's of people, even millionaires, have dropped out of school.

Me: I know that is true. Do you know anyone who has dropped out of school and how they are doing?

Son: No. (He didn't want to talk about the friend who was in jail or the one working in a fast food restaurant.)

Me: What kind of job will you be able to get if you don't have a high school diploma?

Son: I could be a contractor.

Me: Yes, and that is an honorable occupation, and I'm sure you could do that. What have you thought about doing that you wouldn't be able to do without a diploma?

Son, reluctantly: I couldn't be an engineer or a pilot. (This is where I could see his thinking wheels turning before he blurted out this conclusion:) Okay, I'll go, but I'm not going to like it.

Me. That is brilliant thinking. Many successful people know they have to do what they don't like now so they can do what they want in the future.

I stayed out of future power struggles and Mark went to school. The interesting part is how much he loved college. No one lectured him about what to do, so he had to take responsibility for what was required for him to reach his goal to be a graduate.

Notes

Decide What You Will Do and Follow Through
Demo of Siblings Fighting in the Car

Objective:

To help parents understand the value of deciding what they will do instead of what they will try to make children do—and then to follow through with kindness and firmness at the same time.

Materials:

3 chairs set up to represent a car with one seat in the front and two seats in the back. A book to read while following through Characteristics and Life Skills list from the Two Lists activity

Comment:

Too many parents don't say what they mean and mean what they say—and children know this. Children feel much more secure (and don't learn manipulation skills) when they know they can trust their parents to mean what they say—and to follow through with dignity and respect.

Directions

1. Let the group know there are many different ways to solve the problem of sibling fights in the car, such as a family meeting where the kids come up with a plan. However, you are going to demonstrate deciding what you will do, informing in advance, and following through.

2. Ask for two volunteers who will role-play siblings who fight in the back seat of the car while you are driving.

3. Give the volunteers the following instructions out loud so everyone can hear; "I want you to play real kids, and I would also like you to be in the present. In other words, please notice what you feel like doing in response to what I do, not what your kids usually do in response to what you do."

Scene 1:

4. (Let the group know that this scene demonstrates the importance of "Informing in Advance" when deciding what you will do.) Ask the siblings to stand with you a few feet away from "the car". Then inform them what you have decided to do, "It is dangerous for me to drive when you are fighting because I get distracted. So, when you fight, I have decided that I will pull over to the side of the road and I will read my book until you are done fighting. The way I will know you are done is that you will both tell me that you are ready for me to start driving again."

5. Then check out their understanding of what you said by asking, "What is your understanding of what I will do when you fight?"

6. Wait for them both to clarify that they understand you will pull over.

7. Then ask, "And how will I know you are ready for me to drive again? What do I need to hear from both of you?"

8. Wait until they both respond with what they heard you say: "We are ready for you to start driving."

9. Let the rest of the group know you are now going to do Scene 2.

Scene 2:

10. Sit in the front seat and ask the children to sit in the back seats and start fighting. Let them fight for a few seconds and then say the following while getting louder and louder, "Kids, stop fighting right now. I told you that I would pull over if you fight. Don't you know this is dangerous? Why can't you cooperate? Do you want me to pull over and make us late? I mean it. I'm going to pull over. I really mean it. Did you hear me?"

11. Usually, the children continue to fight and get louder as you get louder. Stop this scene and process with the children what they were thinking, feeling and deciding.

12. Announce that you will now demonstrate what kind and firm follow through looks like in Scene 3:

Scene 3:

13. Turn around and whisper to the children that they will need to move their chairs when you move yours (to pull over). Then, in full voice, ask the children to start fighting again.

14. After a few seconds, without saying a word, pull over (move your chair a few feet to the side of the road), pick up your book, and start reading. It is very important that you don't say a word until they BOTH tell you they are ready—no matter how long it takes.

15. Usually the children will keep fighting for a while, but they eventually stop and tell you they are ready. Then you can say, "Thanks. I appreciate your cooperation," and move your chair "back to the road" and start driving.

16. Process by asking the children what they were thinking, feeling, and deciding this time. Ask why they didn't stop fighting in the first role-play and why they did in this one.

17. Show them the list of Characteristics and Life Skills and ask them if they learned anything on the list from the first scene when you lectured. (Usually nothing) Then ask if they learned anything on the list from the second scene when you followed through with what you said you would do. (Usually many things)

18. Process with the whole group about what they learned from watching. Be sure the following points come out:

    - Someone almost always asks, "But what if pulling over makes you late?" Let them know (whether or not someone asks the question) that it is a good idea to start at least 10 minutes early the first time you do this because kids will test to see if you mean what you say. If you do this consistently, kids will stop fighting the minute you start to pull over—or, they won't fight because they know you mean what you say.

    - Another point is that it is sometimes worth it to be late when the results are that you can teach your children valuable characteristics and life skills.

    - Discuss the importance of keeping your mouth shut because words just give children ammunition to argue and defeat you.

    - Point out that it is disrespectful to remind kids once they have told you that they understand what you said because it is assuming they are stupid; and/or it teaches them that they don't have to do anything until they have heard several reminders.

Facilitator's Note:

A good extension is to do the "Follow Up After Agreements" Activity.

Notes

Dependency Dyads

Adapted from an activity by John Taylor. *Person to Person*, available at www.add-plus.com

Objective:

To experience the non-productive feelings and results of enabling and co-dependency

Materials:

Flip chart
Masking tape

Comment:

Once adults realize the results of their enabling, co-dependent behaviors, they may be inspired to learn skills that empower teenagers.

Directions

1. Invite participants to choose a partner. Ask for a volunteer to be your partner and demonstrate the task they will be doing while you explain it: "One of you will be the supporter. The other partner will be the support-ee." In the demonstration, you will be the supportee. Stand behind your volunteer partner (the supporter) and put your arms around his or her neck. (Caution people who have back or neck problems to take care of themselves and decide what they can do.) Ask the volunteer supporter to start walking around the room while you hang on and go semi-limp so she has to support much of your weight. Switch roles. While demon-strating as the supporter, you might want to say, "See how much I'm needed?" Invite the other participants to walk around the room as supporter and supportee until you ask them to stop. Allow about 30 seconds.

2. Write "Supporter" on the flip chart. Ask people who were carrying the weight of the supportees, what they were thinking, feeling, and deciding in that position. Record their comments. Write "Supportee" on another sheet of paper. Ask the supportees what they were feeling and deciding in that position. Record their comments. Ask if this reminds them of any relationships in their lives. Use masking tape to hang both sheets of paper on the wall for later discussion.

3. Demonstrate the next task with your partner while you explain it: "One of you will be the leaner. The other partner will be the leanee." You will demonstrate being the leaner. Stand in front of your volunteer. Ask him or her to put both hands in front of his/her chest with palms out, ready to support your weight when you lean back. Lean back and tell him or her to push you around the room while you depend on him or her for support. It can be fun to make the following comments while you are being pushed around by your partner to demonstrate "Doesn't this look like a teenager saying, 'Look at me. I can go anywhere I want. No one knows I'm secretly supported.' (Caution people to be careful of slippery floors. We don't want anyone to fall.) Invite the other participants to walk around the room as leaner/leanee until you ask them to stop. Allow about 30 seconds.

4. Write "Leanee" on the flip chart. Ask Leanees who were pushing the weight of the leaners what they were thinking, feeling, and deciding. Record their comments.

5. Write "Leaner" on another sheet of paper. Ask the Leaners what they were thinking, feeling and deciding in that position. Record their comments. Use masking tape to hang both sheets of paper on the wall for later discussion.

6. Ask the Leanee: "Why didn't you let go?" Allow them to make comments. Then ask them to assume the Leanee/Leaner positions again. This time instruct the Leanees to walk around for a while supporting the Leaners and then say, "I'm going to let go. I'm sure you can stand on your own two feet." Then let go.

7. Ask participants to discuss their experience. Many things might come out. Some Leaners lean harder after hearing their partner is going to let go in an attempt to manipulate them into not letting go. Many have power struggles about who is in charge. Some are afraid to let go. These are all real life events. It is seldom that anyone falls.

8. Ask, "What if the Leaner did fall?" Allow comments. Ask participants to try one last part of this activity. Tell Leaners to sit on the floor and pretend they did fall down when the Leanee let go. Give Leanees the assignment to empower the Leaners without rescuing them.

Comment:

Jane shares, "I role-played the Leaner sitting on the floor, I was angry and felt abandoned. Then my partner sat on the floor next to me and said, 'What are you going to do?' I wanted to resist, but I felt too empowered. I had to focus on myself and what I was going to do."

---

9. Lead a discussion about what was learned from this activity. Look at the flip charts and ask, "How many of these feelings represent real life in an enabling, co-dependent relationship? Even though this activity focused on teens, do any of you experience co-dependent relationships in other parts of your life? How does any of this relate to their lives with your children? Your partner? Your adult parents? Others?"

Discipline: What Have You Tried?

Objective:

To examine conventional thinking about discipline (punishment) and the long-term results.

Materials:

Flip chart
Marking pens
Chart of the Five Criteria for Effective Discipline (below)

Comment:

Most people think discipline and punishment are synonymous. They are not. The word "discipline" originates from the Latin word disciplina which means "teaching, training, education" and the Latin word discipulus which means "disciple or pupil".

Directions

1. Divide the group into groups of four and give each a flip-chart paper with two columns labeled as follows:

Discipline methods used　　　　　　**What children learn from each method**

2. Allow five minutes or so, and then have each group tape their paper to a wall next to each other. Ask for a member of each group to read their list.

3. In a beginning group, most of the discipline methods used will be punishment such as: spanking, timeout (the naughty chair), taking away privileges, lecturing, yelling, rewards, bribes, threats. If any of these are missing you can ask, "What about _____?"

4. Process by asking what insights people had from participating in this activity.

5. In beginning groups, many may indicate that their children are learning good things from the punishment. They may think their "punishments" are "logical consequences." If so, be sure to discuss how logical consequences are usually poorly disguised punishment and that in Positive Discipline we advocate "No more logical consequences—at least hardly ever". We focus on solutions. Then do the Expanded Version.

EXPANDED VERSION:

6. Have each group choose one behavior from the list of challenges brainstormed earlier. Make sure each group chooses a different challenge.

7. Then have them create a role-play that they will perform in front of the group by choosing one of the discipline methods they brainstormed. Have someone in their group role-play a child doing the challenging behavior they chose and an adult to role-play the discipline method. (It might be more effective to have them do this spontaneously instead of practicing.)

8. Process after each role-play by asking what each role-player was thinking, feeling, and deciding.

9. Ask the group what they learned from this activity.

10. Present the following chart of the Five Criteria for Effective Discipline and ask the group, "How many of the discipline methods fit these criteria?"

Five Criteria for Positive Discipline

1. Helps children feel a sense of connection (belonging and significance)

2. Is kind and firm at the same time (respectful and encouraging)

3. Is effective long-term (punishment works short term, but has negative long-term results)

4. Teaches valuable social and life skills for good character (respect, concern for others, problem solving, cooperation)

5. Invites children to discover how capable they are (encourages the constructive use of personal power and autonomy)

Let participants know that all of the Positive Discipline methods they will be learning will fit all of these criteria.

Divorce

Objective:

To experience different realities of children when faced with divorcing parents, and that the effects of divorce on your children may not be what you think.

Materials:

None

Comment:

Do not introduce the title of this activity to the group before doing it. Only say, "We are going to look at how children and parents often see an experience with very different realities."

Directions

1. Divide the group into dyads: one parent, one child. Tell the "children," "Your parents have an important announcement to share with you." Ask the "children" to choose an age they want to be, making sure there are young children, school-agers, teens, and perhaps even an adult child.

2. Take the parents aside and tell them quietly so that only they can hear what you are saying, "You are going to tell your child that you are getting a divorce." Ask each parent to choose one of the following ideas to try after their "child" responds to the announcement. Encourage the parents to be sure each of the responses gets role-played if possible:

   a. Explain why he or she is leaving the other person.
   b. Bad mouth the other partner.
   c. Say it's not the child's fault.
   d. Say it'll be okay.
   e. Reflect the child's feelings.
   f. Hug the child.
   g. Any others?

3. Ask the parents to go back and sit facing their children. Have each parent simultaneously tell their child "Your mother/father and I are getting a divorce."

4. After they hear the first reaction from their child, they will try the response they chose above. Allow a few minutes.

5. Process by asking the children: "What are you thinking/feeling/deciding? What possible actions might you take as a child just hearing this piece of news? Which parental behavior above helped…which made it worse?"

6. Ask the parents how they are feeling, what are they thinking, and deciding.

7. In another role-play, suggest that the parents role-play their same announcement sharing their feelings and actively listening to the child's feelings.

8. Process by asking about the differences between the first and second role-play.

EXPANDED VERSION

9. Ask the group to share personal examples of times they have discussed difficult topics with their children, or discussed this very topic – divorce.

10. Divide the group into fours and talk about how the ideas in role-play #2 would help.

Don't Back Talk Back

Objective:

To help parents and teachers understand how they often model the opposite of the characteristics and life skills they want to teach.

Materials:

Chart of Characteristics and Life Skills list and Challenges list from Two Lists Activity

Scripts for Parents or for Teachers (3 choices below) laminated and cut into strips

Comment:

This activity provides another example of how a challenging behavior provides an opportunity to model controlling our own behavior and to create a connection that is encouraging and often leads to correction.

Directions

1. Ask for nine volunteers: eight to be parents and one to be a child. (If working with teachers or early childhood educators), ask for seven volunteers: one to be a student and six to be teachers, per statements below.)

2. Give each parent or teacher a "back talk" statement. Suggest that they try to memorize it so they can say it more spontaneously without reading—and it is okay to peek if they need to.

3. Instruct the child to walk down the line, pause in front of each adult with a defiant look on his/her face, and then just listen as each makes their statements. The "child" is not to respond verbally to what the adult says, but is to notice what she is thinking, feeling, and deciding (to do) in response to each statement. (Non-verbal body language is okay.)

4. After all "backtalk" statements have been made, process by asking the child what she is thinking, feeling, and deciding (to do). Take her to the Characteristics and Life Skills list and ask if there is anything on the list that he/she is learning. (Usually nothing)

5. Then take the child to the Challenges list and ask if he or she feels inspired to do any of these. (Usually some)

6. Next, ask the adults to pass back the "backtalk" statements; and pass out the "encouraging statements" while telling the adults that they have just taken a Positive Discipline class. (Ask them to memorize them if possible.)

7. Have the child go down the line of parents or teachers again. This time the adults will make their "encouraging" statements while the "child" just notices what she is thinking, feeling, and deciding.

8. Process by asking the child what she is thinking, feeling, and deciding. Take her to the Characteristics and Life Skills list and ask if there is anything on the list that she is learning. (Usually many things)

9. Process with the adults about what they were thinking, feeling, and deciding while making the "back talk" and the "encouraging" statements. How did they differ? (You do not need to hear from each one, just those who volunteer to share.)

10. Invite everyone to take their seats.

11. Invite the whole group to share what they learned from this activity.

12. If it doesn't come up from the group, point out how the "encouraging" statements represent Positive Discipline (creates connection before correction, is kind and firm, invites the child to think, is respectful, teaches valuable social and life skills), and that modeling is the best teacher.

13. If you have time invite a discussion about what is modeled by "back talk" statements and "encouraging" statements.

Back Talk (Parents Back Talk Statements)

1. Don't talk to me that way young lady!

2. Go to your room and don't come out until you can be respectful!

3. You are grounded for a week!

4. How can you talk to me that way after all I have done for you?

5. You just lost all your privileges.

6. Maybe Military School will teach you to be more respectful of authority.

7. How far do you think that smart mouth is going to take you?

8. You will be respectful if I have to ground you for a year.

Back Talk (Parents Encouraging Statements)

1. I wonder what I did to upset you so much?

2. Wow. You are really angry.

3. I need to take some time out until I can be with you respectfully (Modeling)

4. What would help us right now—some Positive Time-Out or putting this on the family meeting agenda?

5. I can hear that you are really angry right now. Do you feel like telling me more about it?

6. Put your hand over your heart and look lovingly at your child.

7. I need a hug. Please come find me when you feel ready for one.

8. Do you know that I really love you?

Teachers Backtalk Statements

1. Don't talk to me that way young lady!

2. How far do you think that smart mouth is going to take you?

3. You are in detention and don't come back until you can be respectful!

4. No recess for you. You can sit in the thinking chair until you are ready to apologize.

5. You might as well have a red card with your name personally embossed on it.

6. Write "I will be respectful," 500 times before tomorrow morning.

Teachers Encouraging Statements

1. Hmmm. I wonder what I did to upset you so much?

2. Wow. You are really angry. Do you want to tell me more about it?

3. I need to sit quietly and take some deep breaths until I can be with you respectfully. (Modeling)

4. What would help us right now—some Positive Time-Out or putting this on the class meeting agenda?

5. I know how it feels to be so angry. I'm glad we have the skills to work things through when we feel better.

6. Do you know that I really care about you?

Early Childhood Back Talk Statements

1. Don't talk to me that way young lady!

2. I don't care what he did. It is not okay to hit others.

3. Go sit on the naughty chair until you can be respectful!

4. No recess for you. Maybe that will teach you to watch your mouth.

5. You might as well have a red card with your name personally embossed on it.

6. Do I need to put duct tape on your mouth until you quit that back talk?

Early Childhood Encouraging Statements

1. Hmmm. I wonder what I did to upset you so much?

2. Wow. You are really angry. Do you want to tell me more about it?

3. I need to sit quietly and take some deep breaths until I can be with you respectfully. (Modeling)

4. What would help us right now—some Positive Time-Out or finding a solution on the Wheel of Choice?

5. I know how it feels to be so angry. I'm glad we are learning problem-solving skills to work things through when we feel better.

6. Do you know that I really care about you?

Draw a Teen (or a Child)

Objective:
To create an opportunity for a reality check on what is normal and what is not.

Materials:
Two to four large pieces of butcher paper
Six to twelve colored marking pens
Masking tape

Comment:
A picture is worth a thousand words to give parents a reality check on the difference between expectations and normal behavior.

Directions

1. You will need two to four groups of three to ten participants. If you have enough participants for two groups of at least three people, you will have renderings of a typical teen (or child) and a dream teen (or child). If you have enough participants for four groups of at least three people, you will also have renderings of a typical parent and a dream parent from a teenager's (or child's) point of view.

2. Tape the two (or four) sheets of flip chart paper on the wall in different areas of the room where groups can stand around them while an artist depicts their brainstorming ideas. Before they divide into groups ask for two to four volunteers (depending on the number of groups you will have) to be the artists who will quickly draw onto paper the brainstorming ideas of the rest of the group. Explain that you are not looking for Picasso, but people who feel comfortable drawing stick figures or other kinds of renderings. Give each "artist" two or three colored markers. They can also write words (sometimes in cartoon type bubbles), or whatever they want to do.

3. Have the artists come stand by you and ask the rest of the group to "count off" in twos or fours. Go around the circle taking turns calling off one, two; one, two; etc.; or one, two, three, four; one, two, three, four, etc.

4. Assign each group to different areas of the room where pre-labeled flip chart paper is hanging: Typical Teen or Child, Dream Teen or Child, Typical Parent, Dream Parent. Assign an artist to each group and tell the whole group that they will be doing a brainstorming activity and to remember that brainstorming means coming up with as many ideas as they can, as quickly as they can, without analyzing or judging the ideas.

5. Brainstorm as many adjectives as you can think of while your artist quickly draws your ideas to depict the person on the flip chart paper in your group.

6. Allow five to ten minutes for the brainstorming and drawing. Go to each group and let them know when they have one minute to finish. Then have them all bring their pictures to hang next to each other on one wall.

7. Ask for a volunteer from each group to explain the details of the drawing produced by his or her group. Allow a few minutes for each explanation.

8. Invite your group to respond to the following questions. You might want to record their responses on a flip chart:

    What did you learn from participating in this activity?

    Does anyone know a dream teen (or child) or a dream parent?

    If so, how do you feel about him or her?

    As a result of this activity, how are you feeling about your child?

    How are you feeling about yourself?

Encouragement Bouquet

By Rozenn Le Roux-Mion (France)

Objective:

To help parents and teachers understand the power of encouragement, and to feel comfortable giving and receiving encouragement to their children and to themselves.

Materials:

7 flower stickers per person (more if you have a larger group and more than 15 minutes for the activity)

Comment:

Rudolf Dreikurs often said, "A child needs encouragement like a plant needs water." This activity can be a fun and encouraging warm-up or as a closing to any class.

Directions

1. Pass out 7 stickers per person (more if you have a larger group and more than 15 minutes for the activity).

2. Ask the participants to close their eyes and think of two or three encouragements they would like to hear from others. (It might help if they think of a statement they heard from a parent or teacher that helped them feel encouraged when they were children.)

3. After allowing a minute or so, invite them to open their eyes. The task is now to find 6 other people (one at a time), make one of the statements they thought of to these people while pasting a sticker on the back of the person's wrist or arm. They should save one sticker for a later instruction.

4. They should make sure they find a person who doesn't already have 6 stickers. This insures that everyone will get 6 encouragement statements. (They can make the same encouraging statement to each person, or different ones if they thought of more than one.)

5. Allow about 4 minutes or so, and then ask them to stop and invite sharing about what they are learning from this activity (You can ask for thinking, feeling, and deciding or just learning.) Ask if anyone wants to share the most encouraging thing they heard.

6. Now ask them to give themselves the most encouraging thing they can think of while pasting their last sticker on the back of their hands or arms.

Comment:

One reason for asking them what they would like to hear is to help them feel comfortable giving encouragement even when they don't know someone well.

Notes

Encouragement: the Language of Love

Objective:
To experience the value of encouragement as a positive motivator.

Materials:
Marking pens
Flip chart

Comment:
Children DO better when they FEEL better. A misbehaving child is a discouraged child. Therefore, encouragement is the best way to deal with misbehavior. Maintaining dignity and respect while being kind and firm at the same time is the underlying theme of encouragement that forms the foundation of the Positive Discipline philosophy. This activity will give you other specific ideas for encouragement.

Directions

1. Display a chart with the heading Encouragement.

2. Ask participants to think of someone who has been encouraging to them past or present. Why? What does this person do that makes them feel good? Another way is to ask them to think of someone that they know loves them and then to think about how it is they know the person cares. What do they do that shows their love? List all of the responses on a flip chart.

3. Write their responses on the flip chart. Have the participants get into groups of two or three and give the following instructions: Think of the last time you engaged with a child in a discouraging way.

4. Now look at the Encouragement list and choose one you could use in this situation.

5. Take turns role-playing both scenes with your partner—what they did or said that was discouraging, and what they could do or say that would be encouraging. Allow about 5 minutes letting them know that each role-play can be done in about 30 seconds.

6. Process with the group what they were thinking, feeling, and deciding during each role-play in both roles as parents and as children.

7. Discuss what they learned from this activity.

Notes

Encouragement vs. Praise

Adapted from an activity created by Mickie Berry

Objective:

To help people understand the difference between encouragement and praise, and the long-term effects on children of each.

Materials:

"Praise and Encouragement Statements" on 8 ½ x 11 sheets of paper in large colored print and laminated

Characteristics and Life Skills list from the Two Lists activity.

Differences Between Praise and Encouragement handout

Comment:

Praise may seem to work and motivate good behavior temporarily; but what are the long-term results? Praise may "feel good" for the moment but what does it invite children to decide about themselves?

Directions

1. Prepare in advance the praise and encouragement statements on laminated sheets of paper (for the age group you are working with).

2. Do not read the beginning comment. It is meant as your foundational premise.

3. Ask for two volunteers to be children and have them stand on each side of you. One will be given the praise statements, and the other will be given the encouragement statements. (Do not tell them which kind of statements each will be given. That will come out later.)

4. Give the following instructions to the "children" (loud enough so everyone can hear): As you listen to these statements, quietly notice what you are thinking, feeling, and deciding. I will ask you to share later.

5. Say to the whole group: Notice what you would be thinking, feeling, and deciding if you were sitting in these chairs. Later you will be asked to share.

6. Be sincere as you make each statement—as though you really believe it is the best way to be encouraging to your child.

7. As each statement is made verbally, hand it to the child and ask her to hold it facing out so the audience can see it. Alternate the praise and encouragement statements. For example, say, "All A's. You get a big reward," to child

1 (while handing her the laminated statement to hold so the audience can see it), and, "You worked hard; you deserve it," to child # 2. Alternate back and forth until all the statements are made.

8. Process with the two participants by asking what each was thinking, feeling, and deciding while hearing the statements.

9. Ask the observers to share what they would have been thinking, feeling, and deciding if they had been sitting in the chairs?

10. Go back to the volunteers and ask if either would like to trade with the other person, or if they want to keep their statements, and why or why not. (Normally the person who received praise is willing to trade and the person who received encouragement is not.)

Facilitators Note:

Don't be surprised if the person who received the praise liked it. He or she may have learned to be "approval junkies." More often the person who received the praise statements will make comments such as "I felt conditionally loved," or, "It was all about you," or, "I felt pressured to live up to adult expectations."

The person who received encouragement statements usually makes comments such as "I felt empowered to be myself and to improve myself. I felt unconditionally loved and encouraged." Don't discuss any of this now. If these comments are not made by the volunteers, most of them will be brought out in the group discussion.

11. Ask both children to look at the Characteristics and Life Skills list to see if they were learning any of them from the statements they heard.

12. At this point, do not question the volunteers any more, and avoid making too many of your own comments. Let the learning come from the whole group.

13. Ask for a show of hands, from the whole group, how many would prefer the praise and how many would prefer the encouragement.

14. Then ask the whole group what they learned from this process, including what they might have been thinking, feeling, and deciding if they had received the statements.

15. If it hasn't already come out in the discussion, ask what they think would be the long-term effects of excessive praise. (Normally participants will indicate that too much praise can keep children tied in an unhealthy way to their parents or other authority figure and keep them from gaining independence. They also see that praise is enabling—teaching children to become "approval junkies"). Encouragement is designed to support inner validation and empowerment.

16. Point out that it is impossible to give praise when someone is failing; and that is when they need encouragement the most.

17. If it hasn't already come from the group, share the comments above and below.

18. Pass out the Praise and Encouragement handout on the following page as homework, and suggest that they read it and make notes about questions and comments they would like to make at the beginning of the next class.

> **Comment:**
> This exercise is not meant to make us paranoid for giving praise once in awhile. Praise, like candy, can be enjoyable on occasion, but too much can be unhealthy and addictive. Encouragement, however, should be the staple that you give to yourself and your family every day. Encouragement allows your children to see themselves as being capable, and it values their effort rather than focusing on perfection or pleasing others.

Praise and Encouragement Statements

Praise	**Encouragement**
All A's. You get a big reward.	You worked hard; you deserve it.
I'm so proud of you.	You must be proud of yourself.
I'm glad you listened to me.	How do you feel about it?
I like what you did!	You figured it out for yourself.
You did it just like I told you.	I trust your judgment.
You really know how to please me.	You can decide what is best for you.
Great! That's what I expected.	I have faith in you to learn from mistakes.
You are such a good boy/girl.	I love you no matter what.

Two to Three-Year-Olds

(Imagine your child has gone potty, dressed himself, or brought you a picture with mostly scribbles.)

Praise Statements	**Encouragement Statements**
Yay! I'm so proud of you!	You must be so proud of yourself.
Good girl!	Thanks for your help.
Your picture is so awesome.	Looks like you are having fun.
You are so smart.	You figured it out.
You're such a big boy.	You are learning more and more every day.
You make me so happy when you do that.	I love you no matter what.

Differences between Praise and Encouragement
(Revised from a chart by Sacramento parent educators Bonnie G. Smith and Judy Dixon)

Research by Carol Dweck, Ph.D. a professor at Stanford University, has now proven what Adler taught years ago. Praise is not good for children. Praise can create "approval junkies" instead of children with enhanced self-esteem. Dweck has also found that praise can hamper risk-taking. Children who were praised for being smart when they accomplished a task chose easier tasks in the future. They didn't want to risk making mistakes. On the other hand, children who were "encouraged" for their efforts were willing to choose more challenging tasks when given a choice. All of the Positive Discipline books teach the value of encouragement instead of praise. Following is an excerpt from Positive Discipline on the difference between praise and encouragement.

DIFFERENCES BETWEEN PRAISE AND ENCOURAGEMENT

	Praise	Encouragement
Dictionary Definition	1. To express favorable judgment of 2. To glorify, especially by attribution of perfection 3. An expression of approval	1.To inspire with courage 2. To spur on: stimulate
Addresses	The doer; "Good Girl."	The deed; "Good job."
Recognizes	Only complete, perfect product; "You did it right."	Effort and improvement: "You gave it your best." Or, "How do you feel about what you accomplished?"
Attitude	Patronizing, manipulative: "I like the way Suzie is sitting."	Respectful, appreciative: "Who can show me how we should be sitting now?"
"I" message	Judgmental: "I like the way you did that."	Self-directing: "I appreciate your cooperation."
Used most often with	Children: "You're such a good girl."	Adults: "Thanks for helping."
Examples	"I'm proud of you for getting an A" (Robs person of ownership of own achievement.)	"That A reflects your hard work." (Recognizes ownership and responsibility for effort.)
Invites	Children to change for others. "Approval junkies"	Children to change for themselves. "Inner direction."
Locus of control	External: "What do others think?"	Internal: "What do I think?"
Teaches	What to think. Dependence on the evaluation of others.	How to think. Self –evaluation.
Goal	Conformity. "You did it right."	Understanding. "What do you think/learn/feel?"
Effect on sense of worth	Feel worthwhile when others approve	Feel worthwhile without the approval of others
Long-term effect	Dependence of others	Self-confidence, self-reliance

Energetic Encouragement

Objective:

To give parents an alternative for encouragement that does not involve words.

Materials:

Two chairs side by side

Comment:

Many parents have a habit of talking too much—even when it is their intention to be encouraging. This activity could provide some insights about energetic encouragement.

Directions

1. Ask for a volunteer to play a five to nine-year-old who is having a temper tantrum because she can't have her own way.

2. Ask the volunteer to sit in a chair beside you. (Remind the volunteer to be a "child" and to be in the here and now. In other words, to notice what she feels like doing in response to what you are doing, not what her child does in response to what she usually does.) Now ask the child to start having a tantrum.

3. Your role is to sit quietly looking at the child with compassion in your eyes while you send out "supportive energy."

4. It might take a while for the child to realize what you are doing (or to show confusion that you aren't doing what you usually do).

5. If the child gets angry because you are sitting too close, move about one or two feet from the child and continue to send out supportive energy.

6. It may take awhile, but usually the "child" will stop the tantrum. If not, put your hand over your heart as a loving signal, and leave (allowing the child to have his/her feelings).

7. Process with the volunteer by asking what she was thinking, feeling, and deciding while in the role of the five-year-old.

8. If it doesn't come out in the sharing, ask, "Were you feeling frustrated and/or confused that you weren't getting the response you usually get with your tantrums?" "Were you deciding to keep having the tantrum, or to stop because it wasn't getting the response you were used to?

9. Share with the whole group that sometimes a Positive Discipline tool doesn't seem to be working because the child doesn't change his or her behavior right away. However, when a child is frustrated or confused that the behavior isn't getting the usual response, then he or she is ready to consider a new behavior that might not show up until later. It takes a while for a new decision to gel.

10. Ask participants to share what they learned from this activity.

11. You might want to do this activity before or after "I Need a Hug."

Comment:

Share that the point of Positive Discipline tools is not to change behavior, but to provide support for children to work through what is going on for them in a supportive environment.

Many Positive Discipline tools are used by adults with the goal of changing behavior. Behavior change is a fringe benefit, not the goal of Positive Discipline and is more likely to occur when it is clear that the adults goal is not to change the child.

Encouragement often invites children to make changes, but only because they have experienced the love and support (belonging) that invites them to change their belief.

Empowering vs. Discouraging

Objective:

To gain an understanding of the difference between statements that are discouraging (keep children from feeling capable) and those that are empowering (help children feel capable).

Materials:

Empowering and Discouraging scripts at the end of this activity. (Choose the age group for parents or teachers.)

Characteristics and Life Skills list and Challenges list (from Two Lists activity).

Make a handout of the Empowering Statements for the age group you chose for the role-plays.

Comment:

Discouraging behavior from adults may invite rebellion OR an unhealthy dependence in children, preventing them from feeling capable. Discouraging behavior includes rescuing, over-protecting, and controlling.

Empowering behavior from adults invite children to learn the life skills they need to have power over their own lives, and the joy of contributing to others. Empowering behavior means having faith in them to learn and recover from their mistakes in a supportive environment.

Directions

1. Prepare in advance by printing the discouraging and empowering statements below (for whichever age group you want to represent). You might want to laminate them before cutting the statements into strips, and put them in separate envelopes labeled "Discouraging Responses" and "Empowering Responses."

2. Ask for 22 volunteers (11 in each line) to play parents or teachers, and one volunteer to play a child. (These numbers are based on doing the 6-12 age group. If you have fewer participants you can ask for fewer volunteers and use fewer scripts (or give each volunteer more than one script.)

3. Divide the "parents" or "teachers" into two lines with equal numbers—facing each other about 8 feet apart. Hand out the "discouraging" scripts to the adults in one line and the "empowering" scripts to the adults in the other line. Ask them to read their statements and try to memorize them well enough that they can speak directly to the "child" (but that is okay to peek).

4. Instruct the child to adopt an attitude of a normal kid who has done something he or she is not supposed to do, or has not lived up to an adults expectations.

5. Have the "child" walk back and forth between the line of "adults" with the **discouraging statements** and

the adults with the **empowering statements**. The child is to stand in front of each adult, one at a time. (Do not read the comments in parentheses. They are there to name a tool.) The child is not to say anything, but to just notice what he or she is thinking, feeling, and deciding after listening to the statement of an adult in one line, and then walking over to an adult in the other line.

6. Then process with the child by asking what he or she is thinking, feeling, and deciding from the parents or teachers in each line. Then take him or her to the Characteristics and Life Skills list and ask if he or she is learning anything on this list from the adults who gave the **discouraging statements**. (Usually not) Then point to the Challenges list and ask if the child feels invited to engage in any of these. (Usually some)

7. Then ask the child to look at the Characteristics and Life Skills list again and ask if he or she was learning anything on the list from the **empowering statements**. (Usually most of them)

8. Ask the participants who were watching what they noticed about the body language of the child as he or she went back and forth.

9. Process with the participants role-playing adults, "What were you thinking and feeling and deciding while making your statements?"

10. Invite the volunteers to join the whole group and process what they learned from this activity.

Comment:

Many parents and teachers **discourage** their children/students in the name of love or caring. They do not look at the long-term results. They don't consider what their children/students are deciding about themselves and about what to do in the future (based on their decisions). They may be deciding, "I'm not capable." "It is best to let others take care of me." "You can't make me," etc.

Discouraging Statements for Children Ages 6-12

1. "How many times do I have to tell you not to leave your bicycle in the driveway?"

2. "You act like this everyday! What is wrong with you?"

3. "I don't care what you want. Do it now."

4. "Never mind. I'm sure you'll do it later."

5. "If you can't be more responsible, you are grounded."

6. "I am going to set the timer for 10 minutes and your chores better be done when it dings."

7. "I am so tired of nagging at you."

8. "It's okay. I can do it for you this time."

9. "Why can't you just listen to me and do what I ask?"

10. "If you don't want your things thrown away, you'd better pick them up right now!"

11. "Why do you expect me to do every thing for you when you don't do anything for me?"

Empowering Statements for Children Ages 6–12

1. (Show faith with a reminder of what the child/student can do.) "I know you know where your bike goes. Thanks for taking care of that now."

2. (Curiosity question) "What do you need to do to keep your sports equipment safe?"

3. (Acknowledge feelings first.) "It is hard to remember things that are not on your list or priorities. I'm happy to remind you once."

4. (As soon as _____________.) "As soon as your chores are done, I'll give you a ride to your game.

5. (Check the child's knowledge or understanding.) "What is supposed to be happening now?"

6. (Invite cooperation and then a choice.) "I need your help. Do you want to do your chores now or in 30 minutes?"

7. (Connection before correction) "I don't know what I would do without your help. Anything you can do will be appreciated."

8. (I love you AND______[say what you want/mean].) "I love you, and this needs to be done now."

9. (Use non-verbal language.) Put a gentle hand on his or her shoulder and then take the child by the hand, point at what needs to be done, and smile with a knowing look.

10. (Give Power.) "Do you want to set the timer for how much time you think it will take to get it done?"

11. (Connect and redirect.) "It is more fun if we work together. What would you like me to do to help, and what will you do?"

Discouraging Statements for 2-5

1. "No. No. You can't pour the milk into your glass. You might hurt yourself or make a big mess."

2. Pick up the toys now or you will sit in the naughty chair."

3. "Other children pick up their toys. I wonder if you are a baby or a big girl."

4. "I'm going to set the timer for 3 minutes and these toys better be picked up when it dings!"

5. "You are too little. Mommy will do it for you."

6. "We go through this every day. I'm tired of it."

7. "If you don't want your toys thrown away, you'd better pick them up right now!"

8. "Why can't you just listen to me and do what I ask?"

9. "It's okay. Your Grandma or I will do it."

10. "Don't ever ask me to do anything for you."

Empowering Statements for 2-5

1. (Show faith and provide safe exploring environment.) "I know you can do it. This pitcher of milk is just your size."

2.   (Acknowledge feelings first.) "You are so excited to try. Show me how you can do it."

3. (Check the child's understanding.) "What do we need to do with the toys before story time?"

4. (Invite cooperation and then a choice.) "I need your help. Do you want to clean up while singing or silently?"

5. (Share power.) "Here is the timer. See how many toys you can pick up before it rings."

6. (Offer limited choices.) "Do you want to put the big blocks away first or the small blocks?"

7. (Get down to child's level and say what you want/mean.) "Sweetie, It's time to put the blocks away now."

8. (Ask a curiosity question.) "Where does this toy go?"

9. (Connect and redirect.) "It is more fun if we work together. What would you like me to do to help, and what will you do?"

10. (As soon as _____ then _____.) "As soon as the toys are picked up, it will be story time."

Discouraging Statements for Teens

1. "I can't believe you have procrastinated again. What will ever become of you? Okay, I'll do it this time, but next time you'll just have to suffer the consequences."

2. "Honey, I thought you would do your homework after I bought you a car, a cell phone, and gave you a big allowance."

3. "Honey, you hurry and do as much as you can now while I pick out your clothes, and warm up the car so you won't be cold when I drive you to school."

4. "I just don't understand. I excused you from chores. I woke you up early. I drove you everywhere so you would have more time. I made your lunches. How could this be?"

5. "Okay, I'll write a note to the teacher that you were sick this morning, but you'll need to be sure and catch up."

6. "Well then, you are grounded and you lose all your privileges, no car, no video games, no friends, until it is done."

7. "Well no wonder. I saw you wasting your time on video games, and spending too much time with your friends and sleeping in.

8. You should feel ashamed of yourself. You'd better shape up or you'll be shipping out to live on the streets like a bum."

9. "How many times have I told you to get your homework done early? Why can't you be more responsible like your brother?"

Empowering Statements for Teens

1. (Curiosity questions) "What is your picture of what is going on regarding your homework? Would you be willing to hear my concerns? Could we brainstorm together on some possible solutions?"

2. (Show faith) "I can see that you feel bad about getting that poor grade. I have faith in you to learn from this and figure out what you need to do to get the grade you want."

3. (Decide what you will do and inform in advance) "I'm not willing to bail you out. When your teacher calls, I'll hand the phone to you so she can discuss it with you."

4. (Listen) "I would like to hear what this means for you."

5. (Decide what you will do and follow-through) "I'm willing to be available for an hour two nights a week when we agree in advance on a convenient time, but I'm not willing to get involved at the last minute."

6. (Share what you want and listen) "I hope you'll go to college, but I'm not sure it's important to you. I'm happy to talk with you about your thoughts or plans."

7. (Share your feelings, positive time-out, family meeting agenda) "I'm feeling too upset to talk about this right now. Let's put it on the family meeting agenda so we can talk about it when I'm not so emotional."

8. (Joint problem-solving) "Could we sit down and see if we can work on a plan regarding homework that we both can live with?"

9. (Unconditional love and acceptance) "I love you just the way you are and respect you to choose what is right for you."

Discouraging Statements Early Childhood Educators
by Laurie Prusso

1. "It is clean up time. Why are you just sitting there?"

2. "You act like this everyday! What is wrong with you?"

3. "All of your friends are able to help. I wonder if you are a baby—not a big girl?"

4. "Pick up the toys now, or you will sit on the chair instead of joining us at circle."

5. "I am going to set the timer for 3 minutes and these better be picked up when it dings."

6. "We go through this every day! I am tired of it."

7. "Why can't you just listen to me and do what I ask?"

8. "If you don't want your toys thrown away, you'd better pick them up right now!"

9. "Never mind. You can come back and pick them up later."

Empowering Statements Early Childhood Educators

1. (Show faith with a reminder of what the child/student can do.) "I have seen you pick up your toys before. I know you can do it."

2. (Curiosity question) "What ideas do you have to get the toys picked up?"

3. (Acknowledge feelings first.) "You were really having fun. It is hard to stop playing to clean up. How about I pick up the squares and you pick up the rectangles?"

4. (Check the child's understanding.) "What is supposed to be happening now?"

5. (Invite cooperation and then a limited choice.) "I need your help and you are a good helper. Do you want to pick up the red blocks or the green blocks first?"

6. (Say what you want/mean.) Get down at the child's level and with a smile, calmly say, "Sweetie, it is time to put the blocks away now."

7. (Use non-verbal language.) Put a gentle hand on his or her shoulder and then take the child by the hand and lead her to the blocks and smile with a knowing look.

8. (Give Power.) "Do you want to set the timer for how much time you think it will take to pickup your toys?"

9. (As soon as ___________.) "As soon as the toys are picked up, it will be reading time.

Teacher Discouraging Statements

1. "I can't believe you have procrastinated again. This time I'll let you turn it in tomorrow, but next time you'll just have to suffer the consequences."

2. "I'll have to call your parents about this."

3. "You can have a prize from my treasure box if you finish your work by lunch time."

4. "How many times have I told you to pay attention and get your work done? Why can't you be more like your brother?

5. "How come you always forget and never get your work done? Why can't you be more responsible?"

6. "I thought you would do your work after I was so kind to you and let you be my helper and take messages to other teachers in the building. You are so disappointing."

7. "Well, no wonder! I saw you wasting your time, looking out the window. You should feel ashamed of yourself.

8. "You are so irresponsible. You will never amount to anything in this world."

Teacher Encouraging Statements

1. "I'm available to help with homework after school on Tuesdays and Thursdays. I won't be available to help with last minute projects."

2. "Do you know that I care very deeply about you, no matter what – and that you are more important to me than your grades?"

3. "What is your picture of what is going on regarding your work? Would you be willing to hear my concerns?"

4. "Could we brainstorm together on some solutions that might be helpful to you?"

5. "Could we sit down and see if we can work on a plan regarding class work that we both can live with?"

6. "I would like to hear what this means for you. Will you share with me why it isn't important to you to do your assignments?"

7. "I feel upset when you don't do your work because I value education so much. I wish you could see the value to you in your life."

8. "I can see that you feel bad about getting that poor grade. I have faith in you to learn from this and figure out what you need to do to get the grade you would like."

Family Fun

Objective:

To plan for family fun and make a commitment to schedule quality time both for self and for family.

Materials:

Flip chart
Marking pens
Paper (8 1/2 x 11)
Pencils

Comment:

Quality time can provide a sense of well being, self-confidence, significance, and belonging for every family member.

Directions

1. Pass out paper to each participant and have them fold paper into fourths.

2. In the upper left-hand quadrant, have participants write down what they like to do or would like to do for fun by themselves that doesn't cost money. If they can't think of anything, they could think of what they liked to do as a kid for fun and write that down.

3. In the upper right-hand quadrant, have participants write down what they like to do or would like to do themselves that costs money.

4. In the lower left-hand quadrant, have participants write down fun things they like to do or would like to do with their family that doesn't cost money.

5. In the lower right-hand quadrant, have participants write down fun things they like to do or would like to do with their family that cost money.

6. Have participants form groups of four and share what they wrote in their lower left quadrant (what they like to do with their family that doesn't cost money.) Have them comment on what they notice about similarities and differences on this list.

7. If any group member heard something on another person's list that they would like to add to their list, have them do so.

8. Ask each group to decide on one thing they would like to put on their family fun calendar to do the next week.

9. Process by asking if anyone would like to share what they learned from this activity.

10. Ask how many would be willing to make a commitment to do this activity with their families at home.

Notes

Family Meetings (Short Version)

Objective:

To help families and classrooms quickly get the essence of the family/class meeting. This easy format helps solve problems and gain buy-in.

Materials:

Talking stick-or something to represent a talking stick

Notebook or paper for Agenda

Challenges and Characteristics and Life Skills lists from the Two Lists Activity.

Tips for Successful Family Meetings from 9 Steps for Effective Family Meetings Activity (handout)

Comment:

During family meetings and class meetings, children have the opportunity to develop most of the Characteristics and Life Skills parents and teachers hope for them, including a sense of belonging and the belief that they are capable. Parents have the opportunity to avoid power struggles when they invite shared problem-solving instead of lecturing and micromanaging.

Directions

1. Invite five people to make a circle (others will observe).

2. Pick a topic either from the agenda or by asking who has a problem they'd like help with

3. Use a talking stick

4. Ask the person who has the problem to start by holding the talking stick and stating the problem.

5. Pass the talking stick around the circle two times. No one can talk unless it is their turn to hold the talking stick. When they have the talking stick, they can say whatever they think and feel about the problem.

6. After two times around the circle, the parent/teacher either suggests to leave the item on the agenda for another week or to problem solve.

7. If the choice is problem solve, again, pass the talking stick around two times so folks can give suggestions which one of the members writes down.

8. Pick a suggestion to try for one week.

9. Process by asking everyone what they were thinking, feeling, and deciding.

10. Ask participants to look at the Characteristics and Life Skills list and share if they were learning any of them during this family meeting.

11. Invite participants to share what they learned from participating in or observing the demonstration

EXTENSION:

1. Ask group to form groups of three to five.

2. Allow 5 to 8 minutes for them to practice the steps that were demonstrated.

3. Process as per 9-11 above.

9 Steps for Effective Family Meetings

Objective:

To provide practice using the 9 Steps for Effective Family Meetings.

To help parents understand that there is no such thing as a perfect family meeting, and that practice makes better.

Materials:

Talking stick-(or something to represent a talking stick) for each group of 4

Notebook (or paper for Agenda) for each group of 4

Challenges and Characteristics and Life Skills lists from the Two Lists Activity.

9 Steps for Effective Family Meetings and Tips for Successful Family Meetings (back to back handout) for every one.

Comment:

During family meetings children have the opportunity to develop most of the Characteristics and Life Skills parents hope for them, including a sense of belonging and the belief that they are capable. Parents have the opportunity to avoid power struggles and model the characteristics and life skills they hope their children will develop when they invite shared problem-solving instead of lecturing and micromanaging.

Directions

1. Pass out the Tips for Successful Family Meetings and Cautions and invite participants to take turns reading the Tips and the Cautions.

2. Divide into groups of four (one or two groups can include 3 if not enough people to make groups of four) and ask them to decide who will play different roles in their family (two co-parents and two children, 1 parent and 3 children, etc.). The children should be at least 4-years-old and older.

3. Have them turn over the handout to the *9 Steps for Effective Family Meetings* so they can follow along.

4. Provide a "talking stick" and an "agenda" to a parent in each group and ask him or her to go through all of the *9 Steps*—reading each one as though they are in a family meeting, and then doing what the step says to do. (If the children are old enough, an option is to have them take turns reading the steps and then doing what each step says to do.) Allow about 15 minutes.

5. When time is up, ask if anyone would like to share what went on in their family meeting—successes/challenges.

6. Then process with those who role-played kids what they were thinking, feeling, and deciding during the family meeting. Point to the Characteristics and Life Skills list and ask them if they can find things that they were learning. (Usually most of them)

7. Ask the parents what they were thinking, feeling and deciding. Point to the Modeling list and ask them if they can find things that they were teaching.

8. Ask all participants to share what they learned from this activity. (See Facilitators Note below for answers to some typical questions.)

FACILITATORS NOTE:

Instead of answering questions immediately, first ask the rest of the group what they think. If they don't come up with a point that needs to be made, you can then make it. Some of the most common questions:

Q: *What if my spouse can't attend?*

A: Call it a problem-solving session instead of a family meeting.

Q: *What if a child refuses to give a compliment?*

A: Say, "Okay. Maybe you'll want to next time," and continue on around the circle.

ALTERNATE:

9. Ask for four people to demonstrate a family meeting using the 9 Steps for Effective Family Meetings in front of the rest of the group.

10. Interrupt and coach as needed if they miss any of the steps or don't heed the 5 cautions.

11. Process by going though steps 4 through 8 above.

9 Steps for Effective Family Meetings

1. **Introduction:** "We are going to have our first family meeting. We will read these steps and practice each one until we all know them well enough to have family meetings without reading them."

2. **Talking stick:** "This item will be passed around to help everyone remember that only one person can talk at a time, and that everyone gets a turn. Who would like to start with No. 3?" (If children are old enough they can take turns reading the steps.)

3. **Compliments or appreciations:** "Each of us will share one thing we appreciate about each member of the family. I will start. I would like to compliment ____________ for ______________." (Give each family member a compliment, and then have them all do the same.)

4. **Family meeting agenda:** "The agenda will be placed on the refrigerator so every one can write down problems during the week. You'll notice that **everyone not being dressed and ready to go when it is time to leave in the morning** is on the agenda for us to practice problem-solving."

5. **Teach about Focusing on Solutions and Brainstorming:** "Brainstorming means thinking of as many solutions as we can. All ideas are okay (even funny ideas). We will write down every idea without discussion. Let's practice with this problem. Who would like to be our scribe and write down every suggestion?" (If your children aren't old enough, you can take this job.)

6. **Encourage the children to go first:** "Who would like to start with some wild and crazy ideas?" (If no one speaks up, you might need to get them started with some wild and some practical ideas by saying, "What about leaving in our pajamas, or those who aren't ready can walk?" Allow for silence. If someone objects to any ideas, say, "For now we are just brainstorming for solutions. All ideas will be written down." (Be sure you have at least 4 suggestions. 6 are even better.)

7. **Use the 3 R's and an H to assess proposed solutions:** Encouraging solutions must be (1) Related, (2) Reasonable, (3) Respectful, and, (4) Helpful. "Who can see any solutions we need to eliminate because they are not related, reasonable, respectful, or helpful? Our scribe can cross them off after we discuss why."

8. **Choosing the solution:** "Do we want to narrow it to one solution that we can all agree to, or try more than one? We can evaluate how the solution or solutions worked during our next meeting in one week."

9. **Fun activity:** "We will take turns choosing an activity for the end of each family meeting. For tonight I've chosen Charades. Who will volunteer to decide the fun activity for next week?"

TIPS FOR SUCCESSFUL FAMILY MEETINGS

1. Remember the long-term purpose of family meetings: To teach valuable life skills.

2. Have all family members sit around a table (not during a meal time) or in another comfortable space where they can all see each other.

3. Post an agenda where family members can write their concerns or problems.

4. Start with compliments to set the tone by verbalizing positive things about each other.

5. Focus on solutions, not blame.

6. Teach children about brainstorming: Brainstorming means we think of all the possible solutions we could use to solve this challenge. It is okay to have fun and suggest wild and crazy ideas. During the brainstorming time all ideas are okay. We will write down every suggestion without discussion. When we are finished brainstorming we will choose one we can all agree with because it is practical and respectful to everyone.

7. Have fun. Some suggestions can be silly or outrageous.

8. Choose one suggestion (by consensus) that is practical and respectful to everyone and try it for a week. (Or, if several suggestions might work, let each person choose which one he or she would like to use.)

9. When consensus can't be reached (and it is practical to use only one suggestion), table that item for more discussion next week.

10. Calendar a family fun activity for later in the week—and all sports and other activities (including a schedule who need rides where and when).

11. Keep family meetings short,10 to 30 minutes, depending on the ages of your children.

12. End with a family fun activity, game, or dessert.

13. MISTAKES ARE WONDERFUL OPPORTUNITIES TO LEARN.

CAUTIONS

14. AVOID using family meetings as a platform for lectures and parental control.

15. DON'T expect perfection. Celebrate improvement.

16. LEARNING SKILLS TAKES TIME. You wouldn't expect children to learn to read in a day, a week, or a month. Family members need time to learn cooperation and problem solving skills. Even solutions that don't work provide an opportunity to learn and try again to focus on respectful solutions.

17. UNDERSTAND DEVELOPMENTAL READINESS. Children under the age of four may not be developmentally ready to participate in family meetings, but may be content to do a quiet activity such as drawing. If younger children are too distracting, wait until they are asleep.

18. AVOID SKIPPING REGULAR, WEEKLY FAMILY MEETINGS. **Make them the most important date on your calendar.**

Family Work—Whose Job is It?

Objective:

To provide ideas for encouraging children to cooperate in family work.

Materials:

Two paper plates
One brad
Scissors
Colored pen per group

Comment:

Family work is an excellent medium for building relationships and increasing your child's sense of self-esteem through a strong sense of belonging.

Directions

1. Introduce the idea that what's important about family work is working together and building character. The quality of the work is not essential with young, new, or inexperienced workers–their effort is.

2. Explain the steps for training new workers:

   a. First work with them.

   b. Work near them. You work in one area of the room, the child works in another.

   c. Be nearby if needed but not in the same room.

3. Have the group divide into triads. Ask one person to teach the other two how to play pat-a-cake using 2-a through 2-c above.

4. Discuss, "With this experience, what jobs at home can you teach your child to do this way?"

EXPANDED VERSION:

In addition to the above:

5. Brainstorm a list of specific household jobs and have a volunteer record them on a flip chart.

6. Divide the group into fours.

7. Describe the work wheel from a sample. Ask each group to make one per the following instructions:

    a. On the first paper plate, draw lines to divide it like a pie into the number of people in your family. Put one person's name on the top of each divided area.

    b. Cut the rim off of the second paper plate. Divide it the same way as the larger paper plate. In these divisions, take a picture of your child doing the job and paste it onto the plate or simply write the name of the job that any and all members of the family can do.

    c. Attach the plates together with the smaller job plate on top. Press the brad through the center of both plates.

To use: the center wheel is rotated to align a job with a different person's name. The family decides how often the jobs will be changed, daily or once a week.

Feelings: Using them Effectively

Objective:

To go beyond your feelings to find out what you want and how to accomplish what you want in healthy, effective ways.

Materials:

Paper
Pencils
Flip chart
Marking pens
Emotional Honesty handout
"Feeling Faces" handout (in handouts section) for each participant

Comment:

Feelings are emotional responses to a grievance, as well as being diagnostic tools. They give you valuable information about yourself and what's going on around you. When you learn to listen to your feelings and know the names of the feelings you experience, you are taking the first step toward having control over your feelings instead of them controlling you. You can learn to act instead of react, finding more choices in your life.

Directions

1. Have participants write down three feelings they felt today. (refer to feeling faces handout.)

    Today (or recently) I felt

    a. ________________
    b. ________________
    c. ________________

2. Have participants identify: "What do I usually do when I feel this way?"

    a. When I feel ______________ I usually do this:________________

    b. When I feel ______________ I usually do this:________________

    c. When I feel ______________ I usually do this:________________

3.　Have participants identify: "How would I rather feel?" and/or "What do I want?"

　　　I would rather feel _______________________ and/or I want _______________

　　　I would rather feel _______________________ and/or I want _______________

　　　I would rather feel _______________________ and/or I want _______________

4.　Have participants turn to their partners and share steps 1, 2, and 3, keeping in mind: "Does what I usually do get in the way of what I want?"

　　　(The following example is for the facilitator to use only if there are questions from participants about how to complete a cycle from 1 through 3.)

　　　"When I feel angry toward my son for leaving his dishes in the den,

　　　I usually yell at him to, "Get up out of that chair and stop being so lazy–take those dishes to the sink and wash them up right now."

　　　I would rather be in control of my feelings and calmly remind my son of my expectations of his responsibility. That would be much more effective than losing it! I could even ask him, "What would help you remember to take care of your dirty dishes?"

5.　Have partners brainstorm other ways to behave that could help them get the desired results

6.　Discuss, "What was learned through this activity?"

EXPANDED VERSION:

In addition to the above:

7.　Between steps 4 and 5 make a list of options on the board with the group offering ideas under the following captions:

　　　1. Feeling　　　　　　　　　　　　　　2. Usual behavior

　　　3. How I'd rather feel　　　　　　　　　4. Another behavior

　　　5. What I want:

Comment:

It is important to know how we feel without expecting anyone else to feel the same, and to say what we wish or want without expecting anyone to give us our wishes. It is also important to practice feeling our feelings and listening to others express their feelings without thinking we have to fix them. An excellent follow-up activity to this exercise is the "I Feel Process: Emotional Honesty".

---

　　　　　　　　　　　　　　　　　　　　　　　www.positivediscipline.com

Emotional Honesty

Lynn Lott

Emotional honesty is a skill. It can be learned. First, is the emotional part. That means feelings. Feelings are those things that happen inside of us. There are words for feelings, usually one word long. Feeling words sound like "happy," "comfortable," "hungry," "sleepy," "angry," "sad" "hopeless," "irritated," "joyful," etc. They are not words such as "like," "as if," "you," "that," etc. Feelings describe something that is going on inside of us and is information about us. Feelings aren't judgments about others and are different from thoughts. Feelings aren't good or bad, right or wrong, proper or improper. Feelings aren't logical. Feelings aren't actions or behaviors. The feeling of anger or hunger or tired or happy is very different from a display of anger, hunger, tired, or happy. We cannot tell how a person is feeling just from observing his/her behavior. People can smile when they feel angry, eat when they're not hungry, sleep when they're bored and cry from happiness. To really know someone's feelings we must ask him/her tell us. Or we can make guesses out loud about how a person is feeling and he or she can confirm or deny it.

The second part of emotional honesty is the word honesty. Once we know there are feelings, that they are inside of us and that there are words for the feeling, we need to communicate the feeling to those around us. This can be very frightening to do. When we communicate feelings, we are vulnerable, and people around us are not always well-trained and sensitive to listen to feelings without taking them personally or explaining them away or correcting them. It's still worth the risk, for without emotional honesty, there is very little self-acceptance, acceptance of others or growth.

Emotional honesty works two ways. We are emotionally honest when we communicate our feelings and we are emotionally honest when we hear another's feelings without judging, criticizing, fixing, or defending. A family meeting without emotional honesty can be like a grenade ready to go off if someone accidentally steps on it. When I'm emotionally honest, I'm always worried about hurting someone else's feelings, but what I notice is that it usually has the opposite effect. It opens communication and invites closeness.

My emotional honesty takes the stress and tension out of a situation instead of putting them into one. For instance, at one of our family meetings I shared how torn I felt about parenting. On the one hand, I enjoyed not having kids living with us and felt relaxed and comfortable with my physical setting when I could count on it to be neat and clean. I liked coming home from an out-of-town trip and not having to deal with anyone's needs other than my own. I was angry about missing tapes and CD's, spots on the carpet, broken items, and dirty dishes. I liked being a "Disneyland" parent who could be with the kids on vacations and special occasions and come home to a childless house most of the time. I was done raising kids on a day-to-day basis. On the other hand I loved my stepson. I had invited him to live with us and wanted him to be part of our family. I felt good being together much of the time and took great pleasure watching his relationship with his dad blossom. I appreciated all his help and his good-natured attitude. I wasn't thinking of asking him to leave, but I was feeling stuck in my own mixed feelings. I was worried that after sharing all this, my stepson would feel unwanted, that my husband would feel torn and think he had to choose between us, and that they both would think I was petty and selfish. What happened was what almost always happens. They both were grinning and thanking me for telling them how I really felt. My stepson said, "I had no idea you felt that way and I really care about how you feel about things." There was a release of tension in the house for weeks after this meeting. What I've noticed is that quite often when one of us is emotionally honest we don't have to move into a problem solving mode because the problem takes care of itself when the issues are out on the table.

Notes

Fighting Kids and the 3 B's

Objective:

To help parents understand how important it is to put kids in the same boat (treat them the same) instead of taking sides.

To understand possible beliefs kids might form as a result of ineffective interference in their fights.

To provide alternative tools to use when children fight.

Materials:

A chart of "The Three B's"
 Beat it
 Bear it
 Boot 'em out

A chime or a bell to signal for attention

Characteristics and Life Skills list and Challenges list from Two Lists activity

Comment:

Parents encourage sibling rivalry when they decide which child is to blame for the fight, or when they take responsibility to resolve the fight. Taking sides can actually intensify sibling rivalry and invite children to assume the roles of victim and bully.

Directions

1. Keep the chart of the 3 B's hidden until later.

2. Ask the group to divide into groups of three. Within their groups, have them decide who will be the parent and who will be the two children, and which child will be the oldest and the youngest. Then have the kids stay in the middle of the room and the parents come to the front part of the room.

3. Explain to the "kids" (in front of the whole group) that they will engage in a VERBAL fight when you tell them to start fighting.

4. Explain to the "parents" (in front of the whole group) that when you give a signal (a bell or a simple wave of your hand), they will step in to break up the fight—blaming and scolding the oldest.

Facilitator's Note:

The reason for explaining the roles in front of everyone is that the kids already know what is going on. The role-plays will simply emphasize what everyone is thinking feeling and deciding.

---

5. Give a signal for the kids to start fighting.

    - Wait about 10 to 20 seconds before giving the parents a signal to step in and break up the fight, scolding the oldest.

    - Wait 10 to 20 seconds before ringing the chime (or clapping your hands) to signal that they should stop fighting and the parents should come back to the outer part of the room.

    - Repeat two more times: asking the children to start fighting, signaling the parents to step in and break up the fight (picking on the oldest), and ringing the bell for them to stop. (Note: Some facilitators wonder why this should be done three times. It is to help participants experience what children think, feel, and decide when this happens over and over in their lives.)

6. Process by first asking the children what they were thinking, feeling, and deciding. Also ask what they are learning about fighting. Then point to the Characteristics and Life Skills list to see if they are learning anything on the list. Then point to the Challenges list and ask if they are deciding to do any of these.

7. Then ask the parents what they were thinking, feeling, and deciding.

8. Now tell the parents you are taking them to a Positive Discipline Parenting class (at the front of the room), while the children listen in.

9. An alternative is to have a volunteer take the children outside the room while you take the parents to parenting class. The advantage of allowing them to stay in the room is equivalent to "letting kids know in advance" what you are going to do.

10. Show parents the "The Three Bs" chart. Describe these three tools for dealing with fighting to avoid teaching children to become victims or bullies. (They are engaging in victim/bully training when they blame the oldest and "rescue" the youngest.)

    - Beat It (The parent makes sure the children see him or her and then leaves.)

    - Bear It (The parent stays and observes, but doesn't get involved no matter what.)

    - Boot 'Em Out (The parent removes both children from the scene while treating them the same. "If you want to fight, you need to go outside," or, "You can go to separate rooms until you are ready to stop fighting," or, "Go to another room together and come out when you have solved the problem and are ready to stop fighting."

11. Ask each "parent" to choose one of "The Three Bs" to deal with the fight. Ask for a show of hands regarding who is doing each "B" to make sure all are covered. (If the kids are still in the room, they will know what their parent is going to do.)

12. If the kids were sent out, have a volunteer to bring them back in. Ask the kids to start fighting again. Give the parents the signal to move in and use whatever "B" they chose.

13. Tell the kids to start fighting. After about 20 seconds of the parents role-playing whichever "B" they are using, ring a bell to gain their attention. Process by asking the kids first, what they were thinking, feeling, and deciding. Also ask them what they were learning about fighting. Again point to the Characteristics and Life Skills to ask if they are learning any of them.

14. Then ask the parents what they were thinking, feeling, and deciding during the role-play—and what they were teaching about fighting.

15. Point out that the 3 Bs are not the only ways to deal with fights. Invite participants to brainstorm other Positive Discipline tools that might be even more effective for dealing with sibling fights. (Or, let them know they will be learning many alternatives to dealing with fights such as putting the problem on the family meeting agenda, the wheel of choice, or just plain focusing on solutions, etc.) Also see Fighting, Family Meetings, and Focusing on Solutions in Positive Discipline A-Z.

16. Invite a discussion from the whole group about what they learned from this activity.

Comment:

Parents may not realize how they teach the opposite of what they want (love and peace) when they label one child as the bully and another child learns to feel special by being a victim. Often they don't see how the "victim" starts the fight.

Not getting involved in fights is not the same as abandonment. Occasionally adults have memories of their own parents just leaving them at the mercy of their violent siblings. That is not what we are advocating. It is the parent's job to teach that hurting other people is not okay. This is done most effectively by using some of the alternatives mentioned in No. 16 above.

Notes

Follow-Through After Agreements

Objective:

To give parents an alternative to punishment and logical consequences by involving kids in agreements and then taking responsibility for kind and firm follow through.

Materials:

Follow Through Steps Charts (see below) on three separate flip charts.

Characteristics and Life Skills List from the Two Lists Activity.

Comment:

Parents usually try to disguise punishment by calling it a "logical consequence". Children aren't fooled and rebel or comply—but they don't learn the Characteristics and Life Skills parents hope for. These three sets of steps for effective follow-through provide an alternative to avoid this dilemma. With younger children (0-3), non-verbal, kind and firm follow through is more effective.

Directions

1. Start this activity as a demonstration/role-play between you and a volunteer.

2. Ask for a volunteer to play a child who doesn't keep his or her promises (to unload the dishwasher, do his or homework, feed the dog, clean up messes, etc.). Ask the "volunteer child" to decide which of these challenges you will work on together.

3. Display the Four Steps for Respectful Agreements. Scene One: Role-play the first three of these steps as follows:

    For Step 1, Ask the volunteer to share his or her thoughts and feelings around this issue. For your issue, explain: "You have reassured me that you mean to do it, but just forget. I understand and will help in the future by following through on whatever we decide."

    Step 2: Brainstorm solutions including exaggerations, such as paying for someone else to do it—which he or she will pay for." (Have a scribe record what you brainstorm).

    Step 3: Decide together which one solution to try.

    Read Step 4 to the group and let them know that in Scene 2, you will role-play what happens when the child doesn't keep his or her agreement.

4. To set up the role-play let the child know that he or she is now sitting on the couch watching TV at the agreed upon time instead of doing the task. Then you enter the scene and role-play the Four Hints for Effective Follow-Through (but don't show the steps until later). We have never seen it fail that the child decides to keep his or her agreement IF you stick to the steps.

5. After the role-play, display the Four Hints for Effective Follow-Through to show what you did. Others will doubt this will work with their children. To demonstrate why it worked, display the Four Traps that Defeat Follow-Through. Process with the volunteer child by asking him or her if you avoided these traps. For example, "How high on your priority list is unloading the dishwasher?" (Usually not on the list.) "Did you feel any criticism or judgment from me?" "Did I stick to the issue?" "How important was it that you knew we had agreed to a specific time in advance?" "Did you think I maintained dignity and respect for you, for myself, and for what needed to be done?"

6. Take the child to the Characteristics and Life Skills list and ask him or her if there is anything on the list that he learned from this interaction. (Usually many of them.)

7. Invite participants to share what they learned from watching this demo.

Extension:

1. Ask participants to find a partner and choose a situation where their child does not keep agreements, such as mowing the lawn, cleaning up messes, doing laundry, homework, etc. Ask one to role-play a child and one to role-play a parent.

2. Display the chart on the **Four Steps for Effective Follow-Through**. Ask them to role-play a scene where they use the first three steps and come to an agreement. Allow around three to five minutes for this process. Then explain the next round.

3. Share how normal it is that children are willing to make an agreement during a friendly discussion. However it is also normal for children not to keep the agreement. Display the **Four Hints for Effective Follow-Through** chart. For scene two. Ask role-players to pretend that the specific time for the agreement to be completed has arrived and their child is parked in front of the television. The person playing the parent will come into the room and approach the child using these steps. Allow about one or two minutes.

4. Process with both children and parents what they are thinking, feeling, and deciding.

5. Display the chart of the **Four Traps that Defeat Effective Follow-Through** and ask the children if their parents avoided all of these traps.

6. Show the Characteristics and Life Skills list to the "children" and ask if they can find things on the list that they were learning.

7. Remind parents that agreements rarely work without follow-through, and it is their job to follow through. Some will object that they want their kids to be responsible without reminders. Assure them that this will magically happen by the time they are parents—just as it did for them.

8. Ask the participants what they learned from this activity

Four Steps for Respectful Agreements

1. Have a friendly discussion where everyone gets to voice his or her feelings and thoughts around the issue.

2. Brainstorm for possible solutions and choose one that both you and your child agree to.

3. Agree on a specific time deadline (to the minute).

4. Understand children well enough to know that the deadline probably won't be met and simply follow through with your part of the agreement by holding them accountable.

Four Hints for Effective Follow-Through

1. Keep comments simple and concise. "I notice you didn't mow the lawn. Please do that now."

2. In response to objections, ask, "What was our agreement?"

3. In response to further objections, shut your mouth and use nonverbal communication. Point to your watch. Smile knowingly. Give a hug and point to your watch again.

4. When the child concedes to keep the agreement (sometimes obviously annoyed) say, "Thank you for keeping our agreement."

Four Traps that Defeat Effective Follow-Through

1. Wanting children to have the same priorities as adults.

2. Getting into judgments and criticism instead of sticking to the issue.

3. Not getting agreements in advance that include a specific time deadline.

4. Not maintaining dignity and respect for the child and yourself.

Notes

Food Problems with Kids

Objective:

To learn alternatives to badgering so mealtime can be fun.

Materials:

Chart on "Alternative Ideas to Badgering" below

Comment:

What would it be like if you treated dinner guests the way you treat your children? Eating disorders can be caused by parents.

Directions

1. Role-play "adults for dinner." Have two volunteers from the group be a couple coming to dinner. Have a spouse who has been instructed to treat the guests like some people do their children: "Eat all your vegetables or no dessert.""Are your hands washed?""Don't forget to use your napkin""Don't chew with your mouth open.""Just take one bite.""Do you want some potatoes? Are you sure? Wouldn't you like just a little bit?""I worked so hard on this meal and will be very upset if you don't eat it!""Would anyone like me to make them something different if you don't like what I've made?"

2. Process: What were people thinking, feeling, and deciding?

3. Discuss ways we badger our kids about food/eating/mealtimes.

4. Introduce the chart on "Alternative Ideas to Badgering."

Alternative Ideas to Badgering

Each person serves him/herself, eats what he/she wants and doesn't eat what he/she doesn't want.

Dinner conversation can be about anything other than food.

When children get up from the table, parent clears their plates without saying a word.

EXPANDED VERSION:

In addition to the above:

5. Add role-plays to the discussion in step 3 and process thoughts, feelings, and decisions.

6. Ask group members what they learned.

Notes

Four R's of Recovery from Mistakes

Objective:

To learn a process that illustrates that mistakes are learning opportunities.

Materials:

"Four R's of Recovery" handout for each participant.

Flip chart listing the Four R's of Recovery (without the details)

Characteristics and Life Skills list and Challenges list from the Two Lists activity.

Comment:

Using the "Four R's of Recovery" is a great way to create a connection before correction, and can make your relationships with your children better than it was before the mistake.

Directions

1. Ask participants to find a partner.

2. Ask them to describe to their partner a situation when they were disrespectful to their child so the partner can role-play the part of the child.

3. Scene I. Let them know they will each have 60 seconds or less to role-play the mistake they made, while the child notices what he/she is thinking feeling and deciding.

4. After 60 seconds ask them to switch roles.

5. Allow another 60 seconds and ask them to stop. Process by asking the children what they were thinking, feeling, and deciding.

6. Point to the Characteristics and Life Skills list and ask the children if they can find anything on the list that they are learning. (Probably none of them.)

7. Point to the Challenges list and ask if the children are feeling motivated to do any of them. (They will probably list several.)

8. Process with the parents what they were thinking, feeling, and deciding.

9. Scene II. Role-play the "Four R's of Recovery" as described on your handout: (Use the suggested words or your own.)

10. Allow about 60 seconds for each partner to role-play. Let them know when it's time to switch.

11.   Process by asking the children what they were thinking, feeling, and deciding.

12.   Point to the Characteristics and Life Skills list and ask the children if they can find anything on the list that they are learning. (Probably many of them.)

13.   Process with the parents what they were thinking, feeling, and deciding.

14.   Invite participants to share what they learned from this activity.

Four R's of Recovery From Mistakes (Handout)

1. Recognize that you made a mistake:

Share your part of the mistake with your child. (Avoid blame or guilt and focus on what you can learn from it.)

2. Responsibility:

Be specific in taking responsibility for your part: "I yelled at you instead of telling you my feelings."

3. Reconcile:

Apologize. Children are so forgiving when you let them know you are sorry.

4. Resolve by focusing on solutions:

Brainstorm for an agreement that will be respectful to fix the problem or prevent it in the future such as:

"I would appreciate your help finding a solution to this problem."

If one or both of you isn't ready, "Could we make an appointment to work together on a solution when we feel better?"

"What could I do that would be helpful to you now?"

"Could we choose a Positive Discipline tool card and see if we pick one that would work for us?

Iceberg Activity
From Discouragement to Encouragement

Objective:

To help parents comprehend the deeper purpose of misbehavior (expressions of discouragement), and how to use encouragement to motivate emotionally healthy behavior. To explore the Mistaken Goal Chart, the Jungle, and Encouragement in one activity.

Comment:

Positive Discipline is based on an encouragement model instead of medical model. A medical model asks, "What causes this behavior," and looks for an illness, a label, a disease—and a pill to fix the problem. An encouragement model asks, "What is the purpose of this behavior, and how can we use encouragement to change the purpose?"

The purpose of the misbehavior is almost always a mistaken way to find belonging and significance. When children feel discouraged about belonging and significance, they find mistaken ways (misbehavior) to seek belonging.

Positive Discipline teaches adults how to respond to the belief below the surface of the behavior to invite behavior change through connection, encouragement, and capability skills that invites children to seek belonging through socially acceptable ways.

Materials:

"Characteristics and Life Skills" and "Challenges" lists from Two Lists Activity.

A Mistaken Goal Chart for each person.

A hat to represent each mistaken goal (per Read My Hat Activity) or costume glasses to represent each mistaken goal

Iceberg Posters for each goal (From the Iceberg Deep activity), enlarged to 11"x 17".

Small sticky note strips packets, in four colors.

Encouragement Statements (for each mistaken goal-from the Iceberg Deep activity): laminated, cut into strips, and saved in appropriately labeled envelopes.

Pencils or pens for each group.

A copy of "Group Instructions" for each group (4).

Six sturdy chairs. (Or fewer if the groups are smaller and some "adults" will be making more than one statement, for a total of six encouragement statements.)

All Encouraging Statements on one page as a handout from Iceberg Deep activity.

Group Instructions for Iceberg Activity

Choose one person in your group to read these instructions.

Give every one in your group a few sticky notes.

Ask each member of your group to write on the sticky notes behaviors kids do that invite them to feel the feelings listed in column 2 of the Mistaken Goal Chart (MGC) for the Mistaken Goal you are assigned.

Paste the sticky notes on the tip part of the Iceberg Poster.

Prepare to do the following role-play in front of the large group:

Choose one person in your group to role-play a child (who has the belief described in column 5), and has been engaging in one of the behaviors listed on the sticky notes.

Choose up to six people to role-play adults who will stand on chairs and "react" (based on their feelings in Column 2) to any of the behaviors written on the sticky notes. (Check Column 3 of the Mistaken Goal Chart for clues for what the reaction might look like, but it is okay to use your own imagination.)

Note: There is no need to practice in your small group. Once you have some idea of what you are going to do and say it is okay to be spontaneous, exaggerate, and have fun, while role-playing in front of the large group.

When you role-play in front of the group, the "child" will put on the hat or wear the glasses, hold the Iceberg Poster at chest level, walk down the line of adults standing on the chairs, pausing in front of each one to listen to the adult "react". The child will not react back verbally (body language is okay) and will notice what he or she is thinking, feeling, and deciding.

The workshop facilitator will process what each is thinking, feeling, and deciding, starting with the child, and will then proceed to Part 2 of the role-play with your group.

Directions

Part One:

1. Display the "Behavior" iceberg poster and point out that most adults react to the behavior, which is only the tip of the iceberg. The base of the iceberg (much larger than the tip) represents the goal of the behavior (based upon the "mistaken" belief of how to find belonging). This activity teaches adults how to respond to the belief below the surface of the behavior to invite behavior change through encouragement: connection, and teaching capability skills.

2. Divide into four groups—one for each Mistaken Goal: Undue Attention, Misguided Power, Revenge, and Assumed Inadequacy. (If you have a smaller groups, divide into two groups and have each group work on two Mistaken Goals, or have the whole group do one Mistaken Goal a week.)

3. Give each group:

    a. The iceberg poster representing the Mistaken Goal assigned to them.
    b. A Mistaken Goal Chart for each person.
    c. Mistaken goal hat or costume glasses for their mistaken goal.
    d. A packet of small sticky note strips (a different color for each group)

e.   Pens or pencils.

f.   A copy of the "Group Instructions" (previous page). Do not give out Encouragement Statements yet. They will be given out for Part Two.

4.   Let them know they will have 5-7 minutes to prepare Scene One per the "Group Instructions". (See below to make a copy for each group that can be read aloud by one volunteer in their group.)

5.   While the groups are preparing, line up some chairs in the middle of the room (up to 6 for the "adults" in the groups).

6.   Visit each group to see how they are doing and to coach if they have questions.

7.   When the preparation time is up, ask which group would like to go first. Ask the adults to stand on the chairs if they are comfortable doing so. (Ask for "spotters" from the group to help them get up and down.)

8.   Ask the child to wear the hat or glasses, and to hold the Iceberg Poster at chest level, and stand in front of the first adult and listen to the statement (without saying a word—just noticing what he or she is thinking, feeling, and deciding), and then to proceed down the line while the adults make the "reaction" statements they have prepared.

9.   Process with the child what he or she was thinking, feeling, and deciding.

10. Take the child to the list of Characteristics and Life Skills from the Two Lists Activity, and ask if her or she learned anything from the discouraging statements (probably not). Take the child to the "Challenges" list and ask if he/she is feeling inspired to do any of these. (Usually several)

11. Invite the adults to step down from the chairs. Process with the adults what they were thinking, feeling, and deciding during the role-play.

Part Two:

12. Ask the adults to remain standing on the floor and pass out the laminated strips of Encouraging Statements (if the group is small, some may have more than one).

13. Have the child move down the line again, standing in front of each adult long enough to hear the encouraging statement while noticing what he or she is thinking, feeling, and deciding. (If adults have more than one encouraging statement, the child will go down the line again.)

14. Process with the child what he or she was thinking, feeling, and deciding. Take the child to the list of Characteristics and Life Skills and ask if he or she learned anything on the list from the experience of hearing the encouraging statements. (Usually many)

15. Process with the parents or teachers what they were thinking, feeling, and deciding during this part of the role-play.

16. Repeat for each mistaken goal group.

17. Invite the whole group to share what they learned from this activity.

18. Pass out the handout of combined Encouraging Statements, and remind the participants that when we switch from reactive behavior to thoughtful behavior, it takes time and we often need to start with a script.

Notes

Iceberg Deep
Mistaken Goal Encouragement

Objective:

To help parents comprehend the deeper purpose of misbehavior, and how to use encouragement for each of the Four Mistaken Goals. This activity is a condensed version of the Iceberg Activity and can stand alone or be used as part of the Alternate part of The Jungle

Materials:

"Characteristics and Life Skills" and "Challenges" lists from Two Lists Activity.

Party glasses to represent each mistaken goal (per Read My Hat Activity)

Iceberg Posters for each goal (see following pages), enlarged to 11" x 17".

Encouragement Statements (for each mistaken goal): laminated, cut into strips, and saved in appropriately labeled envelopes.

All Encouraging Statements on one page as a handout at the end of the activity.

Comment:

The purpose of misbehavior is almost always a mistaken way to find belonging and significance. When children feel discouraged about belonging and and not feeling capable, they find mistaken ways (misbehavior) to seek belonging.

Positive Discipline teaches adults how to **respond** to the belief below the surface of the behavior and to invite behavior change through connection and encouragement that invites children to seek belonging through socially acceptable ways.

Directions

1. Display the "Behavior" iceberg poster and point out that most parents **react** to the behavior, which is only the tip of the iceberg. The base of the iceberg (much larger than the tip) represents the goal of the behavior (based upon the "mistaken" belief of how to find belonging). This activity provides **responses** to the belief below the surface of the behavior to invite behavior change through encouragement.

2. Invite four participants to role-play children. One will play a child with the mistaken goal of undue attention, one will play misguided power, one will play revenge, and one will play assumed inadequacy. Give each the appropriate Mistaken Goal party glasses.

3. Invite 6 people to role-play parents. Ask them to stand in a line and give them the six laminated encouraging statements for Undue Attention.

4. Ask the child who is playing Undue Attention to pretend he can't do his homework even though he knows he can, but just wants attention. This child (wearing the glasses that represent Undue Attention) will stand in front of each of the six parents and listen to their statements, without responding verbally, but noticing what he/she is thinking, feeling and deciding.

5. Process with the child what he or she was thinking, feeling, and deciding. Take the child to the list of Characteristics and Life Skills and ask if he or she learned anything on the list from the experience of hearing the encouraging statements. (Usually many)

6. Ask the child who is playing Assumed Inadequacy to go next and pretend he can't do this homework, and really believes he can't. (By following Undue Attention, observers and participants are invited to notice the difference when the same behavior is displayed based on different beliefs.) Pass out the encouragement statements for Assumed Inadequacy to the six parents and have the child stand in front of each one and listen to their statements.

7. Process as above. Then pass out the encouraging statements for Misguided Power to the parents.

8. Ask the child who is playing Misguided Power to assume an attitude of "You can't make me" and to go the parents and listen to the encouraging statements.

9. Process as above. Then pass out the encouraging statements for Revenge to the parents.

10. Ask the child who is playing Revenge to assume the attitude of, "I feel hurt and want to hurt back" and go to each parent and listen to the encouraging statements. Process as above.

11. Process with the parents what they were thinking, feeling, and deciding during each of the role-plays.

12. Invite the whole group to share what they were thinking, feeling, and deciding while they observed, and what they learned from this activity.

13. Pass out the handout of combined Encouraging Statements, and remind the participants that it takes time to switch from reactive behavior to thoughtful behavior, and we often need to start with a script.

Parent's Encouraging Statements
Undue Attention

1. **Would you be willing to use this timer to time me for three minutes on the phone?**

2. **Let's make a deal. How about you get your homework done and we can hang out for a few minutes after dinner.**

3. **I'm busy now and I'm looking forward to our special time later.**

4. **Thanks for helping. I appreciate it.**

5. **I know it can be hard to wait without interrupting, and I notice you are being more patient.**

6. **I hear you, and I look forward to connecting with you as soon as I can.**

Encouraging Statements
Power

1. **I need your help. What ideas do you have to solve this problem?**

2. **What is your understanding of our agreement?**

3. **I think we are in a power struggle. Let's take some time to calm down and then start over.**

4. **You are making some good points. It will be easier to listen when we are both calmer.**

5. **I need your help and could really use your brain power.**

6. **What would help you the most—to put this challenge on the family meeting agenda, or to find a solution on the Wheel of Choice?**

Encouraging Statements
Revenge

1. **When you hurt me or others, I know you are hurting. I'm so sorry.**

2. **No wonder you are upset. You always get in trouble, and others walk away without getting caught.**

3. **Why don't we both take a break, cool off, and then come back and try again.**

4. **When you hurt others, I wonder what you feel hurt about. Want to talk about it now–or later?**

5. **Looks like you are having a rough time right now. I want you to know that I'm on your side.**

6. **Do you know I really love you?**

Encouraging Statements
Assumed Inadequacy

1. **Remember when you first tried to tie your shoes, and how long it took till you were good at it?**

2. **How about doing a small step first?**

3. **Let's do it together.**

4. I'll write the first letter and you write the next one. Okay?

5. I can't remember how to use my iPad. I could really use some help.

6. It's okay to make mistakes. That's how we learn.

Iceberg Activity Encouraging Statements Handout
Undue Attention

- Would you be willing to use this timer to time me for three minutes on the phone?
- Let's make a deal. How about you get your homework done and we can hang out for a few minutes after dinner.
- I'm busy now and I'm looking forward to our special time later.
- Thanks for helping. I appreciate it.
- I know it can be hard to wait without interrupting, and I notice you are being more patient.
- I hear you, and I look forward to connecting with you as soon as I can.

Encouraging Statements Power

- I need your help. What ideas do you have to solve this problem?
- What is your understanding of our agreement?
- I think we are in a power struggle. Let's take some time to calm down and then start over.
- You are making some good points. It will be easier to listen when we are both calmer.
- I need your help and could really use your brain power.
- What would help you the most—to put this challenge on the family meeting agenda, or to find a solution on the Wheel of Choice?

Encouraging Statements Revenge

- When you hurt me or others, I know you are hurting. I'm so sorry.
- No wonder you are upset. You always get in trouble, and others walk away without getting caught..
- Why don't we both take a break, cool off, and then come back and try again.
- When you hurt others, I wonder what you feel hurt about. Want to talk about it now–or later?
- Looks like you are having a rough time right now. I want you to know that I'm on your side.
- Do you know I really care love you?

Encouraging Statements Assumed Inadequacy

- Remember when you first tried to tie your shoes, and how long it took till you were good at it?
- How about doing a small step first?
- Let's do it together.
- I'll write the first letter and you write the next one. Okay?
- I can't remember how to use my iPad. I could really use some help.
- It's okay to make mistakes. That's how we learn.

　　　　　www.positivediscipline.com

For Any Mistaken Goal

- Would you be willing to work with me to figure out if you'd like to improve your grade and if so, how you could go about that?
- When you've put away your things, we can move on to the next activity.
- Let's try it this way for a week and then we can re-evaluate.
- You can try again.
- I'll let you know when I'm ready to try again.
- Wow! You're really angry, upset, annoyed, etc. Want to tell me about it?
- I feel ______________ because ______________ and I wish ________________.
- (One word): Towels. Now. Later. Bedtime.
- I can tell this is really important to you.
- I can see how hard you worked on this and how much time went into it.

The iceberg was painted by Doug Bartsch, Visalia School District, CA.
You can create your own illustrations for this activity or have these blown up and laminated.

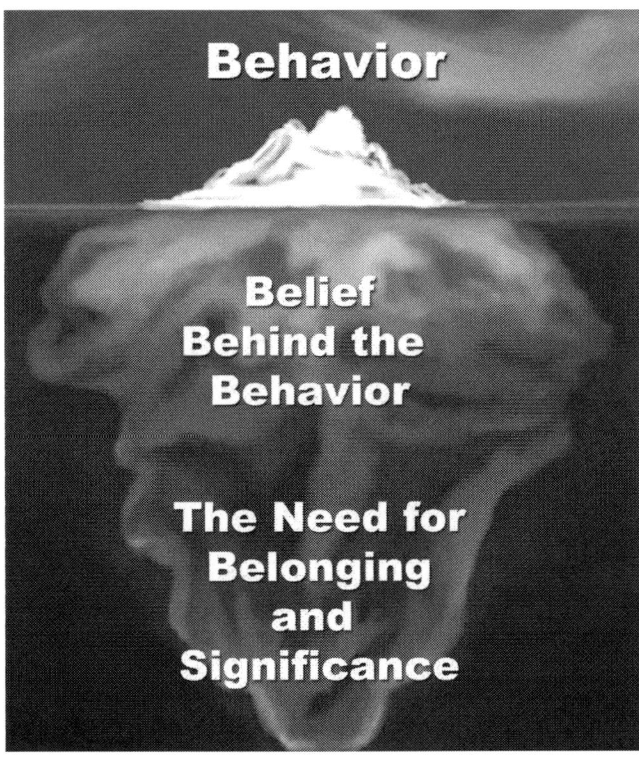

Misguided Power
I belong only when I'm the boss, or at least don't let you boss me.
Let me help.
Give me choices.

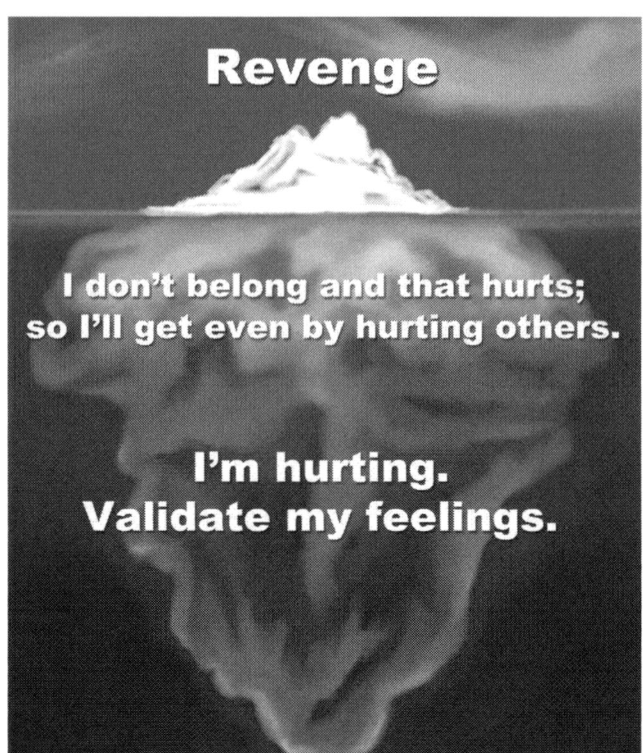
Revenge
I don't belong and that hurts; so I'll get even by hurting others.
I'm hurting.
Validate my feelings.

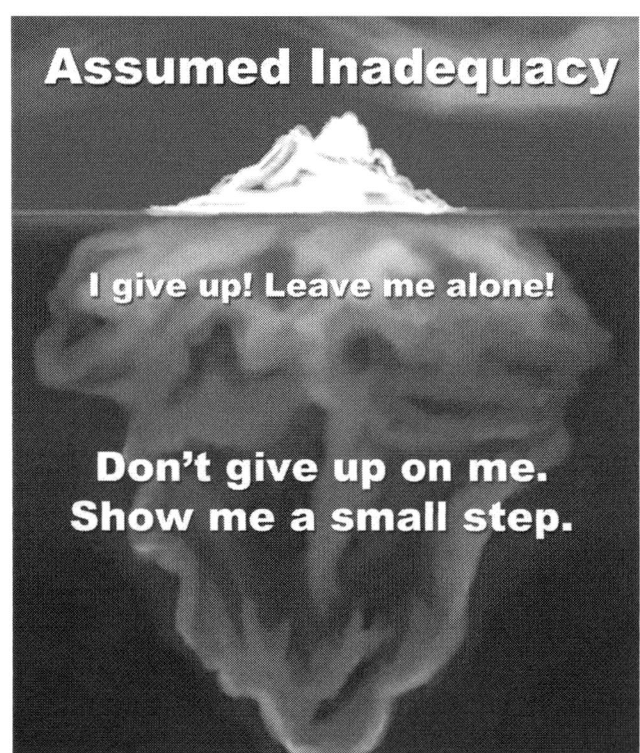
Assumed Inadequacy
I give up! Leave me alone!
Don't give up on me.
Show me a small step.

I Need a Hug

Objective:

To help parents experience the power of asking for a hug to provide connection and encouragement that might change behavior—including their own.

To help parents understand that it is okay to allow their children to have their feelings.

Materials:

Attached Bob Bradbury
and Steven Foster stories

Comment:

Children DO better when they FEEL better Too many people think children must pay for what they have done in the form of blame, shame, or pain (other words for punishment). Try a hug instead.

Directions

1. Wait until the end of the activity to talk about the comment.

2. Ask for 8 volunteers (4 to be children and 4 to be parents).

3. After they decide who will be parents and who will be children, ask the parents to "adopt" a child. (They will then be partners in the activity.)

4. Remind all volunteers that when they role-play children it is important to "play" the child, but to also "be in the present moment"—which means to respond to what is going on now, not how their children respond to a different method at home.

5. Ask for a volunteer to take the children outside the room so they can't hear the instructions given to the parents (but observers can). Let the "children know they can think about what they want to have a tantrum about, (a loud one or a sulky quiet one) while outside.

6. Instruct the parents: "Your children will come to the center of the room and have a temper tantrum. When I give you a signal, go to your child, make eye contact if you can (put your hand on a shoulder if you can't get eye contact) and validate the child's feelings, "I can see your are really upset." Wait a few seconds and then say, "I need a hug." If your child doesn't give you a hug, wait a few seconds and repeat, "I need a hug." If your child still doesn't give you a hug, wait a few seconds and say, "I need a hug, come find me when you are ready," and then walk away.

7. Ask another volunteer get the children who left the room and have them go to the middle of the room. The volunteer parents will be at the side of the room.

8. Tell the children to start their temper tantrums. Let them have their temper tantrums for a few seconds and then signal the parents to intervene per the instructions you gave in No. 6.

9. Allow just enough time to see when the parents have asked 3 times, and then ring a chime or bell to stop the action. Ask the children what happened and what they were thinking, feeling and deciding. Then process with the parents what they were thinking, feeling, and deciding.

10. Ask the observers what they noticed and what they learned. Some report that it is almost funny to watch the bewildered look on the children's faces if their parents leave after saying, "Come find me when you are ready." Many children run after them saying they are ready for a hug.

11. Make the following points if they don't come out during the discussion:

12. Nothing works for every child every time. Sometimes hugs don't work because the child is too upset to give or receive a hug. Discuss the importance of allowing children to have their feelings. If they don't want to give a hug that is fine. Sometimes it might be best to validate their feelings and then leave them alone. Children can develop their resiliency muscles by learning that they can survive being upset and eventually feel more capable by working it through.

13. Why say, "I need a hug," instead of "You need a hug"? Saying, "I need a hug," may speak to the child's innate desire to help and to contribute.

14. It will help if parents understand that the point of this activity is not to change the behavior of children, but to emphasize the importance of connection before correction, and to allow their children to have their feelings. It is paradoxical that behavior is more likely to change when changing them is not your goal or attitude. Children "feel" the difference.

15. Ask for volunteers to read the attached success stories. (You might want to pass these out to 2 volunteers in advance.)

Facilitator's Note:

Some people ask, "After the hug, then what? What about the misbehavior?" Remember, "A misbehaving child is a discouraged child." Hugs can create the encouragement needed to inspire changed behavior. Once children feel encouraged (after the hug and time to calm down), parents might take time for training, ask curiosity questions, give a limited choice, use distraction, engage in joint problem-solving—or to do nothing and see what happens next. It could be that the hug is enough.

I Need a Hug

A father attending Dr. Bob Bradbury's Sanity Circus, an Adlerian Open Forum Counseling in Seattle, WA, asked what to do when his four-year-old son, had a temper tantrum. Dr. Bradbury suggested asking for a hug.

The father was surprised and asked, "Wouldn't that reward the misbehavior?"

Dr. Bradbury asked, "Would you be willing to try and see what happens?"

The father agreed, and the next week he reported the following scene:

His little son, Timothy, started a tantrum because he couldn't have something he wanted. Dad got down on one knee and said, "I need a hug."

Timothy stopped sobbing long enough to ask, "What?"

The father said again, "I need a hug."

Timothy again stopped sobbing and asked incredulously, "Now?!?"

Dad said, "Yes, now."

Timothy begrudgingly said, "Okay," and stiffly gave his father a hug. Soon the stiffness disappeared and they melted into each other's arms.

After a few moments Dad said, "Thanks, I needed that."

Timothy said, with a small tremor on his lips, "So did I."

Story by Steven Foster,
co-author of Positive Discipline for Children with Special Needs

Today a four-year-old boy stormed away from the art table, screaming that he was "mad, frustrated and not happy." My assistant followed him over to our comfy cushion where he had wrapped himself in a blanket, now just screaming wordlessly and kicking the cushion. He refused to talk to the assistant, just continuing to scream.

I sat next to him and whispered, "I need a hug."

He continued screaming and writhing.

After about 15 seconds, I repeated, "I need a hug."

He stopped screaming and flailing but kept his back to me.

10 more seconds. "I need a hug."

Long pause and he turned over, climbed into my lap and hugged me.

I asked him if he wanted to go back to the art table by himself or if he wanted me to go with him. He asked me to go with him. He went back, finished his project happily and left the table.

Notes

Emotional Honesty: The "I Feel" Process

Objective:
To practice sharing feelings rather than judgments.

Materials:
"Feeling Faces" chart in handout section for each participant

Comment:
Many people in our society are not aware of their feelings or how to express them. We are taught that it is not okay to have feelings and to talk from our heads instead of our hearts or guts—our judgments instead of our feelings. (You may want to review the material in chapter seven in Positive Discipline for Teenagers.)

Directions

1. Ask participants to think of an issue where they think they're not getting anywhere and are feeling frustrated with a family member of any age. They are feeling that, no matter how many times they try to communicate, their family members are not getting the message.

2. Have participants choose a partner and demonstrate how they have been handling the situation that concerns them such as lecturing, nagging, guilt tripping, punishing or even avoiding.

3. Now have them go back to the same situation and share their feelings instead of their judgments with the following simple formula.

    4. I feel______________ because ____________and I wish ___________________.

    5. Here's an example, "I feel hurt because you won't talk to me, and I wish we could talk more often."

6. Have them check the "Feeling Faces" chart if they are having trouble using feeling words and are using "like," "that," or "you," because these are not feeling words. (See article on Emotional Honesty in the Using Feeling Effectively activity)

7. Have them ask their partners to share how they were feeling when they demonstrated their usual way of handling the situation, and how they were feeling when they role-played sharing their feelings.

8. Process with the whole group. How did they feel in each situation? What were they thinking and deciding?

Notes

I Love You and the Answer Is No

Objective:

To learn the power of connection followed by a simple, "No."

To learn other ways for saying, "No."

Materials:

Laminated slips of paper with the child questions or requests below for each age group. Use the ones that fit for the parents in your group.

List of Characteristics and Life Skills from Two Lists activity

Flip-chart with the heading, "Other Ways to Say No" (Do not display until ROUND THREE)

Comment:

Most parents can't just say "no." They add anger, criticism, blame, or character defamations; or they want to teach lessons and think the best way is to make their children suffer. Later they may give in instead of kindly and firmly following through.

Child Questions or Requests

Teens

"Can I use the car?"

"Can I borrow $5 for lunch money?"

"Can I wear your new sweater?"

Six to twelve

"Will you do my science project for me?"

"Can I have a TV in my room?"

"Can I go to this concert with my friends?"

Four to six

"Can I go to the park by myself?"

"Can I play computer games all day?"

"Can we go to Disneyland again?"

Three to four

"I want that toy in the store."

"I want a cookie now."

"I want her toy."

Directions

1. Decide which of the four age groups you want to role-play. If it is just one age group, ask for three volunteers to play children and three to play parents. If you have parents with different aged children, ask for one participant to represent each of the four age groups as the child, and three to represent each of the groups as the parent. Let them know you will be doing THREE ROUNDS.

2. ROUND ONE: Let the child role-players choose a slip of paper with one of the questions from the envelope for their age. Let them know that their role will be to ask the question, and then coax their parent to say, "Yes." They can rehearse how they will coax while you take the parents aside.

3. Take the parent role-players aside and instruct them to say, "No," and then add some kind of "piggy back" lecture that might include criticism or disappointment, "Do you think I'm made of money?" "Do you think the world revolves around you?" "Why should I do anything for you, when you don't do anything for me?"

4. Have the parents go their child, and instruct the children to start with their request. In 30 seconds (more or less), stop the role-playing with a pleasant sounding bell.

5. Ask the volunteers (first children and then parents) to share what they were thinking, how they were feeling and what they were deciding. Ask the children if they are learning anything on the Characteristics and Life Skills list. (Usually not.)

6. ROUND TWO: This might be a good time to remind child role-players to "play children" and to also "be in the present." In other words, to play children who are responding to what they are experiencing now, not to what their children do at home when they are experiencing different reactions from their parents.

7. Take the parents aside again and give them the following instructions: After your child asks or demands, make a connection by taking your child by the hand and saying, "I love you and the answer is no." If the child keeps coaxing, just smile.

8. In 30 seconds (more or less), stop the role-playing with a pleasant sounding bell.

9. Ask the volunteers (first children and then parents) to share what they were thinking, how they were feeling and what they were learning. How important was it to "make a connection" before saying, "No?" How important was it to use non-verbals if they continued to try to coax?

10. Ask the "children" to look at the list of Characteristics and Life Skills to see if there is anything on the list that they are learning. (If "strong disappointment muscles" isn't on the list, add it.)

11. ROUND THREE: Display flip chart you have prepared in advance: "Other Ways to Say No" and invite participants to take turns reading each of them. Ask the group if they can think of others possibilities.

12. Now have all participants get back into their pairs. The child can ask again, and the parents can respond with one of the "other ways to say no." Allow about 60 seconds each.

13. Process with the children by asking what they were thinking, feeling, and deciding this time—and what they learned on the Characteristics and Life Skills list. Process with the parents what they were thinking, feeling, and deciding this time.

14. After coming back together in the large group, invite a discussion of what they have learned so far from this activity.

15. Very important question: What characteristics and life skills can your children learn from hearing, "I love you and the answer is no," or one of the "Other Ways to Say No"? (Resiliency, delayed gratification, strengthened disappointment muscles, a sense of capability by learning they can survive the ups and downs of life.)

Other Ways to Say, "No."

1. Validate feelings (and allow child to have them without trying to fix or rescue).

2. Suggest that the child put the request on the family meeting agenda to get everyone's ideas.

3. Suggest scheduling a time to brainstorm with the child on how to achieve what he or she wants.

4. Ask the child what he or she can do. (How much money will you need to save to get that?)

5. Say, "I have faith in you to figure out how to achieve that goal."

6. Say, "Yes, as soon as _______________."

7. Follow through. (What was our agreement?)

8. Use "the look" with humor. ("Nice try.")

Notes

Johnny Said the "F" Word

Objective:
To learn the difference between effective and ineffective ways to deal with potty talk and profanity.

Materials:
Flip chart
Marking pens

Comment:
Because parents tend to overreact, they invite children to use profanity as misbehavior. Potty talk is extremely popular during the preschool years, and many attempts to stop it fall on deaf ears.

Directions

1. Ask the group what messages they got as children about "bad" words.

2. Ask participants to remember a personal experience when a child used potty talk or profanity.

3. Have the group share feelings experienced during the episode and how adults responded.

4. Ask,"How did that response effect what the child did?"

5. Give a few ideas on how a parent can respond in a way that won't invite misbehavior, e.g. ignore or ask the child to say it someplace else. Ask the group for more ideas and list them on the flip chart.

EXPANDED VERSION:

6. Divide the group into small groups and have the participants help each other with a different way of handling their own situations.

7. Ask a small group to role-play both situations for the larger group.

8. Process by asking both the parents and the children what they were thinking, what they were feeling, and what they were deciding.

9. Ask a volunteer to read the following essay:

Potty talk through the Ages
By Lynn Lott

When I was a kid, if we used "bad" language we were threatened to have our mouths washed out with soap. I'm not sure our parents ever did the dastardly deed, but I've certainly worked with enough clients who experienced the soapy bubbles as a punishment for swearing.

When my nephews were little, my sister and I spent hours with them in the car trying to get them to stop using potty talk. All of our attempts failed until we decided to join them and talk like a couple of four year olds. They were so disgusted and annoyed with us they stopped.

My grandson discovered that when he talked potty talk at school he had to sit in a special place and take some space until he was ready to try again using better language. The word "stupid" made the rounds at preschool and was considered a bad and hurtful word. Any kid using that word got a lot of attention, even if the attention was negative. The attention didn't seem to diminish the use of the word. One day my daughter asked if I could talk to my grandson about the use of that word. Here's our discussion:

Me: Z, I understand that you like to say the word "stupid" and that it gets you in trouble at home and at school.

Z: Yes, Grandma. That's a bad word and we're not supposed to say it.

Me: You know, I don't think words are good or bad. I think the problem is in where and how you use them. If you say, "Stupid" to hurt someone's feelings, that's a problem. If you say "stupid" around people who don't like to hear that word, that's a problem, too. Personally, I don't mind if you say the word around me, but I have discovered something that happens whenever I hear the word.

Z: What's that, Grandma?

Me: It makes my hands need to tickle someone and I can't seem to make them stop till the person stops saying that word. Want to try it out?

Z: Okay.

Z said, "Stupid" and I tickled him till he asked me to stop. Eventually he decided that he wouldn't use that word around me. It was his choice.

On another occasion he burst out with a flood of potty talk which he calls potty mouth. He looked at me and said, "Grandma, I can say those words around you, right?" I think he got the message about appropriate places to use certain language. When he tried out the "F" word on me (age 4), saying he was sure he could use that word around me, I said, "You could use that word, but I prefer "Holy Schlamoley." We spent the rest of the day saying "Holy Schlamoley" to everything and that was the end of the "F" word.

Joint Problem Solving

<table>
<tr><td>

Objective:

To learn a process for solving problems with your child that you both can live with.

</td><td>

Materials:

A copy of the "Joint Problem Solving Steps" chart below for each participant

</td></tr>
</table>

Comment:

When we live the principle of mutual respect, we learn that parents and kids have different issues and different feelings about the same subject. If adults try to force their way on children or give in to their demands, any solution is short-lived. It is only when every one feels understood that resolution is possible.

Directions

1. Ask the participants to think of a disagreement they have with their child such as getting chores done, cleaning rooms, use of the family car, telephone use, curfew, etc.

2. Have them pick a partner and share their issue. The partners can decide which problem to work on if there isn't time for both.

3. Have the partners decide who will be the parent and who will be the child. The parent says to the child,

   "I notice we have a problem with _____________ (fill in the blank with whatever the problem is). I'd like it if we could work out another way to deal with this that we both can live with. Would you be willing to have a discussion without attacking, blaming, or hurting each other?"

4. After getting an agreement to have a respectful discussion, have the parent ask the child what his view of the problem is and how he feels. The person playing the child will have to "make up" what the child's issues are. When the child has finished, have the parent feed back to him what he just said using the following format: "You feel _________ because ___________ and you wish_________."

5. Next have the parent ask the child if he is willing to hear what the parent's issues are. Let the child know that it's okay if they see things differently. The idea is just to understand each other, not to see it the same way Then have the parent tell the child his or her thoughts and feelings about the problem and ask the child to tell the parent what he or she heard.

6. Acknowledge that you have different ideas about the problem and suggest brainstorming some ideas so you can find a solution you can both live with for one week. (It helps the brainstorming process if the parent comes up with wild and crazy ideas to create a sense of fun.)

7. Ask the participants to choose a suggestion they're both willing to try for one week.

8. Have them appreciate each other for listening. Agree on a review date.

9. With the whole group, talk about areas where the process broke down and why they think it happened. What did it feel like to negotiate with your child instead of arguing, giving orders, or giving in?

10. Suggest that they try joint problem solving at home and report the results to the group next time.

Joint Problem Solving Steps

1. State an observation, "I notice ___________ and I'd like it if we could work out another way to deal with this that we both can live with. I'd like us to agree to take each other seriously and not attack or hurt each other."

2. Ask the child what is his or her view of the problem and how he or she feels. Listen without interrupting, unless it is to ask, "Is there more? Anything else?" Don't argue. When your child has finished, feed back to him what he just said using the following format, "You feel _________ because ___________ and you wish_________."

3. State your feelings and views of the problem. Ask him or her to feed back what you said.

4. Express appreciation, "Thank you for sharing your thoughts and feelings."

5. Ask, "Have you thought of something else you might do?" If not, brainstorm for alternatives.

6. Choose an alternative that you can all live with for a short time — one day, one week etc. Role-play the alternative if there is enough time.

7. Agree on a review date and share appreciations.

The Jungle

Adapted from an activity by John Taylor, Person to Person, available at *www.add-plus.com*

Objective:

To become aware of the thoughts, feelings, and decisions children could be making in response to parenting styles; and to get a better feeling for the statement by Rudolf Dreikurs, "A misbehaving child is a discouraged child." *Children: The Challenge*, Rudolf Dreikurs and Vicki Soltz..

Materials:

Eight sturdy chairs in a circle facing out (toward the larger group circle)

Flip-chart with the heading, "Encouraging Statements"

Party glasses to represent each of the 4 Mistaken Goals for the Alternate version

If doing the Alternate version: Two Lists

Encouraging statements for Iceberg Deep Activity

Comment:

This activity can be very powerful and emotional. It is best to use it after the group has established a sense of trust and rapport. Let them know that this activity will make a huge impression that they will never forget.

Directions

1. Prepare in advance by having 8 chairs set up in a circle facing out.

2. Start by sharing that this can be a very emotional activity. Jokingly (and seriously) suggest that they may not want to volunteer if they are feeling emotionally fragile. However, they may want to volunteer to "get into the child's world" to experientially increase their understanding of how a child's sense of belonging can be damaged.

3. Ask for eight volunteers (to play adults) who are willing to stand on chairs in a circle. Ask for "spotters" to help them get up on the chairs.

4. Then ask for two participants to be children.

5. Explain that the two "children" will each stand in front of an adult on opposite sides (outside) of the circle. Moving at the same time and in the same direction (clockwise or counter clockwise), they will rotate slowly around the circle, pausing to look up at each adult to say, "I am a child and I just want to belong."

6. The adult will look down at the child and respond by making discouraging statements such as: "Why can't you ever __________?" "How come you never __________?" "How many times have I told you __________?" "When will you ever learn __________?" "I'm so disappointed in you." "I can't believe you did that." "You are so lazy." "You will belong when your grades improve." (Let them know that they will need to pretend that the child is misbehaving instead of saying, "I am a child and I just want to belong.") The children will go around the circle three times.

7. After you share the instructions, give them another chance to "back out." People, usually don't; but if they do, ask if anyone is willing to take their place. If not, just remove a chair.

8. Ask the children, positioned at opposite sides of the circle, to start moving around the circle saying to each adult, "I'm a child and I just want to belong."

9. As a surprise, you might want to whisper in the ear of one "adult" to suggest he/she turn his or her back and be silent after the child says, "I'm a child and I just want to belong."

10. Pay close attention to the mood. If you feel people "get it," and are becoming too emotional, stop before the "children" go around three times.

11. Ask the spotters to help the "adults" get down from the chairs and ask the "adults" to sit down in the same chairs they were standing on.

12. Then have the two children come and stand with you and process by asking, "What were you thinking, feeling, and deciding during this activity?"

13. Ask the children, "Without mentioning names (because the parents already feel bad enough), what statements were hardest for you to hear?"

14. Assuming the group has learned about the mistaken goals, you can ask the children, "Do you feel like choosing undue attention, misguided power, revenge, or giving up?"

15. You might want to add, "If I told you I had something that would make you feel real good (implying that you have some drugs), would you like to meet me behind the building and try it?" (This makes the point that kids might be tempted to use drugs if they are feeling discouraged.)

16. Ask the "adults" what they were thinking, feeling, and deciding.

17. Then ask the whole group, "Please share one word to express how you feel after watching this activity." You will hear, angry, sad, hurt, etc. Ask, "How many of you felt a little guilty?" Share how you felt the first time you watched this activity. (Some leaders have said, "I wanted to cry for two reasons. First, it broke my heart to know that children hear these statements. Second, I felt guilty because I know I have said some of them.") Emphasize that the purpose of this activity is not about guilt. Ask, "What do you think is the point of this activity? What did you learn from it?"

18. Finally, ask, "If a child came to you and said, 'I'm a child and I just want to belong,' how many of you could make a humiliating remark to that child?" Of course, no one would. So the next question is, "What is the hidden message of a misbehaving child? **I'm a child and I just want to belong."**

19. Go to the flip-chart paper with the heading, "Encouragement." Ask the group to brainstorm some encouraging things that could be said or done, even if kids are misbehaving. If the following don't come up, you can add them.

> "You are so important to me."
> "How can I help?"
> "What would help you feel better right now?"
> "I'm looking forward to our special time."

"I'm so sorry. Can we start over and work out a solution together?"
"I love you so much. I need a hug as soon as you are ready."
"I really need your help. Are you willing to help me think of solutions?"
Open your arms for a hug without saying a word.
"I'm so sorry for what I said. I hope you can forgive me."

20. Then ask the eight "adults" to stand in front of the chairs (at eye level with the "children") Have the two "child" volunteers go around the circle again saying, "I'm a child and I just want to belong." This time have the adults make encouraging, celebrating, respecting statements to the children.

21. Then repeat the "process" about thoughts, feelings, and decisions with the two "children: and eight "adult" volunteers.

22. Invite sharing from the whole group about what they learned from this activity.

Alternate to Incorporate the Four Mistaken Goals

1. The same as No. 1 above.

2. Ask for 4 participants to be children and give each one of the Mistaken Goal glasses to wear.

3. Explain that the four "children" will walk around the circle (spread out evenly) three times, pausing to look up at each adult to say, "I am a child and I just want to belong." The adult will look down at the child and respond by making discouraging statements such as in No. 6 above. (Let them know that they will need to pretend that the child is misbehaving instead of saying, "I am a child and I just want to belong, and they might be motivated to respond to the glasses instead of the child.")

4. When you feel they have experienced enough, stop the circling (even if they haven't gone around 3 times) and ask the spotters to help the "adults" get down so they can sit in the chairs they were standing on while processing.

5. Then have the children come and stand next to you and process by asking, "What were you thinking, feeling, and deciding during this activity?"

6. Process with the adults what they were thinking, feeling, and deciding.

7. Follow immediately with the **Encouraging Statements** from the Iceberg Deep Activity to make sure the children and adults are left with feelings of encouragement. To do this, pass out the six encouragement statements for Undue Attention to six of the parents who are now standing on the floor in front of the 8 chairs. Have the child who played Undue attention, walk around and stand in front of each of these parents until they hear the six encouragement statements.

8. Then process with this child what he/she is thinking feeling, deciding, and if he/she is now learning anything on the Characteristics and Life Skills List.

9. Repeat this process by giving the Encouraging statements for Misguided Power to the parents, starting with the two who didn't get statements for the first child, and to the next four parents. By repeating this process with Revenge and Assumed Inadequacy, each parent will make three encouraging statements, and each child will hear six encouraging statements. Be sure to take each child to the Characteristics and Life Skills List to share what they are learning.

10. Process with the parents about what they are thinking, feeling, and deciding.

11. Invite all the participants to share what they learned from this activity.

Notes

Kid Power Demonstrations

Objective:

To understand how sharing power with children helps avoid discouragement and power struggles.

Materials:

4 Markers

The Characteristics and Life Skills and the Challenges Lists from the Two Lists activity

Comment:

This activity can help adults realize how often they create power struggles and how they can develops feelings of competence and self-worth in children by sharing power.

Directions

1. Ask for a volunteer to play the child (a teen or a younger child, depending on the statements you want to use in Nos. 5 or 6, or Nos. 12 or 13). You will be doing two rounds.

2. **Round One:** Hold out one of the markers to the child and say, *"This marker represents your power. Do you want it?"*

3. As the child starts to take it, pull it back and say, *"I don't know. Maybe you are not ready for this."*

4. Whatever the child says, start to give the marker again. Let the child hang on to one end for a second and then pull it back saying, *"But, what if you make a mistake?"*

5. Continue this back and forth two more times, saying things like the following to a younger child:

   "You're too slow and I'm in a hurry."
   "I'm not sure you can do it well enough."
   "I'm not ready for you to try."

6. For teens you might say things like:

   "I'm not sure I can trust you."
   "I don't know. Remember that really stupid thing you did last time?"
   "Even if I did trust you, I don't trust your friends."

7. Finally, let the child have the marker and keep it while you count slowly to five. Then grab it back from him/her, saying, *"Okay, that's enough for now."*

8. Once you think the point has been made, process with the child, "What were you thinking? What were you feeling? What decisions were you making about yourself and your ability to handle things? How are you going to use your power? (Probably sneaky, underground behavior)

9. Point to the Characteristics and Life Skills list and ask, "Are you learning anything on this list? (Usually not.) Point to the Challenges list and ask if the child is deciding to do any of these? (Usually a few.)

10. Ask the observers what they noticed.

11. **Round two**: Tell the child you would like to try again and do something different.

12. This time, offer the marker, and say, *"I have faith in you to handle this new venture."* Then offer the other three markers, one at a time, while saying to a younger child:

    "If you make a mess, we can clean it up."
    "I can wait; I have time."
    "Isn't it fun to learn from mistakes!"

13. For teens say things like:

    "I trust you."
    "If you make a mistake I have faith in you to learn from it.
    "I'm here if you need me to talk things over."

14. Process again as in No. 8-10 above, omitting the Challenges list part.

15. Be sure to ask, "How will you use your power now?" (Probably, "Be responsible," or "Live up to your trust.")

16. Invite everyone to share what they learned from this activity.

Comment:

Parents often are afraid to let go and allow their kids to experiment with their personal power. Kids will experiment anyway—they just go underground. This means lots of lying and sneaking around so they can do what they want while trying to avoid punishment and/or disappointment from their parents.

Sometimes the "child" gives up trying to take the marker. This tells us that continual thwarting of bids for power can result not only in "underground" behavior, but in giving up.

Kind AND Firm at the SAME Time

Objective:

To teach parents how to avoid being too firm or too kind while learning several statements for being both kind **and** firm at the same time.

Materials:

Characteristics and Life Skills and Challenges from Two Lists Activity

Chart of Too Kind and Too Firm (Laminated copies for half of your group)

Kind and Firm Statements cut into strips and laminated (and a full page as a handout)

Copies of Kind and Firm Practice Questionnaire for each participant

Comment:

Parents struggle with developing a style that combines kindness **and** firmness. Many are more prone to one than the other. Positive Discipline teaches that it is most effective to be both **Kind And Firm** at the same time.

Directions

1. Start by asking, "How many of you have a difficult time being kind and firm at the same time?" Most will raise their hand. Then ask, "Why do you think that is?" They will come up with many ideas which you may want to have someone write on a flip chart. (Too angry, reacting, afraid firm will sound mean, think it is my job to be firm.)

2. "Today you are going to learn how to use the "magic word." Who knows what it might be?" (Someone might guess that it is AND.) We will be doing three rounds.

(Round One)

3. Invite participants to find a partner and choose who will be a P (for parent) and C (for child) and to stand about 3 feet from each other. Ask them to find a place in the room where they aren't too close to another pair.

4. Point to the Characteristics and Life Skills list and ask the children to notice if what is being done or said invites them to learn any of these Characteristics and Life Skills. Ask parents to notice if what they are doing or saying is teaching the Characteristics and Life Skills.

5. Pass out the Chart of Too Kind and Too Firm only to P's. (You might want to laminate these statements folded back to back (so one side is upside down)

6. Let P's know they have some typical statements that many parents use in the hopes of motivating their children to cooperate.

7. Instruct the C's to listen and to move a few inches closer to the parents if they feel motivated to learn the Characteristics and Life Skills after they hear each statement, and to move a few inches back if they don't feel motivated to learn them. (You might want to model this with a volunteer to demonstrate just a few inches.)

8. Instruct P's to first make the Too Firm comments from the Too Kind and Too Firm chart, pausing between each statement to give C's a chance to move a few inches forward or backward. They will all be doing this at the same time, so it can get noisy, but experience has demonstrated that they don't mind.

9. When they have time to finish, process with C's by asking what they are thinking, feeling, and deciding.

10. Point to the Characteristics and Life Skills list and ask if they are learning anything on the list. (Usually not.) (If you have a large group, don't process with each person—just those who volunteer to share.)

11. Then point to the Challenges list and ask the C's if they are feeling motivated to do any of these? (Usually some of them.)

12. Process with P's by asking them what they are thinking, feeling, and deciding. (If you have a large group, don't process with each person—just those who volunteer to share.)

Directions (Round Two)

13. Ask P's and C's to stand about three feet apart again. P's will now make the Too Kind statements in an attempt to motivate the C's. Again, C's are to move a few inches closer if they are learning anything on the Characteristics and Life Skills list, and a few inches back if they aren't.

14. When they finish, process with C's what they were thinking, feeling, and deciding. What was different in their thinking, feeling, and deciding while listening to the Too Firm statements, and then to the Too Kind statements?

15. Point to the Characteristics and Life Skills list and ask if, as children, they were learning any of these? (Usually nothing)

16. Process with P's what they were thinking, feeling, and deciding. What was different for them while saying the Too Kind statements after saying the Two Firm statements? Did one feel better, or more comfortable, than the other? Sometimes children might like the Too Kind statements, so be sure to ask if they are learning the Characteristics and Life Skills. Ask parents if they think they were teaching any of the Characteristics and Life Skills while making any of these statements.

17. Ask what they have learned so far. (There is usually some rich discussion as they absorb and share what they are learning)

Directions: (Round Three)

18. Now invite one C and 6 P's to remain standing and invite the rest to sit down and be observers. Ask them as observers to still notice what they would be thinking, feeling, and deciding if they were actively participating in one of the roles.

19. Pass out the laminated Kind AND Firm Statements to the P's (one to each parent) Instruct the parents to read just the bolded part of the statement, not the small words in parentheses. Also, ask them to take a minute to look at their statements to see if they can say them without reading them so that they can make eye contact with their child, (and it is okay to look if they need to).

20. Instruct the "child" to walk down the line of P's and stand in front of each parent to listen to his or her statement without responding verbally—just noticing what he or she is thinking, feeling, and deciding.

21. When they are finished, process with the child what he or she was thinking, feeling, and deciding. Then point to the Characteristics and Life Skills List and ask if he or she was learning anything on this list.

22. Process with the parents what they were thinking, feeling, and deciding while making their Kind AND Firm Statements.

23. Invite all participants to discuss what they learned from this activity.

Extension:

24. Pass out the "Kind AND Firm PRACTICE Questionnaire" and have parents fill it out or use it as homework. If it is part of the class, when they have time to finish, ask them to get with a partner to practice. If assigned as homework, request that they bring it, completed, to the next class to share what they learned.

Chart of Too Kind and Too Firm

Too Firm

I'm not going to tell you again. Stop playing right now or your toys are going in the garbage!

If you don't stop doing that, you are in time out.

You had better cooperate or you'll lose all your privileges.

I don't care if you don't want to brush your teeth. March into the bathroom and get going, Mister! (or Miss!)

If you don't brush your teeth, you'll never have sugar again, and I mean it.

You said you would unload the dishwasher and I don't want to hear any back talk. Get going now.

Hand me your game boy this minute.

I'm not going to buy you something every time we go to the store.

Too Kind

I don't know why you don't listen. I feel so sad.

Fine. Go ahead, Sweetie, but this is the last time.

Please stop crying. You can have something from the store this time, but remember you can't have something every time we come to the store.

I'm worried that you'll get cavities if you don't brush your teeth.

I'm sure you can fix your own sandwich; but I'll do it this time.

I wish you would eat your dinner. Think of all the starving children in the world.

You promised you would not play video games so much if we bought that game player for you.

Okay, I'll give you five more minutes again.

Kind AND Firm At the Same Time Statements
(Parents)

(Validate feelings) **I know it is hard to stop playing, AND it is time for dinner.**

(Show understanding) **I can understand why you would rather watch TV than do your homework, AND homework needs to be done first.**

(Redirection) **You don't want to brush your teeth, AND I don't want to pay dentist bills. I'll race you to the bathroom.**

(Follow through on advance agreement) **I know you don't want to do your chores, AND what was our agreement about when they would be done? (Kindly and quietly wait for the answer)**

(Provide a choice) **You don't want to go to bed, AND it is bedtime. Is it your turn to read a story, or mine?**

(A choice and then follow through by deciding what you will do) **I know you want to keep playing video games, AND your time is up. You can turn it off now, or it will be put in my closet.**

Kind AND Firm At the Same Time Statements
(Early Childhood Teachers)

(Validate feelings) **I know you really enjoy playing and don't want to stop, AND it's now story time.**

(Show understanding-and "as soon as") **I know you would rather stay outside and play, AND it is nap time. As soon as nap time is over, you can go outside again.**

(Redirection and choice) **I know you don't want to pick up the toys AND it is pick up time. Do you want to set the timer or shall we sing our pick up song?**

(Kindly and quietly wait for the answer—assuming you and the kids have come up with an agreement together in advance.) **I know you don't want to take turns on the bikes, AND what was our agreement about taking turns?**

(Provide a choice) **You don't want to take a nap, AND it's quiet time on the cots. Do you want to quietly read a book or listen to the relaxing music?**

(Validate feeling and ask a curiosity question) **I know you want that toy. How long do you think it will take to save enough money from your allowance to buy it?**

Kind AND Firm At the Same Time Statements
(Teachers)

(Validate feelings) **I can tell you are upset about something, AND it is time to be working on your project. I'm available after school if you would like to talk about what you are upset about.**

(Show understanding) **I can understand why you would rather be doing something else right now, AND your assignment needs to be done first.**

(Redirection) **You don't want to do your homework, AND I don't want you to fail. Let's find time to talk about what you need to do to succeed.**

(Follow through on advance agreement) **I know you don't want to hand in your assignments on time, AND what was our agreement about when they would be done? (Kindly and quietly wait for the answer)**

(Provide a choice) **I know you would prefer to play games now, and it is quiet work time now. Do you want me to hold your phone until after class, or can you keep it in your backpack?**

(A choice and then follow through by deciding what you will do) **I know you want to keep talking with your friends, AND it is time for ______. I will start teaching when you are ready.**

The "And" in Kind AND Firm Practice Questionnaire

1. Think of a recent power struggle you experienced with a child who resisted what you wanted him or her to do or to stop doing. Describe what happened: who said what and who did what—and then what happened?

    ____

    ____

    ____

    ____

2. When you look at what you have written, underline what you did or said that could be interpreted as firm, but not kind. Then circle what you did or said that could be interpreted as kind, but not firm.

3. Get into your child's world and make a guess about what he or she was thinking, feeling, and deciding to do in response to what you said or did.

    ____

    ____

    ____

    ____

4. Now rewrite the scene where you are kind AND firm. (Use the Kind and Firm Statements handout for clues.) In the first blank KINDLY validate your child's feelings and/or verbalize understanding of what he or she wants. In the second blank, FIRMLY state what needs to be done. In the third blank (if you think it would help) add a choice, a redirection, or a kind AND firm statement about what you will do.

    ____

    AND ____

    ____

    (Keep in mind that the last blank may not be necessary.)

5. If this form is used for "homework", please have this Practice Questionnaire completed and ready to share at our next class.

Focus ONLY on Kind OR Firm

(Adapted from an activity by Terry Chadsey, based on the work of Barry Johnson on Polarities)

Objective:

To help parents and teachers understand the results of being too kind or too firm, and the value of being kind and firm at the same time.

Materials:

Flip chart paper and marking pens

4 flip charts prepared as per direction No. 1

Both "Challenges" and "Characteristics and Life Skills" lists from Two Lists activity

Comment:

Being kind and firm creates an important balance—as does breathing in and breathing out.

Directions

1. In advance, prepare flip chart papers with the following headings:

    Positive Results of a Focus only on Kind
    Negative Results of a Focus only on Kind
    Positive Results of a Focus only on Firm
    Negative Results of a Focus only on Firm

2. Discuss the information in the comment by asking, "What would happen if you had to choose between breathing in or breathing out?" Breathing is one example of how things don't work out too well when you choose one or the other.

3. Divide into four groups. Give each group one of the prepared in advance flip charts and ask each group to brainstorm the results per the heading on their charts.

4. Allow about 3 to 5 minutes. Walk around to check how they are doing to help you know if they need more time.

5. When they have finished brainstorming, place the flip chart sheets on the floor per example at the end of this activity, including the "Challenges" and "Characteristics and Life Skills" lists from the Two Lists activity.

6. Ask everyone to stand in a circle around the configuration of flip charts on the floor. Then ask for a volunteer from each group to read what their group brainstormed on their flip chart.

7. Invite participants to share what they are learning—what insights whey are having from doing this activity so far. Don't be afraid of silence while people are processing what they are learning. Eventually they will start sharing.

8. Invite people to move close to the charts on the floor that represent their tendencies. In other words, if they tend to be too kind, have them move to that side of the charts. If they tend to be too firm, have them move to that side of the charts. Ask how many vacillate back and forth. Invite them to stand in the middle (at the top or bottom of the configuration). Ask the group, what did you notice? what did you learn?

9. If someone hasn't mentioned it, point out that people who choose to focus only on firmness may do so because they want to avoid the negative results of a focus only on kindness. People who choose to focus only on kindness may do so because they are afraid of the results of a focus only on firmness.

10. Share that you placed the "Characteristics and Life Skills" list at the top, and the "Challenges" list at the bottom because the positive results of both kindness and firmness invite children to develop the Characteristics and Life skills, and that the negative results of either just kindness or just firmness may invite the Challenging behaviors. (Point this out only if someone else hasn't.)

11. Invite people to go back to their seats and again ask what they learned from this activity. You might want to follow up with the Kind and Firm activity that provides examples of kind AND firm statements.

Example of what one class brainstormed and how it looked when spread out on the floor.

Characteristics and Life Skills

Self Confidence * Morals
Good Judgment * Respect for Self and Others
Kind/Compassion * Internal Compass
Independence/Interdependence
Cooperation/Problem Solving * Hopefulness
Leadership * Courage * Motivation
Faith * Self-Reliance * Self-Discipline
Gemeinschaftsgefuel –Sense of Contribution or "Social Awareness"

Positive Results of a Focus Only On Kind

Good example, model
Self worth, show you care
Trust, empower
Learn kindness, like you
Safe environment
Compassion

Positive Results of a Focus Only on Firm

Order, students know where they stand
Obedience/Compliance
Disciplined child
Predictability
Focus on responsibility, not excuses

Negative Results of a Focus Only On Kind

Entitlement
Pushover
Spoiled
No accountability
Lack of reliance
Lack of good judgment
Not prepared for adversity

Negative Results of a Focus Only on Firm

Rebellion, resistance, revenge
Tuning out, alienation
Fear or power struggles
Lack of felt love
Alienation, anxiety
Distance and hostility
Lack of feeling safe

Challenges

Messy Rooms * Procrastination
Siblings (?) Issues/Fights * Not Listening
Back Talking/ Sassiness * Lack of Focus
Electronic/Media * Communication
Moodiness * Temper
Different Parenting Styles
Over Scheduling * Homework * Nutrition
Expectation of Undue Service
Defiance * Accountability

Notes

Labels and Their Impact

Objective:

To understand the importance of avoiding labels for children.

Comment:

Labels, positive and negative, block both the parent's and the child's ability to experience, express, and/or acknowledge the whole person. Belonging and significance are enhanced by believing that someone knows WHO you are, not WHAT you do.

Materials:

Characteristic and Life Skills List and Challenge List from the Two lists activity

Sticky notes for half the group with descriptive words such as smart, lazy, cute, rebellious, selfish, angel, brat, hyperactive, shy, forgetful, athletic, clumsy, trouble-maker, demanding, charming, good, bad. etc. If you want to get fancy you can make headbands with the labels written on them.

Choose Positive Discipline Tool cards that would be encouraging to children for any of the behaviors listed above. Be sure there are as many cards as there are parents. (Some possibilities: Curiosity Questions, Validate Feelings, Show Faith, Agreements, Put Kids in Same Boat, I Notice, Family Meetings, Listen, Special Time, Problem-solving, Hugs, Empower, Sense of Humor, etc.)

Directions

1. Divide into two groups.

2. Have one group be children who will wear the sticky notes or headbands on their forehead, with labels such as "smart", "lazy", "cute", "rebellious", "angel," "brat", etc. (Be sure to have the same number of "negative" behaviors as "positive" behaviors.)

3. Have the other group be parents who will walk around and stop before each child and respond to their labels the way many parents do (those who haven't taken a Positive Discipline Class).

4. After a few minutes ask the "children" with labels on their foreheads to go to the right side of the room if they think they have a positive label and to the left if they think they have a negative label.

5. Process by asking the children what they were thinking, feeling, and deciding? How long before you knew how you were labeled?

6. Ask them to look at the Characteristics and Life Skills List and ask if they were learning any of them? Then point to the Challenges List and ask if they are deciding to do any of these?

7. Process with the parents about what they were thinking, feeling, and deciding.

8. Now tell the parents they are going to a Positive Discipline parenting class. Give each one a Positive Discipline Tool card. Ask them to take a few seconds to read the card to themselves to learn the tool so they can go to the children and use it with each one of them without having to read the card—unless they really need to.

9. Have the group start milling again, this time have the parents use the tool with each child.

10. After a few minutes, process by asking the children what they were thinking, feeling, and deciding? How was it different this time?

11. Ask them to look at the Characteristics and Life Skills List and ask if they were learning any of them?

12. Process with the parents about what they were thinking, feeling, and deciding.

13. Process with the whole group by asking them what they learned from this activity.

14. If it doesn't come up in the discussion ask, "What are you learning about your own children? About yourself as a child? What labels did you grow up with? How did those labels impact your life?"

Comment:

This activity is extremely powerful and can be very emotional for some parents either because they felt unsupported growing up or they realize they have labeled their children without meaning to. Either know your group before doing this activity or warn participants in advance that some may feel very emotional as a result of doing this activity. Leave plenty of time for processing.

From Laddership to Leadership

Based on the work of Steve A. Maybell, Jody McVittie, and Lois Ingber

Objective:

To explore the implications of vertical relationships.

To recognize skills necessary for effective leadership in a democratic community.

To recognize the importance of shared visions/agreements.

Materials:

Flip chart and markers

Sample Structure of Power chart below for reference

Optional: toy ladder

Characteristic and Life Skills list from the Two List activity

Comments:

As democratic relationships become more prevalent in families, schools, and organizations, the tools needed for effective leadership change.

The time of transition toward a more horizontal or democratic system can be messy.

The process of developing a shared vision/goal is one of many leadership challenges in this paradigm.

Directions

1. **Set up.**
   - Explain briefly: In the past it was normal and acceptable to have people with superior positions and people with inferior positions.
   - Illustrate this by naming some examples. Using only the top half of the flip chart, write the "superior" positions on the top, and the "inferior" positions at the bottom underneath its corresponding superior position (leaving most of the flip chart blank in between).
   - List the following pairs: kings/peasants, boss/workers, men/women, teachers/students, adults/children, light skinned/dark skinned. See sample below.
   - Comment that there are many more hierarchies that are not on this list.
2. **Identify the tools of power.** Pointing to the row of people on the top ask how these people maintained their position above the people below them.
   - What tools did they use? See sample below.
   - Scribe the answers in the space between the two groups of people.

3. **The impact of vertical relationships.** Let the group know that we call these "vertical relationships." Ask:

   - What do you think the people on the bottom might be thinking, feeling or deciding about the people on the top?
   - What are the people on the bottom thinking, feeling or deciding about themselves?
   - What happens if the people on the bottom try to change the hierarchy? (You can reference historical events if not mentioned: revolutions, labor unions, suffragettes, civil rights movement, etc.). This is the "messy" part.

4. **Change is happening.** People on the bottom have decided they want and deserve to be treated with equal dignity and respect. Ask the following: When people have a sense of worthiness, how effective are the old tools? How do children let us know they want to be treated with equal dignity and respect? (Usually people recognize it is through the behaviors on the "Challenges" list.) This explanation (from "Positive Discipline" p. 14) can be shared: In the 1950's dad said "Jump" and mom jumped. Mom said "Jump" and the kids jumped. Today, dad says jump and mom says, "Excuse me?" So when mom says "Jump," why are we surprised when children don't jump? Rudolf Dreikurs said, *"When dad lost control of mom, they both lost control of the children."*

5. **Horizontal relationships.**

   - Draw a horizontal line across the bottom half of the paper.
   - Ask, "What kinds of tools are needed for people to live and work together effectively?" (Participants will list things like cooperation, respect, responsibility, communication, celebrate differences, collaboration etc). Record these near the line.
   - Ask, "Where do we learn those tools?"
   - "Why does it seem so messy?" The idea that comes out here is that power tools are familiar and part of our language. We are less skilled at the cooperation tools; they often take longer and need to be revised during the change process.

6. **Your parenting compass and teaching tools.**

   - Does this list of tools look familiar? (Compare with the "Skills/Characteristics" from Two Lists activity).
   - For most families the long term vision is growing healthy adults who can contribute, connect and treat others with respect. How do you "lead" that?
   - As your children get older, how do they lead the family (especially for short term projects)?
   - What does this tell us about the importance of making agreements? (Refer to the process of making agreements in this manual)

7. **Reflection/Summary.**

   - You can look at this as a change from "Laddership" (top down) to Leadership (horizontal).
   - Horizontal relationships doesn't mean that everyone is the same or has the same responsibilities but does mean everyone is treated with dignity and respect.
   - Parents, teachers and administrators have clear leadership roles with distinct responsibilities.

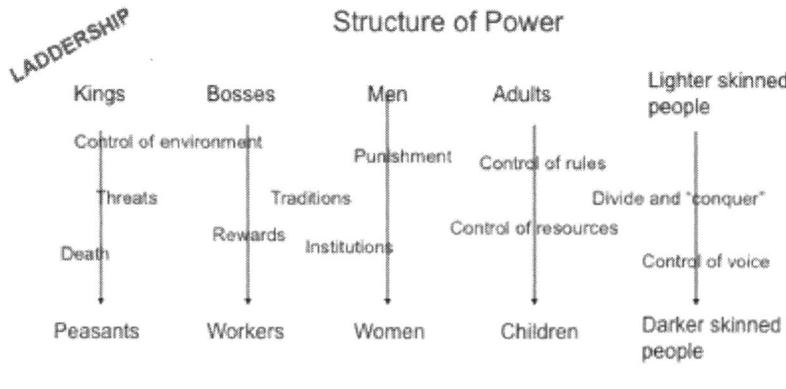

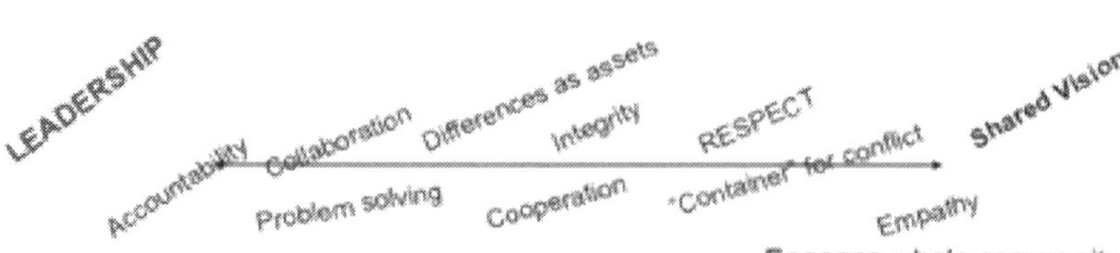

Leadership Styles

Objective:

To discover the leadership style (in homes, classrooms, or businesses) that invites the highest encouragement, creativity, and production.

Comment:

Participants can have fun exaggerating while learning the short-term and the long-term effects of leadership styles.

Materials:

Three large manila envelopes (or sacks) filled with stuff. Each envelope must have exactly the same stuff. Go through your junk drawers and find paper clips, staples, pens, rubber bands; your medicine cabinet for band aids, shampoos samples, q-tips, etc.; the garage for nails, screws, nuts, bolts; other places for puzzle pieces, yarn, macaroni, nuts, rocks, leaves, etc.

Include the appropriate instructions in each envelope

3 flip chart papers and 3 marking pens—one for each group

Characteristics and Life Skills and Challenges lists from the Two Lists

Directions

1. Prepare in advance and include the following written instruction on a piece of laminated paper to include in each envelope:

    The Task: List as many categories as you can for the objects in the envelope.

2. Ask for three volunteers to be leaders and have them stand aside.

3. Divide the rest of the participants into three groups, give each group a flip chart paper and a marking pen and have them settle into three circles as far apart as possible while you take the three volunteers to leadership training.

4. Take the "leaders" aside where others can't hear and tell them they will each be given an envelope filled with stuff. Have the scripts for the three leadership styles on the following page prepared in advance on a laminated piece of paper that can be cut for each leader and ask them each to read their instructions to themselves to get prepared. Let them know it is okay to exaggerate their instructions.

5. Have each "leader" go back to one of the groups and follow his or instructions as a leader.

6. Allow three to five minutes for the category brainstorming. Walk around so you can see how they are doing and judge if they need more time.

7. When the time is up, ask each group to count the number of categories they came up with.

8. Which group had the most?

9. Ask for participants in each group (one group at a time) to share what they were thinking, feeling, and deciding in response to their leader. Ask each group what they were learning from the Characteristics and Life Skills list, or if any were feeling motivated to engage in any of the behaviors on the Challenges list.

10. Ask the group to share what they learned from this activity and how it might relate to leadership styles where they live or work.

Comment:

In most cases, the democratic group will have the most categories. In some cases the permissive group does well because a leader emerges from the group. If the authoritarian group has the most, be sure to take more time processing what the members of that group were thinking, feeling, and deciding.

Authoritarian Leader:

The task instructions are in the envelope. Be sure you read the instructions to your group. Be very controlling. Instruct your group that they are to raise their hands and wait to be called on before they speak. If someone speaks out of turn, send that person to time-out. Let them know that they are not to touch the objects. You will be in charge of that. Once in awhile use discouraging comments such as, "I'm not so sure about that." (Then later suggest the same idea.) Be sure you are the one to record all the suggestions you think are good enough.

Permissive Leader:

The task instructions are in the envelope. When you meet with your group, act unprepared. Indicate that you are not sure you understand the task. Then sit back and let your group see if they can figure it out.

Democratic Leader:

The task instructions are in the envelope. Ask for a volunteer to read them. Then ask for another volunteer to record all the suggestions. Suggest that everyone brainstorm as many classifications (categories) for the stuff as they can think of. Act as an encouraging cheerleader, "Great idea. Very creative. Let's be sure our recorder gets all these great ideas."

Letting Go

Objective:

To deal with our own fears that get in the way of empowering our children by letting go and turning power over to them.

Materials:

"Five Steps for Letting Go" handout, for each participant

Comment:

Letting go is not easy for parents. Our fears often get in the way of allowing children to grow through normal developmental stages. Trying to stop a preadolescent from going to the mall, or a teenager from talking on the phone too much, driving a car, or going to a party is similar to trying to stop a toddler from walking because he/she might hurt him/herself. If our goal is to empower our kids and help them grow, these "Five Steps to Letting Go" can help.

Directions

1. Pass out the Five Steps for Letting Go handout and allow three to five minutes for participants to fill out the first three steps on their own.

2. Sometimes it is hard to figure out the smallest step you can take. Form groups of four and allow time for participants to present their concern and get suggestions from their group on small steps they could take. Each participant can write down all the suggestions they receive and then choose one to complete step 5 on the form. Ask them to brainstorm quickly as each person will have about three to four minutes.

3. Ask participants:

   a. What insights did you gain from completing this activity?
   b. What new understanding did you gain about your issues?
   c. What new understanding did you gain about your child's issues?
   d. What uncomfortable feeling did you experience? What benefits do you see for you and for your child when you let go?

Comment:

Letting go is not something you need to tell our children you are doing. This is a process you can continue to work on in your own quiet moments.

Five Steps for Letting Go

1. Think of an area where you are having a hard time letting go with one of your kids (an area where you know in your heart you are holding on too tight).

2. What are the issues?

    a. Yours (usually your fears)
    b. Theirs (usually what they want)

3. Are you willing to let go? There is no point in going on to the next two steps if you know you are not willing to let go.

4. What is a small step you could take to let go? Be specific.

5. When would you be willing to start your small step of letting go, and how long are you willing to do it even though it may be a little uncomfortable for you?

6. Ask a volunteer to read the following essay:

Letting Go with Love

Lynn Lott

The first time my son wanted to climb to the top of the slide was the first time I remember experiencing the feeling of letting go. He was ready, but I was not. He was a careful kid who didn't try things unless he thought he could do them. I remembered Dreikur's words, "A bruised knee can mend, but bruised courage lasts a lifetime." I took a deep breath and moved away from the slide—far enough to give him a sense of confidence and close enough to grab onto him if he fell. Of course he did just fine, and so did I.

That event wasn't any easier than the time he was late for school and I hid in the bushes while he walked crying into the building, or the time he was ready to cross the alley without my help and I hid behind the plants watching from a safe distance, ready to leap in front of him if a car should happen along. As he got older the letting go opportunities multiplied along with his courage and self-confidence and my faith that he would grow to be an old man. Of course I did create an imaginary golden net to protect him when I wasn't nearby, and so far it's working just fine!

Listening: Effective and Ineffective

Objective:

To experience the difference between
effective and ineffective listening.

Materials:

None

Comment:

How we listen can encourage or discourage further communication and interaction with children.

Directions

1. Have the group divide into partners to role-play where "A" shares a problem and "B" gives advice. Suggest that they think of a time one of their children came to them with a problem and they gave advice such as, "I think you should _____." They can then role-play that scene with their partner.

2. Process by asking how they felt in each role, starting with the ones who had to listen to the advice. Ask what they were thinking, feeling, and what they were deciding.

3. Next have "As" share problems and "Bs" put down, criticize, or get angry such as, "I can't believe you _______.". Again, they might first think of a time when this happened with one of their children—or they heard it happen with one of their neighbors. Process as above.

4. For the third round, have "As" share one of the same problems from above and "Bs" validate their partners feelings using this format, making sure that the word after "feel" is a feeling word (see feeling faces chart in handouts section):

5. "You feel _________ because __________ and you wish _______________

6. Process as above.

7. Discuss, "Which of these response styles would your prefer? Which would you prefer if you were a child?

8. How do these styles apply to what happens at home?

EXPANDED VERSION:

Include more examples for partners to role-play with each other:

9. Have "As" share a problem and "Bs" listen without speaking. Process as above.

10. Have "As" share a problem while "Bs" walk away. Process as above.

11. Have "As" share a problem while "Bs" use the curiosity questions, process as above.

Love Cup

Adapted from an activity by John Taylor. *Person to Person*, available at www.add-plus.com

Objective:

To learn preventive measures to avoid the pot boiling over on those we love.

Materials:

Clear plastic or glass pitcher

A number of clear glasses to equal imaginary family members

Red food coloring

Water and towels, just in case

Comment:

This activity can be a follow up to the anger activities. You can also do "The Brain in the Palm of your Hand" activity prior to this one, which quickly teaches parents the value
of understanding themselves so they are more careful with their families.

Directions

1. Have a pitcher full of red colored water before you start. Set the pitcher and glasses up on a stand or table so all present can see this demonstration. (It is also wise to have a towel or two handy, just in case.)

2. Begin by describing that the red colored water represents love energy, warmth, and feelings of peace, joy and harmony.

3. Pour love energy into one cup until it is almost full. Say, "When your love cup is full you feel happy; you have patience; you remember how to behave so that you get the long term results that you want for your children; you feel confident; you really appreciate your family and each child. This is the way you want to feel at each moment you are called upon to be a parent, partner or employee."

4. Then begin to un-stack the other cups as you discuss each person's needs that seem to need to be met by you. From your cup pour into one cup and say something like, "This is your oldest child coming to you for the fourth time this morning asking where he or she left things needed for school." As the child responds saying, "Gee, Mom, you are the greatest!" pour some portion of the love energy back into your cup. Into the next cup pour more of your love energy and say, "You have just mopped the kitchen floor and your 3 year old attempted to get the gallon jug out of the fridge to pour her own juice and dropped it. You stop your routine and help the child clean up the mess. As you finish, your child says how much he enjoys working with you." Then pour a little back in. Say, "Your partner calls from the office saying someone important is in

from out of town and would you mind giving up your trip to the gym to cover?" The love energy pours out and then your partner says, "Hey, I really appreciate your support." Some pours in from the other's cup. Begin to ad lib at any time. Then your friend, the church group, your parents, etc. And so the love energy continues to pour out. Say, "When you are on 'low energy' how do you speak, feel, respond?"

5. Who is responsible for filling your love cup? How important is it? What can you do? Turn to a person next to you and share several things you could do to keep your love energy up and when was the last time that you did this. Now make an agreement to check with this partner next week and report on your love cup filling progress. Teachers can use the love cup to demonstrate the love energy in the class. What does it take to keep the love cup full in room 3? How do we drain it?

6. Let's share these ideas by going around the circle. Feel free to borrow ideas from each other. Each person say one thing you might do to fill your love cup. Demonstrate by filling the cup as they make suggestions.

7. Stress the fact we are all doing the best at every moment with what we know, how life experiences are now, etc. No one sets out to ruin their day.

8. Stress the importance of putting yourself at the top of the list so you will be more effective in all of your needed roles.

Misbehavior in Public

> ## Objective:
> To learn and practice effective options for dealing with misbehavior in public.

> ## Materials:
> None

> ## Comment:
> Prior training (at home) for public outings frees a family to enjoy their time together. This activity may be done as a demonstration or as small group role-plays.

Directions

1. Ask for five volunteers to role-play a typical family in a restaurant (Mom, Dad, a typical three-year-old boy, a seven-year-old girl, and a 13-year-old girl). Invite each to exaggerate what they imagine to be typical behaviors for their age and role. Remind them to exaggerate and have fun.

2. Process by asking what each family member was thinking, feeling, and what they were deciding. It is important to hear how the parents were feeling in this situation. Focus on the feelings of embarrassment and anger that they express. Emphasize understanding of how their own feelings fuel how they respond to their child's behaviors.

3. Ask the audience what they were thinking, feeling, and learning.

4. Suggest the family role-play a training situation at home (during a family meeting) where they talk about appropriate restaurant behavior and let the kids know that if their plan doesn't work they'll all leave and try again another day.

5. Process as above.

6. Emphasize the following attitudes that are needed to make this work. Training is not a one shot deal— it's important for kids to know what to expect and what is expected of them and what the needs of the situation are.

EXPANDED VERSION:
In addition to the above:

7. Ask if participants have witnessed or experienced public misbehavior in other settings and how they felt when it happened.

8. Have the group role-play situations they have witnessed and then replace with training—as many scenes as they have time for.

Notes

Mistaken Goal Chart Introduction

Objective:

To introduce the goal chart by helping parents become familiar with feelings they experience in reaction to certain behaviors.

Materials:

Mistaken Goal Chart, tab

Flip chart

Marking pens

Comment:

This activity helps parents understand that what they feel in response to a child's behavior is their first clue to understand the child's mistaken goal. You read this right. It is the parent's feeling that is the clue to the child's belief that leads to the "misbehavior."

Directions

1. Have the following prepared in advance on a flip chart: make a line down the middle and across the middle of a page. Then write "Attention" at the top of the upper left quadrant, "Power" at the top of the upper right quadrant, "Revenge" at the top of the lower left quadrant, and "Assumed Inadequacy" at the top of the lower right quadrant.

2. Give each participant a copy of the Mistaken Goal Chart.

3. Ask the group to look at the feelings listed in the second column of the goal chart after "Undue Attention." Then invite them to brainstorm behaviors that invite them to feel "annoyed, irritated, worried, or guilty." Ask a volunteer to record these behaviors under "Attention" on the flip chart.

4. Repeat the above procedure for each of the goals.

> **Comment:**
> Several behaviors may be for any of the four goals. Not doing homework is a good example. Make sure that behavior is listed in every quadrant. Then point out that some children may not do their homework because that is a good way to keep you busy with them; others may not do their homework because that is a good way to show you that, "You can't make me;" others may not do their homework because they feel hurt and this is a good way to hurt back; still others may not do their homework because they don't believe they can. Obviously, different interventions are effective for each goal.

Notes

Mistaken Goal Detective

Objective:

To help parents and teachers become Mistaken Goal Detectives by using a "real" challenge to become familiar with the Mistaken Goal Chart.

Materials:

Poster or drawing of an iceberg with the words "Behavior" written on the tip of the iceberg, and "Belief Behind the Behavior" written on the base of the iceberg

Mistaken Goal Chart for each participant

Mistaken Goal Detective Clue Form (following page) for each participant

Comment:

This can be an effective way to teach the Mistaken Goal Chart while warming people up for the PHPPSS. It has many of the components of the PHPPSS, but not all, since the main goal is to become familiar with the Mistaken Goal Chart.

Directions

1. Introduce the activity by displaying the iceberg poster and sharing that a child's behavior represents the equivalent to the top of the iceberg. A primary difference between Positive Discipline and many other parenting programs is that we know there is a belief behind every behavior. For this reason we seek to understand and address the belief, as well as the behavior. Many parenting programs deal only with the behavior—which misses the biggest part of the iceberg, (the belief behind the behavior). Just as we don't see the foundation of the iceberg, we don't see the foundation of behavior, (the belief); and many parents and teachers do not even know it exists.

2. Point out that, "A misbehaving child is a discouraged child" (has discouraging beliefs about his or her belonging and significance). In most cases, the behavior changes only when the belief about how to find belonging and significance changes.

3. Hand out the Mistaken Goal Detective Clue Form and the Mistaken Goal Chart to each participant. Have them write numbers above each column (1-7)

4. Allow 5 minutes for participants to fill out their forms. Caution them to not think too hard, but to write the first thing that comes to mind. (Notice when most are done and ask if the rest could finish in one or two more minutes.)

5. When everyone is finished, ask for a volunteer who would be willing to share what he or she has written, and to be guided through some brief role-playing.

6. Have the volunteer come sit next to you and share his or her challenge. Ask for a show of hands from those who can relate to the challenge.

7. Have the volunteer share the rest of what he or she has filled out on the Mistaken Goal Detective Clue Form, one question at a time. (You may have to interrupt to keep the volunteer focused on answering the questions, and not wandering to explanations.)

8. When you have finished through No. 10, help the volunteer clarify his or her action plan by asking exactly what he or she is going to do and say. Ask for another volunteer to role-play the child.

9. Ask the "child" to act out the challenging behavior so the volunteer can practice the plan of action.

10. The parent may need coaching. For example, if the volunteer's plan was to, Validate feelings, and then show faith in the child to do what is needed, but instead starts lecturing, interrupt and say, "Excuse me, what did you say you were going to do"

11. Allow about 60 seconds for the role-play and then process with each person (starting with the child) what each was thinking feeling, and deciding.

12. Ask members of the group to share what they learned from this activity.

Facilitator Notes:

One way to involve the whole group is to ask them, "If you had been the child (or other person) in this role-play, what would you be thinking, feeling, or deciding?" Allow sharing. This demonstrates that, just as in real life, different children might make different decisions. And, if you have a child role-player who keeps playing a "misbehaving child," even when the parent did a good job of using a respectful and encouraging tool, it can be helpful for the group to hear that others would respond differently.

If the role-play did not seem "successful" do not repeat. Trust the process. Point out that it is just as important to learn what doesn't work as what does work, and that guessing the mistaken goal is just a hypothesis.

Alternate Activity:

1. After the first 3 steps above, have participants find a partner and decide which one will be the facilitator to lead the other through the process of filling out the Mistaken Goal Detective Clue Form. (Allow 5 minutes.)

2. Ask if anyone would like to share their example.

3. If you have time, facilitate a role-play of the volunteer's plan of action by inviting the volunteer to role-play the child, and including others to role-play others described in the challenge.

4. Process thinking, feeling, deciding of each of the role-players

5. Invite sharing of what all participants learned.

Mistaken Goal Detective Clue Form

1. Think of a recent challenge you had with a child. Write it down. Describe what occurred as though you are writing a script: What did the child do? How did you react? What happened next?

2. What were you feeling when you were in the middle of this challenge? (Choose a feeling from Column 2 of the Mistaken Goal Chart.) Write it down.

3. Now move your finger over to Column 3 of the Mistaken Goal Chart to see if your behavior, as you described it in your challenge, comes close to any of these typical adult responses. If what you did is described better in a different row, double-check to see if there is a feeling in another row in Column 2 that better represents how you were feeling at a deeper level. (For example, we often say we are feeling annoyed when, at a deeper level, we are feeling challenged or hurt, or we might say we feel hopeless and helpless when we really feel challenged or defeated in a power struggle.) How you react is a clue to your deeper feelings.

4. Move your finger across to Column 4. Do any of these descriptions come close to what the child did in response to your reaction?

5. Now move your finger to the left to Column No, 1 of the Mistaken Goal Chart? It is likely that this is your child's mistaken goal. Write it down.

6. Move your finger to the right to Column 5 of the Mistaken Goal Chart. You have just discovered what may be the discouraging belief of the child. Write it down.

7. Move your finger to Column 6. Does this come close to a belief you have that may contribute to the child's misbehavior? (Remember, this is not about blame, only about awareness.) While you are learning skills to encourage the child, you will also change your own belief! Try it now by writing down a response that would be more encouraging to the child. You'll find clues in the last two columns.

8. Move your finger to Column 7, where you will find the coded message the child is sending about what he/she needs in order to feel encouraged.

9. Move once more to Column 8, the last one, to find some ideas you could try the next time the child presents this challenging behavior. You can also use the deck of parent or teacher tool cards, and your own wisdom to think of what to do or say that would speak to the coded message in Column 7. Write down your plan.

10. How did it go? Record in your journal exactly what you discovered and what happened. Did the child's behavior change? Did yours? If your plan isn't successful the first time, try another tool. Make certain that in every effort you begin by making a connection before you attempt a correction.

Notes

Mistaken Goals (Short Role-Plays)

Objective:
To get into the child's world and understand four perceptions (mistaken goals) that lead to misbehavior.

Materials:
A Mistaken Goal chart for each participant

Comment:
The primary goal of all children is to belong and feel significant. When they believe they don't belong, they feel discouraged and will often find mistaken ways (misbehavior) based on one of the four mistaken goals to seek belonging and significance.

Directions

1. UNDUE ATTENTION: Ask for three volunteers—two adults and one child. Have the two adults engage in a conversation. The child interrupts (starts and stops when asked to stop, but soon interrupts again). Process by asking each volunteer how he/she was feeling and what he/she was thinking and deciding.

2. MISGUIDED POWER: Have one volunteer and the leader face one another with palms touching at head level. The leader (the parent) orders the volunteer (the child) to do something (for example, "Go clean your room."), and simultaneously pushes against his or her hands. The child refuses and pushes back. The parent repeats. The child repeats. The action intensifies. Process as above.

3. REVENGE: Ask for two volunteers. Ask them to take turns slapping each other on the leg starting softly and getting harder with each slap until either partner says, "Enough." Process as above.

4. ASSUMED INADEQUACY: The leader can be a child who has the mistaken notion that he/she is not capable of succeeding at anything. A volunteer tries to get the child to do the task at hand (for example, homework. The child continually withdraws as the parent coaxes). Process as above.

EXPANDED VERSION:
Instead of previous steps:

5. Ask the group to role-play steps 1 through 4 in dyads.

6. Process by asking how they were feeling, what they were thinking, and what they were deciding.

7. Redo the role-play with corrective measures.

> For Undue Attention the parent gently strokes the child's arm while continuing the conversation.
>
> For Misguided Power the parent drops hands and walks away saying, "I can't make you, but I'd like your help."
>
> For Revenge the parent makes a guess about what might be hurting the child's feelings and validate the hurt feelings. For example, "I wonder if you feel hurt because you think I don't have enough time for you." The parent shows empathy, which is usually enough to defuse the child's hurt feelings because she feels understood. Parent could add, "Let's talk about this a little later when we both feel better."
>
> For Assumed Inadequacy the parent lets the child know he or she has faith in him and you are there to help if he comes and asks.

8. Refer to the Mistaken Goal Chart for further possible corrective measures.

9. Process as above.

　　　　　　　　　　　　　　

Mistaken Goals and Positive Discipline Tool Cards

Objective:

To help parents and teachers become more aware of how many tools there are to encourage a child who is operating from a mistaken goal.

To give parents and teachers an opportunity to practice encouraging tools for each mistaken goal.

Materials:

A copy of the Mistaken Goal Chart for each participant

4 decks of Positive Discipline Tool Cards

Coded Message signs for each Mistaken Goal (attached) printed & laminated with yarn to hang around necks

List of Characteristics and Life Skills from Two Lists Activity

Comment:

Parents and teachers can have fun while learning through role-plays that help them get into the child's world. The Positive Discipline Tool Cards provide visual clues to emphasize the fact that there are many different tools that can be effective.

Directions

1. Divide the large group into four groups. Each group will receive a deck of Positive Discipline Tool Cards and one of the four laminated Mistaken Goal Coded Message signs.

2. Instruct each group to go through their deck of cards and make a pile of as many as they can that will address the Coded Message for their group. (Allow 5 minutes.)

3. Ask each group to share how many they found, but not to read each one—just how many. (This might raise the curiosity of others to find the possible tool cards for each mistaken goal on their own.)

4. Role-plays. Ask each group to choose a "typical misbehavior" for the Mistaken Goal they are discussing. (A few are listed on the neck hanging signs you gave to each group.)

5. Then ask them to choose just one of the tools they think could be encouraging, and to plan a one-minute role-play using that tool with a child. The role-play will consist of at least one adult and one child—and as many other role-players as they need for their scene. The child will hang the coded message sign around his or her neck. (Allow just 5 minutes for planning the role-play reminding them to have fun and to have the courage to be imperfect—and that the role-play should be 60 seconds or less.)

6. At the end of each role-play scene, starting with the child, process what he or she is thinking, feeling, and deciding. Point to the "Characteristics and Life Skills chart" from the Two Lists activity and ask if there is anything he or she is learning. Then process with the adult and other role-players what they are thinking, feeling and deciding.

7. At the end of the activity, ask the large group to share what insights they had from participating in this activity.

8. Ask for a member of each group to be responsible for collecting all of the tool cards and returning them to you (to use another time.)

Undue Attention

Belief: "I belong when you pay attention to me."

Typical behaviors: Interrupting, talking out of turn, constant noises, won't do work.

Notice me-
involve me usefully

Misguided Power

Belief: "I'm the boss—or at least won't let you boss me."

Typical behaviors: "You can't make me," says "yes" but doesn't do it, defiant behavior, won't do work.

Let me help-
give me choices

Revenge

Belief: "I don't belong and that hurts, so I'll hurt back."

Typical behaviors: Destroys property, hurts others, calls adults names, won't do work.

I'm hurting-
Validate my feelings

Assumed Inadequacy

Belief: "I can't belong, so why try."

Typical behaviors: Won't try, withdraws, gives up, won't do work.

Don't give up
on me;
show me a small step

Mistakes are Wonderful Opportunities to Learn. REALLY?

Objective:

To help parents explore whether or not they really believe in mistakes as opportunities to learn.

To provide, experientially, the short-term and long-term benefits of allowing (and supporting) children in making mistakes.

Materials:

Flip chart as described in No. 2 below.

Markers.

The Two Lists: Challenge and Characteristics and Life Skills (from Two Lists Activity)

Flip charts with the following headings:
- Long and Short-term Benefits of Learning From Mistakes
- Typical Discouraging Responses to Mistakes

Flip Chart or Poster of the following:

Hints for Being Supportive and Encouraging Regarding Mistakes:
- Validate child's feelings.
- Ask curiosity questions.
- Brainstorm together for solutions.
- Show faith in child to handle the situation.

Directions

1. Ask the group, "How many of you believe that mistakes are opportunities to learn?"

2. On a flip chart labeled, "Long and Short-term Benefits of Learning from Mistakes" invite the group to brainstorm. Examples might be:

    Children learn they are okay no matter what.

    Eliminates perfectionism.

    Increases curiosity.

    Creates confidence and risk taking.

    Helps children learn how capable they are.

    Creates a strong sense of belonging and connection.

3. Display another flipchart labeled Typical Discouraging Responses to Mistakes. Ask the group to brainstorm what many parents say and do when their children make a mistake such as getting a poor grade or forget-

ting their coat when it is cold outside. For example:

> You are grounded until your grades improve.
>
> You lose the privilege of _________ until your grades improve.
>
> No more having fun after school. Come right home and study.
>
> How do you think you'll ever get a job if you don't get good grades in school?
>
> How many times do I have to tell you?
>
> Why can't you just trust that I know what I'm talking about and I'm trying to save you from future pain and disappointment?
>
> Don't you care what other people think?

4. Divide the group into 4's and ask them to do the following role-play in their small groups.

    Scene One: Ask for a volunteer to play a child who gets a poor grade in school. Ask for three volunteers to take turns responding the way most parents do when they don't want their child to make a mistake. (Often children hear these comments from more than one parent and a teacher.) They can use any of the brainstormed Typical Responses or be spontaneous.

5. Allow about 3 or 4 minutes and then ask a few of the "children" to share what they were thinking, feeling, and deciding in response to what their parents said. Point to the Characteristics and Life Skills list and ask if they are learning any of these. (Probably not.) Then point to Challenges list and as if they are motivated to learn any of these? Which ones?

6. **Scene Two:** Display the flip chart of Hints for Being Supportive and Encouraging Regarding Mistakes.

7. Then ask them to role-play any or all of the four hints: the same three playing parents to the one child.

8. Allow about 3 or 4 minutes and then ask a few (or all of them if you have a small group) of the "children" to share what they were thinking, feeling, and deciding in response to what their parents said. Point to the Characteristics and Life Skills list and ask if they are learning any of these. (Probably several. Which ones?)

9. Invite a discussion of what they learned from this activity. How could they use the Hints in another situation where they have been trying to prevent a child for making a mistake?

Mistakes as Wonderful Opportunities to Learn

Objective:

To help participants replace negative beliefs about mistakes with beliefs about the value of mistakes.

Materials:

Pencils

Mistakes Interview Form for each participant

Comment:

Parents usually mean well when they try to motivate their children to do better by making them feel bad about their mistakes. However, they fail to check out the results of their good intentions. When they see the fallacy of their misguided intentions they are open to see with a new perspective how empowering it is to view mistakes as wonderful opportunities to learn.

Directions

1. Ask the group to choose partners and take turns interviewing each other using the "Mistakes Interview Form." Allow five minutes for each partner. Let them know when the first five minutes is up and it is time to switch interviewer and interviewee positions.

2. Ask the group:

   a. What insights did you gain from participating in this activity?

   b. Are you willing to make some new decisions about mistakes?

   c. What are they?

   d. Would you be willing to change your thinking about mistakes and tell yourself that mistakes are opportunities to learn and that your child can try again, and so can you?

Mistakes Interview Form

1. What are the messages you heard from your parents about mistakes either stated or implied? Based on the messages you heard about mistakes, what did you decide about mistakes and about yourself?

2. Based on that decision, what kind of behaviors do you do to either avoid making mistakes or keep others from knowing if you do?

3. What do you think mistakes might mean for your child/children?

4. Think of a time when your child made a mistake and you were supportive and encouraging.

   a. What did you do?

   b. What was the result of what you did?

   c. What do you think your child learned from that experience?

   d. What perceptions?

   e. What skills?

   d. What did you learn?

5. Think of a time when your child made a mistake and you were not supportive and encouraging.

   a. What did you do?

   b. What was the result of what you did?

   c. What do you think your child learned from that experience?

   d. What perceptions?

   e. What skills?

   f. What did you learn?

Mom Said–and Other Messages from Childhood

Objective:

To become aware of some of the messages we heard in our childhood, how we felt about them, and the decisions we made that affect our lives today.

Materials:

Flip chart

Marking pens

Comment:

Too often we perpetuate with our children the messages from our parents that were not helpful to us.

Directions

1. Ask participants to find a blank page in their journal and write down answers to the following:

    My mother always said ____.

    I decided ____

    How does that decision affect the way I parent my children?

2. Ask participants to find a partner and take turns sharing their answers.

3. Bring everyone back to the large group and process by asking what they learned from doing this activity so far.

4. Ask for a volunteer who would like to work on changing the decision. Have the volunteer share what he or she wrote.

5. Ask the volunteer if he or she can think of a different decision that would make more sense and be more helpful in his or her life today.

6. Ask how this decision could make a difference in his or her life—and especially regarding parenting.

7. You might want to extend the activity by going through the same process with what your father always said.

8. Discuss with whole group:

a. What did you learn from this activity?

b. Do your decisions from the past help you or hurt you?

c. How might a new decision change your parenting methods?

Money

<table>
<tr><td>

Objective:

To understand the importance of allowing children to learn the value of money from personal experience.

</td><td>

Materials:

What Does Your Child Know About Money? Article for each participant

Flip chart

Marking pens

</td></tr>
</table>

Comment:

Children learn many life skills from their personal experiences around money. Too many children are learning manipulative skills (whining or coaxing) rather than budgeting skills. They are learning that "money grows on trees" rather than "money is something I earn and save for certain goals." They are learning that adults will take care of the mistakes they make (after lectures and put-downs) rather than allowing them to experience the consequences of their mistakes with dignity and respect.

Directions

1. Ask participants to form groups of four. Give them a sheet of flip chart paper with the heading "Childhood Experiences with Money" and ask them to use a marking pen to divide the sheet into four quadrants. In the upper left quadrant have them record their answers to a. In the upper right quadrant have them record their answers to b. In the lower left quadrant, have them record their answers to c. In the lower right quadrant have them record their answers to d.

   a. What did you do to obtain money when you were a child (6-18)?
   b. What did you learn from how you obtained money?
   c. How do your children obtain money today?
   d. What do you think they are learning from the way they obtain money?

2. Invite each group to share their answers with the whole group.

3. Process by asking the group to share what insights they gained from doing this activity.

4. Pass out the article "What Does Your Child Know About Money?" Invite them to take turns reading a few paragraphs out loud.

EXPANDED VERSION:

5. Ask the same groups of four to come up with a plan they will be able to implement with their children based on the insights they gained from their discussions and the material they read.

6. Invite sharing of the plans with the large group.

7. Follow up next week by allowing a few minutes for sharing of how the plans are going.

What Does Your Child Know About Money?

Riki Intner, Jane Nelsen, and Lynn Lott

The Johnson family was about to complete their weekly grocery shopping when five-year-old Jimmy started coaxing for a toy car.

Mom asked politely, "Have you saved enough money from your allowance to buy it?"

Jimmy looked sad and said "No."

Mom suggested, "Maybe you would like to save your money so you can buy that car."

Of course Jimmy never saved enough money to buy the car. He wanted it bad enough to spend Mom's money, but not enough to save his own money.

Five-year-old Sally wanted a new bicycle. Dad worked out a plan with Sally that as soon as she could save $5 toward a bicycle, he would pay the rest. They got a glass jar, pasted a picture of a bicycle on it and Sally put her whole allowance (four quarters) in the jar the first week.

Since Sally's allowance was only $1 a week and it was difficult for her to resist the ice cream truck it took her three months to save $5. This seemed like an eternity to Sally, but every time she brought up the subject of a new bike, her Dad would ask, "How much have you saved?" They would go to the jar and count the quarters. They would figure out how many more quarters she needed to reach her goal of $5 and Dad would encourage her that she could do it.

In the sixth grade, Amy was given a school clothing allowance. Mom and Amy went through her closet together to figure out what she needed and then sat down to work on a budget to see how much she could spend for each item she wanted to purchase. Amy had to make decisions such as: would she buy two pair of expensive jeans or four pair of less expensive jeans. During their shopping expedition, many times Mom heard Amy say, "I like this a little bit but I don't like it `a lot.' I'm not going to buy anything I don't really like a lot."

In the seventh grade, Sam started saving diligently for a car because his parents had taken the time to discuss with him that they would not be willing to buy him a car when he was 16 unless he put in as much effort as they did. They agreed to match what he saved by the time he was ready for a car, if he had a job so he could buy the gas and insurance. Together they investigated the cost of insurance and Sam learned that it was much less expensive if he had a "B" average on his report cards. Sam decided he would work hard to maintain a "B" average.

Jimmy, Sally, Amy, and Sam are all learning the value of money. They are learning delayed gratification, goal setting, and the need to work and plan for what they want. They are also learning many side benefits such as cooperation, responsibility, and appreciating what they get. They all made poor decisions along the way. Amy learned to buy only what she "really liked" after buying some things she didn't like so much and then not having money left for things she really liked.

Sally finally learned that she wanted a bicycle more than she wanted ice cream. Sam did not save enough money for the car of his dreams but learned to fix the clunker he purchased because he was too impatient to wait and save a little longer.

Providing allowances is a tool parents can use to teach children many valuable lessons. Too many parents give "handouts" instead of allowances. Handouts are often based on the whims of parents and/or the ability of kids to coax, whine, and manipulate. Kids believe that checks and credit cards provide an unlimited supply of money. It is a very disrespectful system that leaves everyone feeling bad—parents who feel manipulated by coaxing, crying, or other forms of demand for money, which is never appreciated by their children; and children who do not learn the confidence and self-respect that comes from dealing with money responsibly.

The allowance system is respectful to all concerned. It is negotiated in advance based on what the family can afford and on the needs of the kids. If the children's needs are greater than the family budget, they can be encouraged to supplement their income by baby-sitting, washing cars or mowing lawns. Many problems can be avoided when allowances are not tied to chores. A four-year-old may enthusiastically make her bed for 10 cents, but will ask for 50 cents by the time she is eight. By the time she is 14 she won't want to do it even for a dollar.

Connecting chores to allowances offers too many opportunities for punishment, reward, bribery, and other forms of disrespectful manipulation. Each child gets an allowance just because he/she is a member of the family, and each child does chores just because he/she is a member of the family. It can be helpful to offer special jobs for pay that are beyond regular chore routines such as weeding for $4 an hour or washing the car for $5. This offers opportunities for kids who want to earn extra money, but does not cause problems if they choose not to take the opportunity.

Allowances can be started when children first become aware of the need for money when they start wanting toys at the supermarket or treats from the ice cream truck. Some families start with a quarter, a dime, a nickel, five pennies, and a piggy bank. A small child loves the variety and enjoys putting the money in the piggy bank. As children get older, allowances can be based on need. Children learn budgeting when parents take time to go over their needs with them. A child of six may want $1 for candy and $2 for savings. A child of 15 may need $15 a week for a movie, $10 for school lunches and $10 for savings and or incidentals.

If kids run out of money before the end of the week it is important to empathize but not rescue. They need the freedom to spend their allowance as they wish. If they spend it all at once they have the opportunity to learn from that experience as long as parents don't interfere or make judgments. This does not mean that allowances cannot be renegotiated. Renegotiation is an important part of the learning process as kids get older and their needs change. Birthdays or the start of a new school year are good times to sit down together and look at needs and go over budget planning.

A clothing allowance is a good addition to a regular allowance as soon as kids are old enough to be aware of fashion and want more clothing than is really necessary. A clothing allowance provides limits and encourages responsible decision making. When children are younger there may be two shopping trips each year — one in the spring and one in the fall, each with a certain dollar amount allotted. As children get older they may get a certain amount each month for them to budget.

Allowance and clothing budgets help children learn what their values are, to make decisions and live with the results, and to use money responsibly. By the time they leave home they are ready to manage their finances entirely.

Notes

Mr. Punishment

Objective:

To help parents become aware, experientially, of the long-term results of different discipline methods.

Role-playing is one of the best ways for parents to "get into the child's world" to experience what works and what doesn't work to encourage children to be responsible for their choices.

Comment:

Participants usually struggle to understand the difference between natural consequences and logical consequences. Experimenting with them through role-plays provides an opportunity for more discussion about how difficult it is to allow a natural consequence (the child just won't have clean clothes when she wants them); and how difficult it is to avoid having logical consequences sound and feel like a punishment that invites a power struggle. They may discover why a new theme of Positive Discipline is "No more logical consequences—at least hardly ever."

Materials:

The following props and cue cards (laminated with punch holes for yarn so participants can hang them around their necks):

For Mr. or Mrs. Punishment: Black mask or dark sunglasses, a belt for hitting, a black cape, and a cue card that says: **Threaten to use the belt, or grounding, or taking away privileges, or, Wait until your dad/mom gets home.**

For Mr. or Mrs. Reward: A crown, a magic wand, a bag of goodies including stickers, money, M & Ms, and a cue card that says: **Offer money, candy, and stickers as a reward if behavior will change.**

For Mr. or Mrs. Natural Consequences: A cue card with the words, **I wonder what you will do when you don't have clean clothes tomorrow?**

For Mr. or Mrs. Logical Consequences: A cue card with the following: **Clothes not in the laundry don't get washed.**

For Mr. or Mrs. Focusing on Solutions: Small pen and notebook, and a cue card that says, **What would help you right now—to put this on the family meeting agenda or for us to brainstorm together for a solution?**

Some dirty clothes (a few socks and t-shirt might be enough)

Directions

1. Ask for five volunteers to play Mr./Mrs. Punishment, Mr./Mrs. Rewards, Mr./Mrs. Logical Consequences, Mr./Mrs. Natural Consequences, and Mr./Mrs. Focusing on Solutions, and one volunteer to be the child. Let them know this is a time for them to exaggerate and have fun while role-playing, and that they will be given specific scripts for what to do and say.

2. In front of the whole group assign each a role and give them the props described above for their roles. Only Mr./Mrs. Punishment, Mr./Mrs. Reward, and Mr./Mrs. Focusing on Solutions have props.(Some facilitators prefer to take volunteers out of the room to give them their roles. See comment below.)

3. Explain that each parent will follow the role directions that will be hanging around their necks (so observers can see) to interact with a volunteer child regarding the challenge of not putting dirty clothes in the dirty clothes hamper (or unloading the dishwasher). Read the instructions on their role signs out loud so observers can hear, and will know what is happening.

4. Instruct the child to stand by the dirty clothes looking frustrated (or sitting on the couch ignoring the dirty clothes). Each parent will take turns approaching the child to role-play according to their scripts in the following order: Punishment, Rewards, Logical Consequences, Natural Consequences, Focusing on Solutions.

5. The child is not to say anything—just to notice what he/she is thinking, feeling, deciding.

6. After each role-play, process with the child what he/she is thinking, feeling, deciding (to do); and then take the child to the Characteristics and Life Skills list from the Two Lists activity and ask, "Did you learn any of these characteristic and life skills from this parent? Now look at the Challenges list. Did you feel inspired to do any of these?" (If you have less time, you can wait until after all 5 role-plays before you process.) It is helpful to focus on what the child is learning before processing with the parents.

7. Process with the parents about what they were thinking, feeling, and deciding in their roles.

8. Process with the whole group by asking what they learned from this activity.

9. Pass out the handout of Logical Consequences. You might ask them to read it and then invite more discussion, or assign it as homework and invite them to bring their questions, comments, and sharing next week.

EXTENSION:

10. You might want to ask participants to share childhood experiences of how punishments and rewards were used in their families, and what they learned from these experiences.

Facilitator Note:

As a facilitator, you might prefer to have the role-plays be a surprise to observers by taking them out of the room to give them their costumes and scripts. This can be fun and effective. However, sometimes observers are confused—not quite sure what the role-players are doing. It can be just as effective (if not more) when everyone knows what is going to happen (and fun to watch the role-players get their roles), and then learn at a deeper level as they observe it happening. Experiment with what works for you.

Facilitator Note:

Some facilitators don't use natural consequences in the role-plays because for the parent to say, "I wonder what you will do if you don't have clean clothes tomorrow," is not a natural consequence—it is a curiosity question. Of course, a curiosity question can be very effective—and this is fine. However, it is important to share this during the discussion and make sure they know that Dreikurs taught that Natural Consequences means that the parent does not interfere in any way—which is very difficult for most parents.

　　　　　　　　　　　　　　　　　　　　　　www.positivediscipline.com

Alternatives to Logical Consequences

Jane Nelsen
www.positivediscipline.com

Punishment (even when a poorly disguised as a consequence) is designed to make kids PAY for the past.

Positive Discipline is designed to help children LEARN for the future.

1. Focus on the future instead of the past.

One clue that we are more interested in punishment (in the name of consequences) is when the focus is on the past rather than the future. The focus is on making kids "pay" for what they have done (poorly disguised punishment) instead of looking for solutions that would help them "learn" for the future.

2. Focus on solutions instead of consequences.

Instead of imposing logical consequences, involve children in thinking of solutions. It is a mistake to think there must be a logical consequence for every behavior, or that a logical consequence will solve every problem.

3. Get kids involved in solutions.

Kids are our greatest, untapped, resource. They have a wealth of wisdom and talent for solving problems when we invite them to do so. The benefits are numerous. They have the opportunity to use and strengthen their skills; and they are more likely to keep agreements in which they have ownership. They develop self-confidence and healthy self-esteem when they are listened to, taken seriously, and valued for their contribution. They experience belonging (connection) and significance. When they feel belonging and significance they feel less inclined to misbehave and more willing to learn from their mistakes with optimism.

4. Help children explore the consequences of their choices through curiosity questions (instead of imposing consequences on them).

Exploring is very different from imposing. Curiosity questions help a child explore the consequences of his or her choices in a way that leads to solutions. What happened? What do you think caused it to happen? How do you feel about it? How do you think others feel? What have you learned from this? How can you use what you have learned in the future? What ideas do you have to solve the problem now? These are just examples, not to be used as a script. Be in the now and be curious about "getting into the child's world."
This is very different from adults telling children what happened, what caused it to happen, how they should feel about it, and what they should do about it. Education is derived from the root educarè, which means, "to draw forth." Too often adults try to "stuff in" and then wonder why their words go in one ear and out the other.

5. Allow consequences instead of imposing consequences (punishment).

If a child doesn't study, failing may be the obvious consequence. Allow the child to experience his or her feelings. Avoid rescuing. Show empathy. When the child is ready, use curiosity questions to help the child explore what the consequences mean to him or her. What does he/she want for the future? What does he/she need to do to accomplish what he/she wants?

6. Allow suffering.

Adults should never make children suffer, but allow them to suffer. Through the suffering they can build their "disappointment muscles" and gain a sense of capability in the process. For example, if children don't get the toys they want, they may "suffer." This will not hurt them and may have great benefits. The great benefits come from using the many Positive Discipline tools we teach: validating feelings without rescuing, allowing a cooling off time and then involving children in solutions, in advance through family/class meetings, routine charts, wheels of choice, deciding what you will do and letting kids know what you are going to do and then following through, asking curiosity questions, to name a few.

7. **Decide what you will do. Inform in advance.** "I will read when everyone is ready to listen." "I will listen when you speak in a soft voice."

8. **Follow through (Shut your mouth and act with kindness and firmness)**

9. **As soon as _________ then ______** " As soon as you clean up, then you can go outside."

10. **At least hardly ever! When consequences are appropriate, use the formula: Opportunity = Responsibility = Consequence**

For every opportunity children have there is a responsibility. The obvious consequence for not wanting the responsibility is to lose the opportunity. Students have the opportunity of using the school playground equipment during recess. The responsibility is to treat the equipment and other people with respect. When people or things are treated disrespectfully it would be a logical consequence for that student to lose the opportunity of using the playground equipment until he or she is ready to be respectful again. These consequences will be effective only if they are enforced respectfully and children have another chance to have the opportunity to use the equipment as soon as they are ready for the responsibility. This does not mean they should lose recess, just do something else that doesn't require respectful use of equipment. (See No. 11)

However, even in this case it might be more effective to focus on an immediate solutions: What was our agreement regarding respectful use of playground equipment? Could you two find a solutions to your conflict on the Wheel of Choice? Would you be willing to put this problem on the class meeting agenda?

11. Take time for training

Provide many opportunities for skills training. Family/class meetings are a great opportunity to get children involved in sharing their ideas on how to treat equipment and people respectful. It is quite amazing to hear them say many of the things they have been "lectured about" that seemed to go in one ear and out the other. It is so much more powerful when the ideas come from them.

12. Observe and wait

Kids often solve their own problems if allowed time. If not, wait for a "no conflict" time. Then focus on solutions.

A Logical Consequence by Some Other Name does Smell Sweeter. Following are several alternative names for Logical Consequences

- Curiosity questions to help children "explore" the consequences of their choices
- Decide what you will do
- Shut your mouth and act
- Family meeting agenda
- As soon as ______, then ______
- Follow-through

- Mistakes as opportunities to learn
- Time for training
- Letting go
- Allowing children to experience consequences (different from imposing consequences)
- Avoiding pampering, fixing, rescuing

Logical Consequences
Quotes from *Children the Challenge* by Rudolf Dreikurs

When we use the term "logical consequences," parents so frequently misinterpret it as a new way to impose their demands upon children. The children see this for what it is – disguised punishment. (Children the Challenge, P. 80)

If logical consequences are used as a threat or "imposed" in anger, they cease being consequences and become punishment. Children are quick to discern the difference. They respond to logical consequences; they fight back when punished. (Children the Challenge, P. 79)

Logical consequences cannot be applied in a power struggle except with extreme caution because they usually deteriorate into punitive acts of retaliation. For this reason, natural consequences are always beneficial but logical consequences may backfire. (Children the Challenge, P. 84)

If, however, the parent is engaged in a power struggle with the child, he is inclined to use logical consequences as punishment and thereby forfeit the effectiveness of this method. P. 85

There is no logical connection if Mother denies Bobbie a favorite television program because he failed to take out the garbage…On the other hand, if Bobbie fails to complete his Saturday chores by the time the ball team gathers, it is quite logical that he cannot join the play until he finishes the job. (Children the Challenge, P. 85) **(As soon as…)**

If, however, Mother were to add, "Maybe this will be a lesson to you," she would immediately turn the "consequence" into a punishment. (Children the Challenge, P. 77) **(Avoid piggybacking)**

There is always a misbehaving parent when a child becomes a feeding problem. (Children the Challenge, P.78) **(Attitude and Decide What You Will Do)**

Many times a logical consequence to fit the act will occur to us after a little thought. We merely need to ask ourselves, "What would happen if I didn't interfere?" (Children the Challenge, P. 81) **(Natural Consequences)**

Sometimes the problem can even by solved by discussing it with the children and seeing what they have to offer. (Children the Challenge, P. 85) **(Getting children involved.)**

Notes

My Way, Your Way

Modified by Lois Ingber, LCSW, CPDLT and Susie Zhang, CPDT

Objective:

To learn effective strategies for encouragement when parents/caregivers don't agree on discipline methods.

Materials:

Marking Pens

The Characteristics and Life Skills and Challenges lists from the Two Lists activity

Four flip chart sheets prepared in advance per the headings below:

1. Typical Topics for Parent/Caregivers Disagreements

2. Possible Effects of Disagreeing in front of the children
   On the Relationship of the Adults   On the Child   On the Adults Individually

3. Respectful Alternatives When Parents/Caregivers Disagree

4. Possible Effects of Respectful Alternatives
   On the Relationship of the Adults   On the Child   On the Adults Individually

Comment:

Two parents or caregivers (perhaps grandparents) in the same home can see situations very differently. Since disagreeing in front of the children can promote confusion and manipulation in children, and resentment and hurt feelings in adults, it is important for adults to learn how to respect their differences in ways that promote cooperation.

It can increase effectiveness to do the Top Card activity first.

Directions

1. Display flip chart No. 1. Have the class participants brainstorm a list of things parents/caregivers disagree about. Some suggestions: Homework, Curfew, Money, Cell phone, Food, Candy.

2. Divide the class into two groups. Assign one of the brainstormed topics to each group to create a role-play (NOTE: Be sure each group has a different topic so they will be able to see that it isn't the topic of disagreement that is unpleasant—it is how the disagreement is handled that makes the difference in the effects on family members).

3.   Each group can decide how many people they want in their role-play. It could be two parents and two or more children, or two parents, two grandparents and one child, (or any combination they choose). Whatever the combination, the parents/caregivers openly (in front of the children), disagree on how to deal with the topic they chose.

4.   Let the participants know that they will have 3-5 minutes to plan the role-play they will perform for the whole class; and that the actual role-play does not need to last longer that 60 seconds or less. With humor, encourage the group to exaggerate and have fun. They can pretend they are role-playing what their neighbors do.

5.   After each group does their role-play, process by asking what each role-player was thinking, feeling, and deciding. Ask the "child/children" if they are learning anything on the Characteristics and Life Skills list.

6.   Display the flip chart No. 2 on "The Possible Effects of Disagreeing in Front of the Children". Ask the group to brainstorm the effects in the appropriate columns while a volunteer records on the flip chart.

7.   Next, display flip chart No. 3 and brainstorm "Respectful Alternatives When Parents/Caregivers Disagree". If not mentioned, include these:

   -   The disagreeing parent says nothing, talks to spouse later.
   -   The disagreeing parent quietly leaves the area and lets the other parent deal with the consequences of his or her behavior.
   -   The children have to get a "yes" from both parents before they can act.
   -   If a parent is in the middle of the other parent and child, step out of the middle.
   -   Have a family meeting.
   -   Parents sit next to each other and hold hands.

8.   Have each group role-play the situation again, using one of the alternatives listed.

9.   At the end of each role-play, process thinking, feeling, deciding of each role-player. Ask the "child/children" if they are learning anything on the Characteristics and Life Skills list.

10. Display flip chart No. 4. Ask the group to brainstorm how these changes affect the couple, child, individual. Record in appropriate columns.

11. Ask the group to share what they learned from this activity.

EXPANDED VERSION:

Discuss: "How did your parents handle situations where they disagreed when you were children? What did you learn as children? How have these early decisions impacted you as an adult about how two people handle differing opinions?"

Nurturing a Plant

Objective:

To help parents appreciate the individual nature of each child and to provide the nurturing that helps that child become the best of who he or she is.

Materials:

A variety of small plants (one for each participant), including some that look great, some a little wilted, some in bloom, a cactus and perhaps some weeds. It can be fun to have two or three plants, to represent twins or triplets, for one participant.

Flip chart

Marking pens

Comment:

Many parents are so busy trying to mold their children into what they want them to be that they don't discover the beauty of who they are and how to nurture them to be the best they can be.

Directions

1. Place a plant in front of each chair for participants before they arrive. Notice the reactions as people come in so that you can comment later. Some may change their chairs to get the plant they want. Note the comments some make.

2. Stimulate a discussion by asking some of the following questions:

   You have just been given custody of a plant that will be your responsibility for the rest of your life.
   How do you feel about the plant you have received?
   How many of you got your favorite plant? If you received a petunia but wanted a rose, is there anything you can do to turn your petunia into a rose?

3. Record responses to the following question on a flip chart, "Since you got the plant you got, what do you need to do to help your plant develop into its full potential?" Possible responses: water, light, good soil, shade or sum, learn about it to find out how much of the preceding it needs, talk to it.

Record responses to this question, "What do children need to develop into their full potential?"

Comment:

The general concepts that cover all we have brainstormed are: (1) knowledge about what is needed and (2) nurturing to provide what is needed.

---

4. What have you learned from this exercise that could help you with your children?

    In what ways do you go against the concept of gaining knowledge about what your children need? For example, do you take time to "get into the world of your child" to find out what he or she needs? Are you open to the value of parenting education? Have you forgotten what you learned from your own childhood and continue doing the things that you hated when your parents did them?

    In what ways do you violate the concept of nurturing your children by not providing what is needed? For example, do you encourage your children to be who they are, or do you try to mold them into your image? Do you try to change a petunia into a rose?

5. Take a few minutes to think about something specific you would like to do differently due to your increased insight from this activity. Write it down in your notebook. Be specific about what you want to do, why you want to do it and exactly when you will do it.

6. Allow time for any who would like to share their new commitment.

3 Parenting Styles

Objective:

To help parents understand the difference between three styles of parenting: Authoritarian, Permissive, and Respectful (Positive Discipline)

Materials:

Flip-chart prepared in advance with Graph at the end of this activity

A brick

A Koosh ball or marshmallow

Flex blocks

Characteristics and Life Skills list from the Two Lists Activity

Comment:

The debate goes on and on about which is best: excessive control or permissiveness. Positive Discipline advocates something in the middle: Respectful parenting.

Directions

1. Create the graph at the end of this activity on a flip chart.

2. Ask the group in which column (kind or firm) would they add a check mark for the Authoritarian parent? (Firm)

3. In which column would they add a check mark for the Permissive parent? (Kind)

4. Where would the check marks go for the Positive Discipline parent? (Both kind and firm)

5. Pass around the brick, the Koosh ball (or marshmallow), and the flex blocks and invite them to feel them and think about their characteristics.

6. Ask which item represents the authoritarian parent. (The brick) Then ask for words that would describe the brick that might also describe an authoritarian parent. Add those words in the "Firm" column across from "Authoritarian".

7. Ask which item represents the permissive parent. (The Koosh ball or marshmallow) Then ask for words that would describe this item that might also describe a permissive parent. Add those words in the "Kind" column across from "Permissive".

8. Ask which item represents the Positive Discipline parent. (The flex block) Then ask for words that would describe this item that might also describe a Positive Discipline parent. Add those words in both the "Kind" and the "Firm" columns across from "Positive Discipline Parent".

9. Display the Characteristics and Life Skills List from the Two Lists Activity and ask, "Which parenting style is most likely to help children develop these characteristics and life skills, and why?"

10. What they have learned from this activity has most likely already come out of the discussion.

Comment:

You might want to follow this activity with one of the following activities:

Parenting Styles: What is Yours?

Kind and Firm at the Same Time

Parenting Style	Kind	Firm
Authoritarian Order without freedom		
Permissive Freedom without order		
Respectful (Positive Discipline) Freedom with order		

Parenting Styles: What is Yours?

Objective:
To demonstrate the effectiveness and/or ineffectiveness of different parenting styles.

Materials:
Characteristics and Life Skills
and
Challenges lists from the Two Lists Activity

Comment:
Autocratic and permissive styles of parenting are short-sighted, discouraging, and ineffective. Kind and firm, respectful parenting is effective long-term, and empowering to children. It is sometimes difficult for parents to understand this except through direct experience.

Directions

1. Ask for four to six volunteers to be parents and stand in a line. Invite four to six more volunteers to be teens who stand in a line facing the parents. Invite the parents to "adopt" the "teen" standing across from them. Then have them each step back until there is about 7 feet between them.

2. Tell the volunteers there will be three rounds. In each round the volunteers playing the kids will do exactly the same thing. The parents will have different instructions each time.

> **Facilitator's Note:**
> It is okay to give the following instructions in front of the whole group. It does not take away from the experience when everyone hears exactly what is going to happen, and can make the activity less confusing.

3. Tell the teens that in all three rounds they will walk toward their parents saying drug words such as, "crack, high, loaded, coke, eight ball, cannabis, smashed, alcohol, beer." (Demonstrate what this looks like.)

4. In round one of the activity, the parents will approach the teens saying "controlling" things such as, "No child of mine is going to use drugs. I won't allow it. If you do you are grounded. I will take away your car. I will search your room. You will lose all your privileges." (Demonstrate what this looks like.)

5.   After demonstrating, tell them to start walking toward each other saying what they have been told to say. Let them know you will ring a bell when it is time to stop.

6.   After 30 seconds or so, ring the bell for them to stop.

7.   Process by asking the teens first, then the parents, what they were thinking, how they were feeling, and what they were deciding. (You might want to ask the teens if they are learning anything on the Characteristics and Life Skills List, or if they are feeling motivated to do things on the Challenges list.)

8.   Then ask them to move 7 feet apart again.

9.   During the second round, when the teens walk toward their parents saying the same words, the parents are to talk about something else, or look at their cell phones, or put their hands over their ears, or turn their backs, to simulate parents who try to deal with the situation by denying the problem, and putting their heads in the sand. (Demonstrate this.)

10. Signal them to start. Let the round go for 30 seconds, or so, and then ring a bell to get them to stop.

11. Process by asking the teens first, then the parents, what they were thinking, how they were feeling, and what they were deciding. (You might want to ask the teens if they are learning anything on the Characteristics and Life Skills List, or if they are feeling motivated to do things on the Challenges list.)

12. Have them move 7 feet apart again.

13. In the third round, as the teens walk toward the parents saying the drug words, the parents are to put their arms across the shoulders of the teens and start walking with them while saying, "This scares me; and I'd like to hear what is going on for you"—and then be quiet and listen. It is very important that parents make a short statement and then shut up and listen. It also seems more effective if they walk slowly, with their arm around teens shoulder, while listening. (Demonstrate this with one of the teens.)

14. Signal for them to start. Let the round go for 30 seconds or so and then a bell to get them to stop.

15. Process by asking the teens first, then the parents, what they were thinking, how they were feeling, and what they were deciding. (You might want to ask the teens if they are learning anything on the Characteristics and Life Skills List, or if they are feeling motivated to do things on the Challenges list.)

16. Be sure to let the participants know that we are not implying that the third style is enough to stop a drug problem. (This requires professional help.) However, ask them which of the three styles at least provides an opening for communication and positive influence.

17. Invite participants to discuss what they learned from this activity.

Comment:

Using the example of drugs can be very dramatic (and fun), but the point is to exaggerate the different parenting styles so parents can really see the difference. For this reason it can be very valuable to repeat the activity with less threatening and more common challenges such as homework hassles or chores.

"PD Tools Bingo"

Glenda Montgomery

Objective:

To review core ideas and strategies from a set of parenting classes on the last day of class.

Materials:

A Bingo sheet

A marker or pen for each person in class

Comment:

This is a fun way to review the main strategies we've talked about throughout the seven weeks. It is light and lively and is a friendly way to remind people of some concepts which they might not have tried yet.

Directions

1. Hand everyone a bingo sheet and a marker.

2. Explain that we are going to play bingo.

3. When you have finished with the directions, everyone will rise and will step into the middle of the circle and will approach people one by one.

4. For each person that they approach, they will choose a square and ask that person a question beginning with "Have you….." In other words for the first square, they may ask, "Have you decided what YOU will do? Have you let your child know ahead of time and silently followed through?"

5. If the person they asked says, "Yes" then they can put a big X on that box.

6. They now get to receive a question from the person they approached and must answer honestly. If ever the answer is "no", it is no big deal, they just move on to the next encounter. (But the person who asked, won't get to fill in an X)

7. People can start asking from anywhere on the bingo sheet.

8. As soon as someone gets a straight row of 5 Xs in any direction, they yell "BINGO!!"

I let it go until 3 or 4 people have yelled bingo and then we sit down. People seem to really like the reminder of the tools in this form so I often will hand out a "clean" bingo score card and people circle one or two strategies that they want to commit to trying in the next week.

Positive Discipline BINGO!!

Decide what YOU will do! Let your child know ahead of time and then SILENTLY follow through	Use LIMITED CHOICES to provide options within strong boundaries	Allow kids to learn from their mistakes WITHOUT lectures or "I told you so"	Take the time for training…and RE-training	Use statements of ENCOURGEMENT more often than statements of PRAISE
Hold regular family meetings	Be kind and firm… at the SAME TIME	Disengage from power struggles. Return after self soothing	Teach (and model) self soothing. (Put together a comfort basket with your child)	Commit to regular special one on one time with each child.
NUTRURE YOURSELF! Proactive, conscious parenting takes ENERGY!	Remember to offer messages of love, especially at neutral times	Boost your child's sense of significance and belonging through training for chores	"As soon as you ___________ then you may__________" (Use the firm language of kindness.)	Let the routine be the boss! Together with your child, create routine charts.
When you "blow it" model for your children the 3 Rs of recovery	Use non verbal signals	Refrain from lecturing! Use 10 words or less.	Have a meeting with your child to discuss the problem when you are both calm. Let your child be the #1 problem solver.	Remember the 4 Rs of punishment. Work to find solutions instead of using punishment.
Be proactive. Work to find strategies ahead of time. Refrain from triggering your anger response	Use natural or logical consequences. Even better: FOCUS ON FINDING SOLUTIONS!	Discover the belief BEHIND the behavior. Use the Mistaken Goal Chart!	Trust….not that your child won't make mistakes, but that they can learn from them	Listen well. Listen spelled another way is "silent". Use the template " You feel ___________ because ___________ and you wish ____________ "

Positive Time-Out

Objective:

To help parents understand the negative results of punitive time-out, and the encouraging results of Positive Time-Out.

Materials:

Copy of the demonstration role-play

Flip-chart and markers

Jared's Cool Out Space by Jane Nelsen and Bill Schorr

A copy of the Hints for Using Positive Time-Out

Demonstration Role-play

Volunteer: Hi Honey!

Spouse: Don't 'Hi Honey' me! You left your socks on the floor again! How many times do I have to tell you to pick up your socks? Do you think I'm your maid? Go sit in your den and think about what you did.

Facilitator: After pausing to put on your facilitator hat, ask the volunteer, "What are you thinking?"

Volunteer: Bitch, (or something a little more socially acceptable such as, "Witch").

Facilitator: What are you feeling?

Volunteer: Angry.

Facilitator: What are you deciding?

Volunteer: Divorce, or, to stay in my den as much as possible.

Comment:

Most parents don't realize that their children are always making decisions about themselves and about what to do in the future based on what they think and feel in response to their experiences in life. What decisions do you think children might be making while in punitive time out?

Directions

1. This activity is most powerful when Brain in the Palm of the Hand has been done first.

2. Before class, find a volunteer to role-play your spouse who comes home from work and greets you at the door. (It is best for you to play the main part so the volunteer doesn't have to remember much.) Give a copy of the Demonstration Role-play to the volunteer and take a few minutes to practice where others can't see you. Tell the volunteer you will let him or her know when you are ready for the demonstration.

3. Start the activity by asking the participants if they have ever wondered what a child is thinking, feeling, and deciding (about him or herself and about what to do in the future) when sent to time-out as a punishment.

4. Ask them to think about it now and to share what they think the child might be thinking and deciding. Ask for a volunteer to record their thoughts on a flip chart.

5. Let them know you are now going to do a little role-play with a special guest from Hollywood. Invite the volunteer to now join you for the demonstration.

6. Process by asking the group, "How might this represent what children are thinking, feeling, and deciding when sent to punitive time out—to think about what they did?"

7. Invite the group to close their eyes and give the following instructions: "Pretend you are a 2 ½ year-old who has just grabbed a toy from your six-month-old baby brother, and I am your mom. Pause and say, "I can't believe you did such a thing. He is just a baby. You can just go sit on the naughty chair and think about what you did. And don't get up until I say you can."

8. Process with the group by asking, "As a child, what are you thinking, feeling, and deciding?" Allow a minute or two of discussion.

9. Then ask, "Are any of you thinking, 'Oh thank you. This is so helpful. I'm learning so much about how to be kind to others?' Or, are you feeling humiliated and thinking, 'This is not fair,' and deciding you must be a bad person, and that you'll get even and hurt baby brother every chance you get?"

10. Invite sharing of what they have learned about Positive Time-Out so far.

11. Ask for a volunteer to read Jared's Cool Out Space to the whole group as though they are children. (It might be best if you ask someone before class so they can look through it and be prepared.)

12. Divide the group by the ages of the children. In each group have them choose on person to be the parent, and the rest to be children, Have the parents involve their children in creating a positive time-out space; and to allow their children to brainstorm a special name for it.

13. Invite someone to read the Hints for using Positive Time-Out.

14. Suggest as homework that they all create their own Positive Time-Out space and help their children create theirs. Point out that it is very important to encourage their children to create their own special name for their positive time-out space.

　　　　　　　　　　　　　www.positivediscipline.com

Hints for using Positive Time-Out:

1. Even when children have created their own special time-out place, it is not a good idea to send them. It is better to validate feelings and then ask, "Would it help you to go to _______?"

2. If they don't want to go to their special place, go to your own and let them have their feelings.

3. It might be even more effective to give them a choice once they have learned more tools: "What would help you the most right now, to go to your special place, or to get the Wheel of Choice?" (Or to put this on the family meeting agenda, or to just feel what you feel for a while.)

Extension:

1. Invite a volunteer to come to the front of the room to be a child who wants to create a Positive Time-Out area. Ask what age child the volunteer wants to be (at least 4-years-old or older).

2. Say to the child, "I'm going to help you create a place that feels special to you—a place where you can go when you feel mad or sad, or just need time to calm down. Would you like that place to be in your room or in the living room?"

3. After the child chooses, say, "Okay, where in the room can your special place be, and what kinds of things would you like to have in your special place that will help you feel better?"

4. Write everything the child suggests on a flip-chart paper. If the child is having a hard time thinking of things, you could say, "What about a pillow, a stuffed animal, some books, a special toy that stays in your special place?" (If the child wants a tablet, or any kind of screen, say, "Screens are now allowed. What else?")

5. Ask the child what he or she would like to call this special place—what special name. Write it at the top of the flip-chart.

6. Set up a role-play. Ask the volunteer to think of something that invites him to feel hurt, sad, or mad, and to get into that mind set. Then validate feelings and ask, "Would it help you to go to your special place (name he/she gave it) right now?" If he or she says, "No," ask, "Would you like me to go with you?" "If he or she still says, "No," say, "Okay, I think I'll go to my special place. I would love to be with you when you are ready." Then walk away.

7. Process with the child what he or she was thinking, feeling, and deciding. Process the same with the parent.

8. Ask the rest of the group to share what they learned from this activity.

9. Share the following hints.

Notes

Punishment Results

Objective:

To invite participants to consider the results of punishment from their own collective experience.

Materials:

Flip chart (Labeled per instructions in No. 1)

Flip chart or poster as described below

Flip chart labeled Alternatives to Punishment

Characteristics and Life Skills from Two Lists activity

Challenges List from Two Lists activity

Directions

1. Invite participants to think of a time they were punished. It could have been last week, or many years ago. Invite them to remember who was involved and what they were thinking, feeling, and deciding after they were punished.

2. Divide the flip chart into three columns and write THINKING at the top of the first column, FEELING over the top of the second, and DECIDING over the top of the third.

3. Invite participants to share what they were thinking, feeling, and deciding. It is helpful to collect the thoughts, feelings, and decisions from each volunteer (instead of collecting a list of feelings, then a list of thoughts etc.) because it helps everyone understand that how we are thinking and what we are feeling is connected to what we decide.

4. After people share ask them to discuss what they are learning so far about the results of punishment. Point to the Characteristics and Life Skills list. "Were you learning any of these?" Point to the Challenge list and ask, "Were you feeling inspired to do any of these?"

5. Now display the pre – prepared chart of the results of punishment. Usually most of those results will have been on the lists generated by the participants of what they were Thinking, Feeling, and Deciding.

Revenge: "They are winning now, but I'll get even"

Resentment: "This is unfair. I can't trust adults"

Rebellion: "I'll show them I can do what ever I want"

Retreat: either

        Sneaky – "I won't get caught next time or"

        Reduced self esteem – "I'm a bad person"

---

6. The next obvious question is: "If not punishment, then what?"

7. Display another flip chart with the heading, "Alternatives to Punishment".

8. Invite participants to brainstorm Positive Discipline tools they wish parents or teachers had used with them, instead of the punishment they received in the example they thought of in No. 1.

9. Invite participants to share what they learned from this activity.

Facilitator Note: You might want to follow up with the Punishment Alternatives activity and another time, or combine that activity with this one.

Punishment Alternatives

Objective:
To learn respectful discipline skills that are more effective than punishment.

Materials:
Alternatives to Punishment Chart below
Role-play statements below on cards

Comment:
It is difficult to give up punitive skills until you have alternative skills that are more effective.

Directions

1. Display the following chart:

   Punishment Alternatives

   - Decide what you will do, not what you will make your child do.
   - Set a limit and follow through.
   - Say how you feel.
   - Take care of your own needs.
   - Trust him/her to be who he/she is.
   - Say, "I can't make you, and I would like your help."
   - Work on an agreement and follow through.

2. Ask participants to form three groups. Give each group a role-play statement card (see below). Ask them to choose an alternative to punishment from the chart and set up a demonstration of how they would handle the problem situation with one of these skills.

Role-play Statements

- Your child has been playing the stereo too loud.
- Your child has been coming in after curfew.
- Your child has been spending too much time text messaging and playing video games.
- Your child has been telling you he was studying and then got a report card with the worst grades you have ever seen.

3. Allow time for each group to prepare and demonstrate their role-play.

4. After each demonstration process the activity with the following questions:

   a. As the person playing the child, what were you thinking, feeling, and what were you learning and deciding?

   b. As the person playing the parent, what did you think, what were you feeling and deciding?

   c. As participants watching the demonstrations, what did you learn?

EXPANDED VERSION:

1. Think of a situation where you have used punishment with your child. Write it down.

2. Which of the alternatives to punishment do you think might work better?

3. Share your situation with your group and ask one of them to role-play your child while you practice your new skill.

4. Process as above.

Read My Hat

Adapted from activity by Roslyn Duffy

Objective:

To understand the hidden beliefs behind discouraged behavior and to decode the hidden messages for what the child needs for encouragement.

Comment:

Positive Discipline is one of the few programs that helps parents and teachers understand and deal with the "belief behind the behavior" instead of just the behavior; and that teaches skills for encouragement that can change the belief, and thus the behavior. The logo on the hat provides clues to the hidden message for what the child needs to feel encouraged.

Materials:

Four hats with the following coded messages taped on them.

ATTENTION; A funny hat that draws attention. Notice me. Involve me usefully.

POWER: A construction-hard hat, or any hat that signifies power. Let me help. Give me choices.

REVENGE: A baseball cap in a dark color, turned backwards. I'm hurting. Validate my feelings.

ASSUMED INADEQUACY: A camouflage print hat. Don't give up on me. Show me a small step.

Characteristics and Life Skills and Challenges lists from the Two Lists activity

Laminated Instructions for Group Role-plays for each group (below)

Handout of the Mistaken Goal Chart for each participant

4 decks of PD Tool Cards

Optional: Use novelty eyeglasses instead of hats and make laminated signs as described in No. 3 below.

Directions

1. Divide participants into four groups with at least four people in each group. (If you have fewer people in your class, you may do one or two mistaken goals at a time. For larger groups, there may be more than four people in a group; so they can all participate in the planning, but instruct them to choose no more than four to participate in the role-plays.)

2. Assign one of the four mistaken goals (Attention, Power, Revenge, Assumed Inadequacy) to each group by giving one of the hats to each group.

3. Hand out the Instructions for Group Role-Plays (one for each group), the hat that goes with each Mistaken Goal and a Mistaken Goal Chart for everyone. (An option is to use novelty eyeglasses representing each

Mistaken Goal instead of the hats since some people are reluctant to wear a hat that has been worn by others. In that case, a laminated sign with the coded message could be worn around the neck or just held up during the second role-play).

4. Ask them to have one person in the group read the instructions while everyone listens.

5. Each group is to plan two scenes during the planning time. Each scene should not last much longer than 60 seconds or so, and participants should exaggerate and have fun.

6. Allow five minutes for the groups to plan both of their short role-plays. At the end of five minutes, ask if they need more time. If time allows, give them a few more minutes.

7. Process after scene one by asking each role-player, starting with the child, what each was thinking, feeling, deciding during the role-play.

8. Process after Scene One by asking each role-player, starting with the child, what each was thinking, feeling, and deciding during the role-play.

9. Point to the Characteristics and Life Skills list and ask the child if he or she is learning anything on this list. (Usually none) Then point to the Challenges list and ask if the child is feeling invited to engage in any of these. (Often many)

10. Process after Scene Two by asking each role-player, starting with the child, what each was thinking, feeling, and deciding during the role-play.

11. Take the child to the Characteristics and Life Skills list again and ask if he or she is learning anything on this list. (Usually most of them.)

12. Have each group take turns coming to the center of the room to repeat this process for the remaining three goals.

13. After all groups have had a turn, process by asking the whole group to share what they learned from this activity.

Comment:

There are as many different beliefs as there are people. The Four Mistaken Goals represent "categories" of beliefs with a gazillion variations. When Dreikurs was asked, "How can you keep putting children in these boxes," he said, "I don't put them there, I keep finding them there."

Extension:

Give each group a full deck of Positive Discipline Tool Cards and have them go through the deck and make a pile of all the additional tools that might be effective for the behavior they just role-played. Allow about five minutes and then ask for sharing. Ask each group how many tool cards they found, and what some of them are.

Instructions for Group Role-plays

1. Plan a role-play (with two scenes) for your Mistaken Goal.

2. The first task is to choose a behavior from the Challenges list that fits for the Mistaken Goal you represent—a behavior that invites adults in your group to feel the feelings in Column 2.

3. Decide on characters in each group: One volunteer to role-play a child. (Make sure the same person plays the child in both scenes so they can share how their experience differs.) One volunteer to role-play a parent (or two volunteers to play both parents). All others in your group will be siblings who don't do anything except notice what they are thinking, feeling and deciding. (Point out that a "bystander" member of the family is affected by adult-child interactions, even when they are not directly involved.)

The Mistaken Goal Chart will be your Script Guide

4. The person playing the child is to embody the BELIEF in Column 5 of Mistaken Goal Chart to get into character.

5. The person playing the adult is to embody a FEELING from Column 2 of Mistaken Goal Chart to get into character.

ACTION/SCENE ONE

6. Child puts on the hat and plays the behavior chosen from the Challenges list (or any behavior that invites adults to feel the feelings in Column 1 of the Mistaken Goal Chart.

7. Adult REACTS by doing something from Column 3 of Mistaken Goal Chart.

8. Child responds by doing something from Column 4 of Mistaken Goal Chart.

9. Facilitator will stop the role-play (usually in one minute or less) and will processes what everyone was thinking, feeling, deciding, starting with the child.

ACTION/SCENE TWO

10. Child repeats the same behavior as in Scene One.

11. Adult ACTS by doing something from Column 7 of the Mistaken Goal Chart or another Positive Discipline Tool that responds to the hat message.

12. Child does whatever he/she FEELS like doing in response to what the adult DOES (It is important to play the child AND be in the moment—meaning to respond to what the adult is doing now instead of responding the way children usually do when treated disrespectfully.)

13. Workshop/class facilitator stops the role-play (usually in one minute or less) and processes what everyone was thinking, feeling, deciding, starting first with the child.

Comment:

There are as many different beliefs as there are people. The Four Mistaken Goals represent "categories" of beliefs with a gazillion variations. When Dreikurs was asked, "How can you keep putting children in these boxes, he said, "I don't put them their, I keep finding them there."

Notes

The Results of Rewards

by Lois Ingber, LCSW, CPDLT

Objective:

To demonstrate that rewards, like punishments, are extrinsic motivators and interfere with discipline as teaching. They do not invite development of positive Characteristics/Life Skills. *(This activity can be done immediately following the "Punishment Results" Activity.)*

Materials:

The "Challenges" and "Characteristics/Life Skills" posters from "The Two Lists."

Comment:

Not feeling entirely comfortable with the use of punishments, many parents and teachers turn to the use of rewards believing this is more "kind" to the child. Yet rewards fail to encourage a sense of responsibility and accountability in the child, instead inviting self-centeredness, manipulation for bigger rewards, (or refusing to contribute because they don't care about the reward) and loss of mutual respect. These long-term results get lost when rewards seem to "work," because everyone is "happy" getting what each wants.

Directions

1. **Role Play One.** Invite a volunteer to stand with you and pretend to be your spouse or partner. Say, "I've come up with a new plan! For every night you cook dinner, I'm going to give you a sticker! We'll place the stickers on a chart and at the end of the month, if you fill up the chart, you can have a reward! What would you like it to be?" (Go with their choice if it is something you agree with, or bargain an alternative.)

2. If the volunteer agreed to the plan, ask what he/she was thinking, feeling and deciding. Ask, "Are you learning the responsibility and contribution of cooking dinner? Why or why not?" Ask if the volunteer feels invited to do anything on the Characteristics/Life Skills List, then the Challenges List.

3. If the volunteer did not agree to the plan, ask how come. Draw out thinking, feelings, decisions. Ask if the volunteer feels invited to do anything on the Characteristics/Life Skills List, then the Challenges List. After processing, thank the volunteer and have them take their seat.

   (This part of the activity is designed to show that rewards are used for control in a superior/inferior relationship. Draw out these concepts during processing.)

4. **Role Play Two.** Ask for another volunteer to stand with you. Say, "If I give you $20, would you clap your

hands 10 times?" If he/she agreed, ask how come and draw out thoughts, feelings and decisions. Ask what he/she is learning and deciding about you. Next ask if the volunteer is learning anything on the Characteristics/Life Skills List, then the Challenges list. If the volunteer asked for more money, agree or negotiate, then process the same.

5. If the volunteer did not agree, ask how come and draw out thoughts, feelings, and decisions. Ask what he/she is learning and deciding about you. Ask if the volunteer feels invited to do anything on the Characteristics/Life Skills List.

   (This part of the activity is designed to show that rewards teach people to look for the payoff, rather than doing a task for its own sake. It also shows that the child thinks of rewards differently than we intend: that rewards are really for the 'giver,' i.e., "If you give me something I want, parent or teacher, I will reward you with what you want.")

6. Discuss with the group their reactions, what they are learning.

7. Give the handout "Results of Rewards," read and discuss.

FURTHER DISCUSSION

There is a little understood dynamic that occurs with the use of rewards. By "Doing To" vs. "Doing With" the child, rewards establish a superior/inferior relationship creating a <u>double</u> <u>bind</u> for the child. Since the reward is appealing to the child, by accepting the plan the child <u>agrees</u> to be placed in an inferior position, relinquishing his/her dignity and self-respect. If the child does not agree to the plan, thereby retaining dignity and self-respect, he/she misses out on something he/she would enjoy and risks disappointing the adult or making the situation worse for him/herself with the adult. The child cannot "win" in either scenario, and loses respect for both the adult and him/herself. This is why rewards fail in the long run: because no one can stand to be in the one-down position without compensating in some other way, usually through misbehavior, wanting a greater reward to make it more worthwhile, etc. And all this occurs subconsciously, making it difficult for children (or adults) to sort out what is actually going on.

The above dynamic can be described as a manipulation in which the child and the adult agree to both <u>be manipulated</u> and <u>to manipulate</u> as they each negotiate to get what they want. It is a <u>model</u> <u>that</u> teaches self-interest vs. genuine contribution, cooperation and problem solving to meet the needs of the situation, the key to social interest, socially useful belonging and behavior, and ultimately, the betterment of the world.

The other concern is the message conveyed by the reward about the task or chore. By making the reward the focus of plan, the task or chore is cheapened, de-valued or degraded. It robs children of the opportunity to feel capable and responsible for the contribution they can make by doing something important and useful.

THE RESULTS OF REWARDS

Parents want their children to behave and often choose rewards or positive incentives as a replacement for punishment. Some parents use both. We propose that neither REWARDS nor PUNISHMENTS are helpful in teaching our children to become ethical, caring responsible adults. Why do we say this?

1. Rewards and punishments are two sides of the same coin: they both aim to extrinsically CONTROL behavior instead of focusing on TEACHING. Rewards and punishment model the use of "<u>power</u> <u>over</u>" as a means of solving problems.

2. Rewards and punishments are forms of "DOING TO" and "DOING FOR" children instead of "DOING WITH." children. They don't invite children to learn from within or teach cooperative problem solving, both necessary skills in today's world.

3. Rewards and punishments DISTRACT children from the REAL issues. The child becomes more concerned with avoiding the punishment or gaining the reward than learning the INTRINSIC VALUE of the appropriate decision or activity itself.

4. Rewards and punishments erode our RELATIONSHIPS with our children. Relationships with our children are our most important tool for INFLUENCING our children's development.

REWARDS:

- **Eventually lose their effectiveness.** The child loses interest in "working for" the reward, or may want rewards that are more appealing (bigger, better).

- **May bring temporary "compliance,"** but rarely help a child develop a commitment to a task or action if there is no "payoff."

- **Teach kids to be self-centered.** They learn to think, "What's in it for me?" instead of doing the activity simply because it is worth doing for its own sake or because it is helpful to others.

- **Are discouraging.** They are conditioned on the successful completion of the task. *Without successful completion, the withholding of the reward turns it into a "punishment" because: from the child's perspective the child is denied something promised.*

- **Erode intrinsic motivation.** The child does not have the opportunity to develop an interest or liking in the activity on its own merits. Children are denied the opportunity to make a genuine contribution, the foundation for feeling responsible and capable (belonging and significance).

- De-value or degrade the task or action needed, as the "reward" is presented as more important.

- **Interfere with self-esteem.** They create dependency upon an outside person for approval rather than a conscientious evaluation by the child of her own efforts.

- **Look different from the child's perspective.** We think we are 'rewarding' <u>them</u>; they think, "If you give my what I want, I will '<u>reward</u>' <u>you</u> with what you want."

<u>Instead of rewards...FOCUS ON SOLUTIONS TOGETHER *WITH* YOUR CHILD:</u>

Problem solve together. Make agreements and follow through. Use kindness and firmness. Model "liking what you have to do" vs. "doing what you like." Have regular family meetings. Invite your child to contribute to the family as part of something everyone does (helping make dinner, plan activities together, etc.).

Notes

Rope Activity

(Adapted by Sahara Pirie from activity presented by David Colestock at 2007 NASAP)

Objective:

Build community.

Develop Gemeinschaftsgefühl.

Materials:

One rope 15-20 feet long with a knot tied in the center of it, per 8-10 participants. How elaborate the knot is, is up to you, but more than a simple half hitch is necessary.

Comment:

Many qualities are demonstrated and can be lifted from this activity. Cooperation; leadership; communication and motivation; raise awareness of group dynamics and what is needed for successful problem solving.

If you use multiple ropes and varying degrees of knots, some interesting things can come out about competitiveness, fairness etc.

How you lift out the qualities stated above may depend on your audience - for camp counselors they can witness it for themselves and then see how they can apply it to their campers; for students it can begin a basis for team work, for parents/teachers it may show them the importance of leadership and cooperation and give them an experience of that working, etc.

Directions

1. Lay rope(s) with the knot out on the floor - fully extended.

2. Ask for each participant to find a spot on either side of the knot such that roughly half the participants are to the left of the knot and half are to the right.

3. Ask them to choose to pick the rope up with either one hand or two, and let them know that once they have picked up the rope, they should not let go of it until the activity is complete. They may slide their hand(s) along the rope, but they are not to let go.

4. Ask the participants to untie the knot without letting go of the rope - that is to say if they picked the rope up with one hand, that hand must stay in contact with the rope until the activity is complete. If they picked the rope up with both hands, both hands must stay in contact with the rope until the activity is complete.

5. Optional: Give them a 5 minute time limit. (Not always recommended).

6. Process: What are you feeling? Thinking? Deciding? How did you do it? Who decided? What happened next? What else did you notice?

    Some additional questions you might want to explore:
    How did the time limit effect your behavior? What happened when the other group finished before you? What might have happened if I'd stopped you before you had a chance to be successful? How are you feeling about yourself and your 'teammates' now, in contrast to before the activity?

Alternative: Use a bed sheet laid out flat on the floor; have a group of participants stand on the sheet. Instruct them to turn the sheet over so that they are all standing on the other side of the sheet without any of them ever stepping off the sheet. (I have found this to be a harder activity, and not suitable for younger children.)

Routine Charts

Objective:
To avoid power struggles while helping children feel more capable when they use their power in constructive ways.

Materials:
Flip chart

Marking Pens

Comment:
Children feel empowered and motivated to cooperate when they are respectfully included in problem-solving—including the creation of routine charts.

Directions

1. Ask for a volunteer to role-play a three-year-old (or whatever age you want) to create a bedtime routine.

2. You can role-play the parent.

3. Go to the flip chart and ask the "child" to tell you what he or she needs to do to get ready for bed. Write every task on the flip chart. (Brush teeth, bath, jammies, story, etc.)

4. If the child forgets something, it is okay to say, "What about picking out your clothes for tomorrow?" or whatever else is forgotten. (Having your child lay out clothes for the next day will make your morning routine go much smoother.)

5. If your child wants screen time (or anything else you don't want as part of the routine chart), say something like, "That can't be part of your bedtime routine, but we can put it on our family meeting agenda (or for one-to-one problem-solving) and talk about when you can do that."

6. After getting all the items on the flip chart, ask the child to rank order what needs to be done first, then next until all the tasks have a number.

7. Ask the child if he or she would like to draw pictures of each task or have you take a picture of him or her doing each task that can be glued on to the routine chart later. Process with the volunteer who role-played the child by asking, "What were you thinking, feeling, and deciding while being included in creating a routine chart?" Take the child to the Characteristics and Life Skills chart from the Two Lists Activity and ask if he or she is learning any of these.

8. Let the routine chart be the boss. In other words, instead of nagging, ask, "What is next on your routine chart?"

9. Avoid rewards which take away from the child's inner sense of accomplishment and capability.

10. Ask participants what they learned from this activity.

Comment:

One mother took photos of her child doing each task. Together they went to the craft supply store and purchased a wide ribbon and a stapler and a hook for hanging. Her son then stapled each photo in order (with the first task at the top), and added numbers 1 through 7 (he was learning numbers) and hung it on the back of his bedroom door. He was so proud to show everyone his routine.

School Readiness

By Lois Ingber, LCSW, CPDLT

Objective:

To help adults understand how creating opportunities for contribution in the home combined with mutual respect helps young children develop a sense of belonging and significance, and the belief "I am capable " - all important aspects of school readiness.

Materials:

Small basket of laundry with items of different colors (socks, T-shirts, etc.).

A small electronic device (iPad tablet, or cell phone).

Instructions for role players (below).

List of Challenges and Characteristics/Life Skills from the "Two Lists" activity.

Flip chart and markers.

Decks of "Positive Discipline Parenting Tools."

Copies of handout: "The Five Crucial School Readiness Skills for Preschoolers."

Comment:

Success in school is based on children being able to use causal/sequential thinking, having trust in adults (emotional safety), delaying gratification, having the ability to concentrate, and using social/ emotional skills. The list of "Characteristics and Life Skills" is more predictive of school success than "academic" ability (knowing letters and numbers). Opportunities for contribution in the home, combined with mutual respect, help prepare children for the tasks and relationships of the school environment.

Directions

1. On a flip chart, brainstorm with the group a list of skills children need to be ready for success in school. Post it next to the Characteristics/Life Skills list.

2. Ask for two volunteers, one to be a parent and one to be a preschooler (age 3-6). Explain there will be two Scenes, and give them the role play slips. Say to the group, "While you're observing, notice what you would be thinking, feeling and deciding as the child."

3. **SCENE ONE.** Have the volunteers do the role play using the instructions on the slips. After 20-40 seconds, stop the role play. Ask the child what she/he is thinking, feeling and deciding. Refer the child to the brainstormed list of school readiness skills and the Characteristics/Life Skills list and ask if she/he is learning

any (usually none). Ask if she/he feels like doing anything on the Challenges list (usually many). Process with the parent what she/he is thinking, feeling and deciding.

4. **SCENE TWO.** Have the volunteers do the second role play using the instructions on the slips, again allowing 20-40 seconds. Ask the child what she/he is thinking, feeling and deciding. Refer the child to the brainstormed list of school readiness skills and the Characteristics/Life Skills list and ask if she/he is learning any (usually several). Process with the parent what she/he is thinking, feeling and deciding. Thank the role players and ask them to take their seats.

5. Ask the group what they are noticing and learning. Draw out ways the second role play encouraged school readiness.

6. Form small breakout groups (or as a large group) and give a flip chart, marker and some Tool Cards to each. Brainstorm tools and strategies parents can use every day for children to learn school readiness skills. Ask, "What are some other ways parents can encourage preschoolers to feel connected and capable of contribution in the home? How do these nurture the social and emotional skills needed for success in school?

7. Have each group share their flip chart with the whole group and discuss.

8. Give the Handout, "Five Crucial School Readiness Skills for Preschoolers."

INSTRUCTIONS FOR SLIPS:

PARENT

SCENE ONE: Sort and fold the laundry while your child plays on the electronic device. Ask him/her to help. If he/she refuses, try to make him/her do it.

SCENE TWO: Sit next to your child with the laundry basket and let her/him know you would like his or her help. If your child needs some coaxing, make it fun by asking if he or she would like to play a game such as finding the different colors, counting the items, or asking silly questions: hold up a shirt and ask "Does this go in the kitchen?"

CHILD

SCENE ONE: Play on the electronic device. When your parent asks you to help fold the laundry, keep playing the game, pretend not to hear, or refuse by saying "No," or whining.

SCENE TWO: Play on the electronic device. Respond as you feel inclined based on what your parent is doing.

Five Crucial School Readiness Skills for Preschoolers

By Steven Foster, LCSW, CPDLT

There has been a great deal of concern in the last decade or so that children are starting kindergarten unprepared for academic learning. One unfortunate response has been that preschool programs, such as Head Start, are pressured into placing much greater emphasis on teaching children letters, numbers, and other academic concepts.

These preschool programs would be more effective in actually preparing children for success in kindergarten by creating intriguing environments in which children can explore learning and develop two important beliefs about themselves:

- ***I belong here and I am strongly emotionally connected to significant people who care about me.***

- ***I am capable and my contributions are valuable.***

In the many years that I have worked with preschool children and their families, I have had countless opportunities to connect with kindergarten teachers to consult with them regarding children who will be entering their classrooms. Despite their awareness of the increased emphasis on pre-academic skills, these skills are rarely the ones they want to talk about. They deeply understand that, while they can relatively easily help children who are less well versed in their letters and numbers, it is far more difficult for them to teach children who have not learned how to be part of a group learning community. I have distilled these conversations into the following kindergarten readiness skills for preschoolers:

1. **Delayed Gratification.** They need to be able to stop doing something they are enjoying immensely (like playing) in order to participate in something they probably don't like as much (like circle time).

2. **Cooperation Skills.** They need to be able to share decision making in their play with other children. This, of course, does not mean that the process of decision-making is always smooth.

3. **Emotional Literacy.** They need to be capable of managing strong emotions, such as anger, frustration and disappointment, without routinely being overwhelmed by them. As with many skills, this will look rawer as they start kindergarten and more refined as they grow and develop.

4. **Communication Skills.** They need to be able to use words to solve the problems that inevitably come up in human relationships, with respect for both the other person and for themselves. Again, this is a work in progress.

5. **<u>Courage and Growth Mindset</u>.** They need to believe in their capacity to figure things out and persevere to find answers to problems that are initially challenging. Conversely, they need to be able to ask for help when they feel truly stuck.

Children who feel connection and capability, and who have mastered these five skills to a sufficient degree are ready for Kindergarten, no matter what knowing the letters and numbers suggest.

Notes

Setting Limits with Children

Objective:

To experience effective alternatives for dealing with problem situations.

Materials:

Alternatives to Nagging chart below

Comment:

Action versus talking is often more effective in dealing with problem situations. As Rudolf Dreikurs once said, "Shut your mouth and act."

Directions

1. Pick three groups to role-play the following situations showing ways parents talk by lecturing, reasoning, explaining, begging, etc.

   a. Seven-year-old finicky eater at the dinner table: "I hate beef stew. I won't eat it!"
   b. Four-year-old and mother walking home from the playground. The child wants to stop at her friend's house. Mom says they need to get home. The child then throws a tantrum on the sidewalk.
   c. Mom and friends in the living room trying to have a conversation where the child keeps interrupting with banging noises, asking questions, singing.

2. Process by asking participants what they were thinking, feeling, and deciding.

3. Ask the group if they see themselves in any of these scenes.

4. Ask the group to become familiar with Alternatives to Nagging handout.

5. Ask for volunteers to role-play one of the situations with one alternative and process as above.

Alternatives to Nagging Handout

1. Act without talking. For example, take the child by the hand and continue walking; remove food from table; rub child's back while ignoring behavior.

2. Give a limited choice, "Would you like to walk to the car or have me carry you?" "Would you like to make yourself a peanut butter sandwich or wait until breakfast to eat?" "Would you like to play quietly here or in your room?"

3. Make a reasonable request in 10 words or less. Wait for the child's response.

4. Use one word.

5. Use a signal or note.

6. Say how you feel.

7. Give information.

8. Describe what you see.

Sex: The Questions They Ask

Objective:

To provide practice in answering questions about sex in ways that allow children to feel comfortable about coming to parents with their questions.

Materials:

Paper
Pencils
Excerpt from Positive Discipline A-Z on Sex Education

Comment:

Often your lack of experience, fear, and judgments get in the way of giving your children helpful information about sex.

Directions

1. Ask group members to share briefly how they, as children, got their information regarding sex. Ask how much of it turned out to be accurate.

2. Have the group divide into small groups. Have each member write one question that would be difficult for him or her to answer if asked by his or her child.

3. Ask the participants to throw their questions in the center of the circle.

4. Have one participant select a question slip and ask it as if he or she were a child and it were his or her question. Tell the group members how old the child is.

5. Let the group members practice answering the question.

6. Discuss: Which type of response would encourage a child to ask further questions? Which responses gave encouragement but not too much information? What did you learn?

7. Repeat steps 4 through 6 for each member, or as time permits.

8. Discuss: What will you do to prepare yourself for this at home?

Notes

Solutions vs. Consequences

Objective:
To help parents see the value of focusing on solutions instead of consequences.

Materials:
Flip chart
Marking pens

Comment:
Consequences are often misused. Many parents try to disguise punishment by calling it a consequence. One way to avoid this problem is to focus on solutions instead of consequences.

Directions

1. Read the following to the group: "Serena is an eight year old girl who doesn't get herself ready for school and is frequently late. It is driving you crazy and making other family members late."

2. Ask for a volunteer to be Serena. Give her the instruction to simply listen and notice what she feels.

3. Continue by saying, "Let's list some consequences that will "teach Serena a lesson!" What are some consequences that will do that?" (If the group is familiar with Positive Discipline ask them to role-play more traditional models of parenting. Use a somewhat harsh tone here and emphasize the phrase "teach Serena a lesson.") List the group's ideas on the left side of the flip chart.

4. Now say, "Let's look at this differently. You've had some Positive Discipline training now. Let's think of some solutions that will help Serena develop the skills she needs to get ready for school on time and on her own." List these ideas on the right side of the flip chart.

5. Ask Serena how she was feeling and what she was thinking and deciding as she heard each list. Ask her what "lessons" she was learning from the first list. Ask her which list made her feel more connected. Ask her which list would help her be more successful in developing capability.

6. Discuss the two lists with the whole group. Help the group look for differences (punishment vs. solutions.) Refer to criteria: past-oriented vs. future-oriented, discouraging vs. encouraging, make children pay for their mistakes vs. helps children learn from their mistakes.

7. Point out that many try to disguise punishment by calling it a logical consequence. For this reason Positive Discipline emphasizes, "No more logical consequences—at least hardly ever. Focus on Solutions."

8. Show a chart the Four R's and an H for Solutions:

RELATED

REASONABLE

RESPECTFUL

HELPFUL

Strengths Activity

Debi Sementelli

Objective:

To help children recognize and focus on their strengths, and to make things like being caring, kind, helpful...more concrete in their minds.

Materials:

Butcher paper

Marking pens

Comment:

Parents can help children develop the ability to feel good about themselves without needing external approval or validation.

Directions

1. Ask participants to choose a partner and complete the following directions with each other so they can experience what they will be doing with their children. They will take turns being the child and the parent.

2. Ask your "child" to lie on the butcher paper so you can trace an outline of his or her body.

3. Let your child draw and color in his or her hair and favorite clothes.

4. Around the border of the body, write positive adjectives and talents that describe your child. Brainstorm together on what these might be. To help with this process, ask your child, "What do you think you do really well?" Your child might say things like, "I can run fast, I can fix things, I'm good at soccer, etc." You can help by saying things such as, "What about how helpful you were with dinner tonight, and what about the time you shared with your friend, and how you cheered me up with that big smile?" You can then add "helpful with family work, share with friends, cheerful smile," to the chart.

5. Leave room to keep adding adjectives as you or your child thinks of them. Hang in your child's room so he or she can see it before going to sleep and when he or she wakes up. While tucking your child in bed at night you might ask, "What did you do today that you would like to add to your chart?" You can also suggest things they might not have noticed, such as, "I saw you make the choice to be kind to your friend today when you..."

6. Invite 3 to 5 people (depending on your time) to share their drawing with the whole group.

7. Process with group, "How did this activity help you to see your child and yourself differently?"

FACILITATORS NOTE:

If you are doing this in a large training, divide the participants into groups of 4 to 6 and have them draw one child, and then brainstorm for possible strengths. Invite each group to share their drawing. Let them know this gives them an idea of what the activity will look like when following the directions above with parents.

HOME EXTENSION:

8. Help children to visually see themselves as capable and growing every day. Encourage them to see for themselves that they already have many talents and abilities they can now use in different ways.

9. Suggestions for encouraging children to use these skills in different ways:

"I noticed you...know your colors. Would you like to hear about the "Color Sorter" job that's available in our family?" or, " I noticed you...can climb the monkey bars at the park. That takes strong muscles. There's a job on our family work chart that needs someone with strong muscles. It's vacuuming. Would you like to use your strong muscles to push the vacuum?"

Taking Children's Behavior Personally

Objective:

To realize that what your kids do is about them, not you.

Materials:

Behaviors Chart (see below)

Comment:

When you learn to stop taking your kids' behavior personally, you can stop blaming yourselves for their behavior.

Behaviors

Cutting classes

Spending time in room

Refusing to go on family vacation

Trading outfits you bought for Christmas

Grumpy mood

Forgetting to do chores

Not wanting to sit with you in a movie

Not wanting to go to college

Directions

1. Show the chart of behaviors to the group.

2. Ask each person to choose one behavior that really bugs him/her or to choose another behavior that might not be on the list.

3. Define the following two attitudes to the group:

   a. Taking it personally means, "I tell myself their behavior has something to do with my failures or successes." For example, "I'm a terrible parent. I'm a good parent. What will others think? How could they do this after all I have done for them? They must hate me or they wouldn't behave this way."

b. Not taking it personally means, "I tell myself their behavior has to do with them, not me." For example, "They need to find out for themselves. They are exploring what life and values mean to them. This is important to them. This is not important to them. I have faith that they can learn whatever they need to learn from their mistakes and challenges. I wonder what this means to them?"

4. Ask the participants to form groups of four and discuss their behaviors, attitudes, and feelings when they deal with the behaviors they have chosen.

5. When they come back to the whole group, have them discuss what they learned. Which attitude do they operate from when dealing with behaviors that bug them? How is their attitude helping or hurting them? How is their attitude helping or hurting their children? How can this help them at home with their children this week?

Comment:

Be sure to discuss that not taking it personally does not mean permissiveness. Parents can still use other skills they are learning such a curiosity questions, focusing on solutions, family meetings, and joint problem-solving.

Teen Power Demonstration

Objective:
To understand the importance of turning power over to teens to avoid rebellion (aggressive or passive) and power struggles.

Materials:
A pencil

Comment:
Parents often are afraid to let go and allow their teens to experiment with their personal power. Teens will experiment anyway—they just go underground to do it—which means lots of lying and sneaking around so they can do what they want while trying to avoid punishment and/or disappointment from their parents.

Directions

1. Ask for a volunteer to play a teen (or any age child).

2. Hold out a pen and say to the teen, "This pen represents your power. Do you want it?"

3. When the teen starts to take the pen pull it back and say, "I don't know. Do you think you are ready?"

4. Whatever the teen says, start to give him or her the pen, but then pull it back again and say, "But, what if you make a mistake?"

5. Continue this back and forth, saying things like, "I'm not sure I can trust you?" "I don't know. Remember that really stupid thing you did last time?" "Even if I trust you, I'm not sure I can trust your friends."

6. Optional: Sometimes, after step 5, let the teen volunteer have the "power" for a few seconds and then take it back and say: "That's enough for now." It usually brings up an interesting reaction and insights from the teen volunteer.

7. Once you think the point has been made, process with the teen by asking, "What are you thinking, feeling, and deciding about yourself and what you will do?" Process the same way with the parent.

8. Ask the group what insights they had from watching this demonstration.

9. Be sure to cover the following questions:

   If you don't "give" power to your teens, how do they "take" it openly or by going "underground"?

   How well will your children be prepared to use their personal power when they leave home and you have no more control?

Notes

Teen Secrets

<table>
<tr><td>

Objective:

To have faith in your teenager to pass through a normal growth cycle.

</td><td>

Materials:

Paper
Pencils
Flip chart
Marking pens

</td></tr>
</table>

Comment:

Parents often catastrophize the outcome of normal teenage behavior and believe that how teens are now is how they will be forever. Remembering your own teen years, and that you didn't stay that way forever, can relieve your worries and restore your faith in your teenager.

Directions

1. Ask participants to think of at least three things they did as teenagers that they didn't want their parents to know about. Allow one or two minutes.

2. Ask them to form groups of four to six and make a list of some of the things they did as teens that they preferred to keep secret from their parents. Remind them that they don't have to share anything they don't want to.

3. After a few minutes ask who would be willing to share secrets from their groups list while someone records what is shared on the flip chart.

4. Ask how many have secrets they still don't want their parents to know about. What about items they still don't want anyone to know about?

5. Ask what they learned from participating in this activity.

6. Ask what specific ways they can think of to be supportive and show faith in their teenagers?

Notes

Thermometer

Adapted from an activity by John Taylor, Person to Person, available at *www.add-plus.com*

Objective:

To experience the results of discouragement, and then connection before correction.

Materials:

Flip-chart and markers

Blank sheet of paper and pencil for each participant

Characteristic and Life Skills list from the Two Lists Activity

Comment:

Lectures that sound critical and judgmental invite discouragement (defensiveness and rebellion), thus negating what parents want their children to learn. Connection (from love and understanding) followed by correction through curiosity questions invites openness that can lead to critical thinking, problem solving and cooperation.

Directions

1. Ask for a volunteer to be a child.

2. Ask the volunteer to stand about five feet a way from you and to pretend there is a thermometer on the floor between you. Instruct the volunteer that when you use words that are **discouraging** he or she will move away from you (to the cold end of the thermometer), and when you use words that feel **encouraging** he or she should move closer to you (to the warm end of the thermometer). Let the volunteer know that he of she need not respond with words—just movement indicating discouragement (moving back to the cold end of the thermometer) and encouragement (moving forward to the warm end of the thermometer).

3. Start by using discouraging words (lecturing and blaming) to the volunteer. Use an accusing voice as you say (pausing after each statement to allow the child time to move back). "Your teacher called me today, what did you do? Don't tell me you didn't do anything! Why would the teacher call if you didn't do anything? She said you were talking in class. What are you going to do about this? You can just go to your room and think about what you did."

4. By now the volunteer should be as far as possible to the cold end of the thermometer. Switch to encouraging words and voice, (again pausing after each statement to allow the volunteer time to move forward). "Your teacher called me this morning. I'll bet you felt very embarrassed when she yelled at you in front of

everyone. I remember a time my teacher yelled at me in front of everyone. I felt humiliated and angry. I would really like to hear your version of what happened. Since you can't change your teacher, I'll bet you can think of a way to avoid this problem in the future. Why don't you think about it and let me know what you come up with."

5. By now the "child" should be very close to you.

6. Process with the volunteer "child" what he or she was thinking, feeling, and deciding during both phases of the role-play.

7. Then take the "child" to the Characteristics and Life Skills list and ask if he/she was learning any of these at either end of the thermometer.

8. Invite a discussion about what participants learned from this activity.

9. To extend discussion ask some of the following questions:

    •   Why do you think parents use lectures (criticism and judgment)?
    •   What are the long-term results of criticism? What decisions might children be making that could have a life-long effect on them?
    •   At which end of the thermometer are children open to learning?
    •   Does anyone have an example of a time when they were a child and experienced discouragement or connection in response to a "mistake" they made—and what they were thinking, feeling, and deciding?

Teacher Version (replace Nos. 3 and 4) above with the following:

1. Ask the volunteer teacher to start by using discouraging words (lecturing and blaming) to the volunteer student. Use an accusing voice as you say. "The playground monitor told me that you weren't being cooperative today. What did you do? Don't tell me you didn't do anything! Why would the supervisor call me if you didn't do anything? She said you were pushing in line. What are you going to do about this? You can just go to your desk and think about what you did."

2. Now switch to encouraging words and voice. "The playground monitor told me that you were having a hard time following the rules at the playground today and that she yelled at you in front of everyone. I'll bet you felt very embarrassed when she yelled at you. I remember a time the teacher yelled at me in front of everyone. I felt humiliated and angry. I would really like to hear your version of what happened. I'll bet you can think of a way to avoid this problem in the future. Why don't you think about it and let me know what you come up with. If you need any help with that, let me know."

3. Process as above.

Think Tree

by Jody McVittie, M.D.

Objective:

To embody the sense firmness and kindness at the same time.

Materials:

None needed

Time: about 5 minutes

Comment: This activity can be used alone or after a parenting styles/teaching styles activity.

1. Ask for a volunteer to come stand beside you to "play" a little with how different styles feel.

2. Ask the volunteer to stand next to you and get as rigid as possible. Feet together, muscles tight ALL over (face, shoulder, fists, legs, torso). Ask for permission to gently push the person while they are all tight.

3. Push the person on one shoulder or the other a couple of times. If they are really rigid they will wobble considerably. (This is an exaggerated authoritarian pose).

4. Next ask the person to get really flexible, loose. Again ask permission to push a little and push on a shoulder a couple of times. They usually move quite a bit if they are really flexible.

5. Next ask the person to take a breath and "think tree." Feet shoulder width apart, hands at their sides. Invite the person to think of their legs as a big strong trunk which is held to the earth with very strong roots. Imagine those roots and the trunk. Those are your values. They are what you really care about. Then invite the person to think of the upper part of their body as firmly attached to the trunk. It moves a little in the wind, but not a whole lot. "It knows where it stands" but is not inflexible.

6. After the person appears firmly rooted (sometimes the need to be reminded to breathe and imagine roots) again ask permission to push on their shoulder and push a few times. (This time they will move a little, but come back to center).

7. After the demonstration invite the group to get in pairs and try it themselves. It is helpful to remind them that for the rigid pose they really have to get tight – and for the tree pose to take their time so that they can really feel anchored before they let their partner push.

8. Invite a discussion of what was noticed. When things are stressful at home, how would it feel to "think tree?"

Notes

Positive Discipline Tool Cards for Challenges

Objective:

To help participants gain more awareness of how many tools can be used for challenges, and to become more familiar with using them.

Materials:

A deck of Positive Discipline Tool Cards for each group of 3-6 people (or one tool card for each participant if you use the short version)

The Challenges and Characteristics and Life Skills lists from the Two Lists Activity

A Timer

Time: One Hour (if you have 5 groups)

Directions

1. Display the List of Challenges from the Two Lists Activity. (During class time, when participants ask for help with a personal challenge, you can ask them to add that challenge to the Challenges List so it can be used when it is time for this activity.)

2. Form at least five groups of 3 to 6 people and have each group choose a challenge from the Challenges list. (It is okay if they all choose the same challenge because each group is likely to handle the challenge differently.)

3. Give each group a full deck of cards (one facilitator gave each group just 10 randomly chosen cards from one deck, instead of a whole deck, and found it very successful) and let them know they will have ten minutes for two tasks.

    1) Their first task will be to see how many tools they can find in the deck that could work for the challenge and to put them in a pile (letting them know you will ask for a count).

    2) Their second task is to choose one of the tools to create a role-play to demonstrate how to use it in front of the whole group (Let them know that you are purposely making the preparation time short so they don't have to worry about perfection, but to have fun and to make mistakes that we can all learn from.)

4. At the end of the 10 minute preparation time, they will have 2 minutes to perform the role-play, 2 minutes to process with their role-players what they were thinking, feeling, and deciding—and to see if the child was learning anything from the Characteristics and Life Skills list. (Let them know that their role-plays will provide the basis for follow-up coaching by you so everyone can understand the tool at the deepest level possible.)

5. Invite everyone to share what he or she learned from this activity.

SHORT VERSION

1. Pass out one card to each person.

2. Ask them to look at their card and think about how this tool could work for a challenge they are having in any relationship: child, spouse, friend, or coworker.

3. Have them pair and share the card they received and how they could use it. Let them know they will have one or two minutes each. (Call time up when you can see they are finished.)

4. Ask if anyone is willing to share with the whole group.

Top Card

Lynn Lott's version

Objective:

To help parents understand that people have different perspectives on the world that affect how they respond to life's challenges.

Materials:

Flip chart page with diagram of 4 packages (as illustrated below) and one with an example of the 4 quadrants (see below)

4 more flip chart pages

Markers

Top Cards at Your Best and Worst handout

Comment:

For the purposes of this activity it is important to understand the definition of stress when explaining Top Card (except for the top card Stress and Pain). Stress is the space between how life is and how you think life should be. This is when people go into "only if" thinking. I'll be okay only if ______________ (I'm right, I please others, I'm in control, I avoid conflict, I take care of myself, I'm the best, I'm in charge, others like me, and a million other irrational beliefs.) It is similar to the four mistaken goals of behavior, "I belong only if I get undue attention, I'm the boss, I get even, or I give up."

Directions

1. Introduce this activity by explaining that it is helpful to learn about yourself in order to understand how your actions invite behaviors from others. This is about what you DO, not who you ARE.

2. Show the drawings of the 4 packages. Explain that the UPS delivery truck has just arrived to give you four "wonderful packages." You don't really want any of them, but the driver is willing to take only ONE back. Which one would you return? The boxes carry labels that represent what you most want to avoid in life. They are:

Rejection and Hassles	Stress and Pain	Criticism and Humiliation	Meaninglessness and Unimportance

3. If the participants are struggling a bit to decide which of these things they don't want, ask them to reflect on what they would prefer to avoid when they are feeling stressed.

4. Reassure the participants that there is no right answer and to just make their best guess.

5. Ask them which other box they would send back if they could send two back.

6. After they have decided, label each of the boxes as follows:

   Rejection and Hassles: Pleasing
   Stress and Pain: Comfort
   Criticism and Humiliation: Control
   Meaninglessness and Unimportance: Superiority.

7. We call this Top Card because it is the first card you play during times of stress. This is not about labeling yourself or others, but rather a tool for understanding yourself and others. It is about the direction you choose to take in life when you feel stressed, not who you are.

8. Let participants know that the second box they chose may represent their "method of operation" (what they do when they are feeling secure instead of stressed). For example, if my method of operation is "Pleasing", I will do pleasing in a more rational way, while someone with the top card of Pleasing may have some irrational (only if) thinking going on. "I'm okay only if I'm pleasing." However, if my top card is Superiority, and I start feeling stressed, I don't care if you are pleased or not. "I will be okay only if things are done my way to make them more meaningful."

9. Let the participants know that you will be exploring this a bit further by getting into groups by the package they rejected. When in groups, their task will be to brainstorm and fill in the four quadrants of a flip chart page. Give each group a flip chart page labeled as below, or give them a blank page to make their own.

10. Have the group brainstorm ideas to fill in all four quadrants (this usually takes about 10 minutes.) In their interactions with others, what are their assets? What are their challenges or liabilities? What kinds of responses do they invite from others (especially children)? What kinds of things would they like to improve? Remind them that the "Invites from others" column should include behaviors that might be considered "positive" and those that might be "negative."

11. As their final brainstorming task, ask them to write a bumper sticker that could be used as a motto for the group. (Sometimes they like to do this first to get them into a mood of exaggerating and having fun.) See diagram below.

12. While the groups are brainstorming, walk around the room to offer support as needed, answer questions or assist a little with brainstorming if a group is very small.

13. After 5 to 10 minutes ask them to hang their flip chart paper on a wall next to each other and to choose a representative from each group to read their paper to the rest of the group.

14. Invite them to share what they have learned from this process. (Common responses include noticing that it was fun to be part of a group with people like themselves, enjoying laughing at the similar challenges, noticing how their behavior might invite "misbehavior" from others.)

15. Emphasize again that the negatives of your Top Card represent how you show up when feeling stress. The positives of your Top Card show up when you are feeling secure, but can still have some "only if" thinking attached.

16. Give the group a final reminder that this is not for the purpose of labeling others, but for understanding their own actions so they can begin to focus on their assets, work on liabilities and maintain an awareness of what they invite from others. As parents, teachers, partners, and friends, this awareness can be useful. It can also help you have compassion for others.

Top Card______________________________

Assets	Liabilities

Invites from others　　　　　　　　　　　Would like to improve

Bumper sticker

Hints:

1. It is very helpful to be very familiar with the assets and liabilities of each top card before beginning this activity. Not much needs to be spoken, but as you walk around the room supporting the groups and occasionally making comments can be really helpful.

2. It is helpful to invite the group to exaggerate and have fun with the Assets and Liabilities brainstorming, but then to ask the group to get a more serious for the "Invites from Others" and "Steps for Improvement".

3. Per Adlerian theory, you make decisions when you are young about how you will survive or thrive in the world. These decisions color the way you understand and make meaning of the world around you and influence your behavior.

4. It is common that the box we "avoid" is often what you invite others to feel in your presence when you are feeling stressed.

5. A really fun resource is to go to www.lynnlott.com and click on the Lion that says "Try this." Take the test and get your results. Then go to the bottom of the page and click on "See All Personality Types" for a fabulous handout with much more information on Top Card. Also, Chapter 10 in the 2006 edition of Positive Discipline has a chapter on top card called Personality: How Yours Affects Theirs.

Comment:

Dr. William Pew explains the Adlerian roots of this activity.

"Following the teachings of Adler and Dreikurs we (in our practice) assiduously avoid categorizing or labeling our students. The number one priority (we call this top card) is a bridge to understanding, to helping people understand themselves ... it permits a very rapid insight into the life style, which assists getting at some of the individual's core convictions. It also provides an immediate way to help the person feel understood. The number one priority is a set of convictions that a person gives precedence to; it is a value that takes precedence over other values.... your priority often produces puzzling responses from others. It sometimes interferes with our movement toward self-actualization. It [sometimes] limits our social interest and our courage.

"All people share the same values; the difference is in how people rank the values. Thus, each of us values comfort, pleasing [acceptance], control, and superiority [significance]. But our number one priority indicates our consistent movement, not merely our wishful thinking; movement that we practice every day... The individual with a given priority, in moving toward this goal, always pays a price."

Top Card Designed and Compiled by Lynn Lott, M.A, M.F.T.

IF YOU CHOSE	THEN YOUR PERSONALITY STYLE IS CALLED	AND PERHAPS WHEN YOU ARE STRESSED, YOU DO THE FOLLOWING	WHEN YOU AREN'T STRESSED, YOU HAVE MANY ASSETS AND GIFTS	HERE ARE SOME OF THE PROBLEMS YOU INVITE OR STRUGGLE WITH	WHAT YOU NEED FROM OTHERS WHEN YOU ARE STRESSED IS	WHAT YOU NEED TO WORK ON IS	WHAT YOU LONG FOR IS
Rejection and Hassles	Pleasing (You're like the Chameleon)	Act friendly. Say yes and mean no. Give in. Worry about what others want more than your needs. Gossip instead of confronting directly. Try to fix everything and make everybody happy. Beg for understanding. Complain. Accommodate. Work hard. Catastrophize. Get silent, like a deer in the headlights. Be super-reasonable and avoid your feelings. Whine or feel sorry for yourself. Make lists.	Sensitive to others. Have lots of friends. Considerate. Compromiser. Non threatening. Likely to volunteer. People count on you. Usually see positives in people and things. Can be a loving and lovable person when you aren't seeking approval.	Invite revenge cycles and others to feel rejected. Feel resentful and ignored. Get in trouble for trying to look good while doing bad. Not have things the way you want them. Reduction in personal growth. Loss of sense of self and what pleases self.	Telling you how much they love you. Touching you a lot. Showing approval. Showing appreciation. Letting you know you won't be in trouble if you say how you really feel.	Be more open and honest and say what you are thinking and feeling. Say no and mean it. Let others have their feelings and let their behavior be about them and not you. Spend time alone and give up trying to please everyone. Don't be afraid to ask for help or for another perspective.	To do what you want while others clap. For others to like you, accept you and be flexible. For others to take care of you and make hassles go away.
Criticism and Ridicule	Control (You're like the Eagle)	Hold back. Boss others. Organize. Argue. Get quiet and wait for others to coax you. Do it yourself. Stuff your feelings. Cover all the bases before you make a move. Complain, sigh, get angry. Procrastinate. Explain/defend. Engage in physical activity. Put up a wall.	Good leader and crisis manager. Assertive. Persistent. Well-organized. Productive. Law-abiding. Get what you want. Able to get things done and figure things out. Take charge of situations. Wait patiently. Can be a person of generosity and equanimity when you aren't seeking control.	Lack spontaneity. Social and emotional distance. Want to keep others from finding weak spots. Invite power struggles. End up sick. Avoid dealing with issues when you feel criticized. Get defensive instead of open. Sometimes wait for permission. Critical and fault finding.	Saying OK. Giving you choices. Letting you lead. Asking how you feel. Giving you time and space to sort out your feelings.	Remind yourself that you are not responsible for another. Stop trying to prevent problems you don't have and take a small action step. Stop and listen to others instead of withdrawing. Think about what you want and ask for it. Listen instead of getting defensive. Ask for help and choices. Delegate.	To be in control even though others can be better, smarter. To get respect, cooperation and loyalty. For others to have faith in you and give you permission to do what you want. To have choices and go at your own pace.
Meaninglessness and Unimportance	Superiority (You're like the Lion)	Put down people or things. Knock yourself. Talk about the absurdity of life. Correct others. Overdo. Take on too much. Worry about always doing better. Operate on "shoulds". Sidetrack and shift the playing field. Cry, scream or complain to others. Dig in and get stubborn. Be indecisive. Become the expert. Seek advocates. Fight whether or not it is necessary.	Knowledgeable. Precise. Idealistic. Get a lot done. Make people laugh. Receive a lot of praise, awards and prizes. Don't have to wait for others to tell you what to do to get things done. Have a lot of self-confidence. Can be a person of depth and significance when you aren't seeking status.	Overwhelmed, over-burdened. Invite others to feel incapable and insignificant. Seen as a know-it-all or rude and insulting and don't know it's a problem. Never happy because you could have done more or better. Have to put up with so many imperfect people around you. Sometimes you don't do anything. Spend too much time doubting your worth.	Telling you how significant you are. Thanking you for your contributions. Helping you get started with a small step. Telling you you're right.	Stop looking for blame and start working on solutions. Give credit where credit is due, including to yourself. Look at what you have instead of what you don't have. Show an interest in others and be curious about them. Go for a walk, exercise, eat something healthy.	To prove your worth by being the best. To get appreciation and recognition from others. Spiritual connection. To be recognized for being right and for making a difference.
Stress and Pain	Comfort or Avoidance (You're like the Turtle)	Make jokes. Intellectualize. Do only the things you already do well. Avoid new experiences. Take the path of least resistance. Leave sentences incomplete. Avoid risks. Hide so no one can find you aren't perfect. Overreact. Complain. Cry. Scream. Micromanage and spoil others. Don't ask for help. Tuck back into your shell. Attack like a snapping turtle. Close up your heart.	People enjoy being around you. Flexible. Do what you do well. Easygoing. Look out for self and own needs. Can count on others to help. Make others feel comfortable. Can be a person of courage and grace when you aren't seeking comfort.	Suffer boredom. Lazy, lack of productivity. Hard to motivate. Don't do your share. Invite special attention and service. Worry a lot but no one knows how scared you are. Lose out on the contact of sharing. Juggle uncomfortable situations rather than confront them. Wait to be taken care of instead of becoming independent. Invites others to feel stressed.	Not interrupting. Inviting your comments. Listening quietly. Leaving room for you. Showing faith. Encouraging small steps.	Create a routine for yourself. Show up and stick around, even if all you do at first is watch. Speak up and ask questions or say what you want instead of assuming. Tell others how you are feeling. Ask someone to do things with you at your pace till you feel comfortable. Share your talents with others.	For things to be as easy as they look. To be left alone, to have your own space and pace. You don't want to argue.

Notes

Bumper Stickers (Life Mottos)
Top Card Activity

Jane Nelsen's version

Objective:

To help participants identify their Lifestyle Priority (Top Card) to become more aware of their "only if" thinking; and to appreciate their strengths and to see their challenges as opportunities for improvement.

Materials:

Four posters of bumper stickers or "life mottos" (below) enlarged and laminated if possible—or hand drawn on 4 flip charts. (Colored versions can be found at *www.positivediscipline.com/downloads*)

Top Card labels (Superiority, Control, Pleasing, Comfort) to hang above the appropriate poster. Paper or other material to cover these that is easily removed.

Top Card Worksheet handout for each participant.

Top Card Notes, and **Strengths and Challenges** handout (back to back)

Four flip charts with Top Card _________ at the top, and four quadrants: 1) **Strengths**, 2) **Challenges**, 3) **How Strengths Contribute**, and 4) **Changes for improvement**. At the bottom leave space for: Bumper sticker/Life motto.

Comment:

We all create different beliefs about how to "move" through life. Alfred Adler called this *Private Logic*. Our movement is based on our *private logic* perceptions of how best to "fit in" (to belong) in our many social circles, starting with the family. Some beliefs serve us well in our lives; and others create challenges to our well being and relationships with others. The *private logic* of children can be understood through the Four Mistaken Goals. The *private logic* of adults can be expanded through Top Card (Lifestyle Priorities). **The term "Top Card" is used as being the "first card played" or the "go-to response"** when feeling (or anticipating feeling) insecure or vulnerable and we mistakenly engage in "only if" thinking for how to belong.

Instructions Part One

1. In advance, tape the laminated posters of bumper stickers (life mottos) in four corners of the room. Tape the four labels above the appropriate poster and cover until No. 3 below.)

2. Also tape the four flip charts next to each poster for use in Part Two Instructions.

3. Ask participants to wander to each corner and read all of the posters. After they have read them all, have them "stand" in the corner with the statements that made them laugh because they can identify with some that fit them—even though they may feel a little embarrassed. (This is called a recognition reflex.) If they have difficulty deciding, ask them to just choose one for the moment and that it will become more clear as the activity continues.

4. Then ask someone in each group to uncover the label at the top of each poster that identifies the Top Card.

5. Tell them the Top Card represented by each poster **Superiority** most wants to avoid **Meaninglessness**. **Control** most wants to avoid **Criticism**. **Pleasing** most wants to avoid **Rejection**, and **Comfort** most wants to avoid **Stress**.

6. Ask them to remember the name of their Top Card and take a seat.

Instructions Part Two

7. Pass out the **Top Card Worksheet** and allow a few minutes for them to follow the instructions for Nos. 1 and 2.

8. When they are finished, go over some of the points made on the **Top Card Notes** handout.

9. Pass out the back to back handout with **Top Card Notes** and **Top Card Strengths and Challenges**.

Instructions Part Three

10. Explain that they will now get into groups with others who share their Top Card. They will go back to the flip chart next to the Bumper sticker/Life Mottos and brainstorm according to the four headings. Ask them to choose a scribe to write down what they all brainstorm. Let them know they can look at the **Top Card Notes** and **Strengths/Challenges** handout page for inspiration, but to brainstorm what fits for them as a group. Let them know they will have about 7 minutes, so they should brainstorm quickly.

11. Walk around the room to check in and to notice if they need more time. Then have everyone bring their flip charts and the Life Motto posters to a part of the room where they can be displayed side by side.

12. Have each group come up, one at a time, and share what they have written.

13. At the end of each group sharing, ask for a show of hands of how many have the Top Card of Control, Comfort, Pleasing, and Superiority as their second highest choice. This illustrates how many different combinations there are to create a lifestyle personality (belief system).

14. When back in their seats, invite participants to personalize the last half of the Top Card Worksheet.

15. Invite a discussion about what they learned from this activity.

16. Some additional questions to ask to emphasize that we all may have some strengths and challenges from all Top Cards—and other important points.

 a. Can you name one or two **strengths** you share from another Top Card?

 b. Can you name one or two **challenges** you share from another Top Card?

 c. Name one strength from another Top Card that would help you improve.

 d. Emphasize the importance of not labeling themselves or others. The purpose is to understand—not to label.

 e. Point out that they have just spent 45-60 minutes on this activity just to create awareness. They will find that it "keeps cooking" as their awareness increases.

Top Card and Daily Style Worksheet

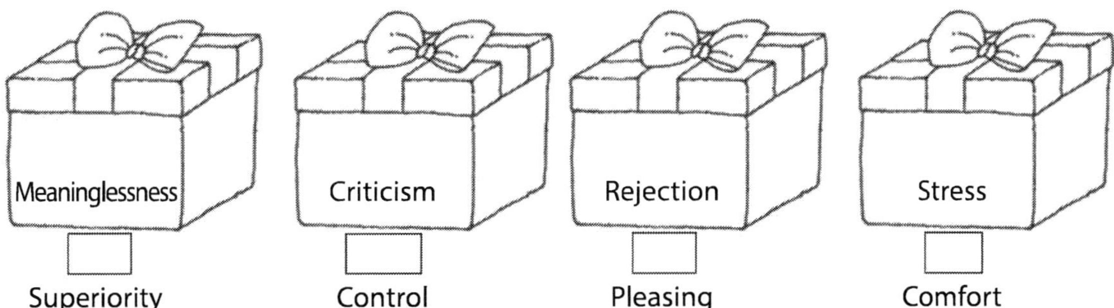

1. Put a "1" in the box under the present that represents your Top Card per the Bumper Sticker/Life Motto activity. This is the present you would like to return—what you most want to avoid.

2. Put a 2 in the box under the present you would return if you could return two. This represents your Daily Style: what you may do with less "only if" thinking when feeling more secure. Don't over think it. Follow your gut reaction.

3. Put a 4 in the box under the present that is the easiest for you to handle (even though you don't like it.) The remaining present gets a 3. These presents represent some influence in your "only if" thinking, but less than the others.

4. From the list of **Strengths and Challenges** handout, (or from your inner wisdom) choose your three best strengths from your **Top Card** and/or your **Daily Style**.

5. From the list of **Strengths and Challenges** handout, (or from your inner wisdom) choose your three top Challenges from your **Top Card** and from your **Daily Style**.

6. How my **Strengths** contribute to my relationship with children.

7. Specific changes I can make to improve my relationship with children based on awareness of my **Challenges**.

PRIORITY LIFE-STYLE (TOP CARD) NOTES

Following is the subconscious, private logic, "only if" thinking of each Top Card about how we may deal with feelings of insecurity.

1) **Superiority:** "I belong only if I'm doing something meaningful; and I feel insecure (and react) when I'm not accomplishing important things and when others don't agree with my opinions about what is meaningful."

2) **Pleasing:** "I belong only if others like me and validate me. I feel hurt and insecure (and react) when others don't appreciate what I do for them and when they don't make an effort to know and do what pleases me."

3) **Control:** "I belong only if I have control over myself, situations (and sometimes others), and feel insecure (and react) when I think I have been criticized, and when others tell me what to do and/or resent and rebel against my efforts to do what I know needs to be done."

4) **Comfort:** "I belong only when I stay within limits that are safe and familiar, and don't want to do anything that is stressful. I feel insecure (and react) when others don't want to join me in comfort, or pressure me to join their agenda."

Most people don't like the name of their Top Card

People with a **Comfort Top Card** may be the exception. They don't understand why anyone would choose anything but comfort (or they may feel defensive about the pressure to change, implying they are not good enough).

Most people with a **Superiority Top Card** do not want to be superior to others. They may have the mistaken belief that they have to be superior in accomplishments to prove (or cover up) their basic feelings of inferiority. It may seem that they need to "be right," but it may be truer to say they have difficulty being "wrong", which they mistakenly interpret as not being good enough.

Most people with a **Control Top Card** usually don't want to have control over others, but of situations and/or themselves, because they mistakenly believe lack of control means not being good enough. This may create the extremes of jumping in to take control, or procrastinating until they feel more secure.

People with a **Pleasing Top Card** may have difficulty saying no to any opportunity to please others—until they feel resentful when others don't appreciate all they do (even when they don't ask what would be pleasing to others). They may feel hurt when others don't "read their minds" to know how to please them (because it isn't special if they have to tell them). They mistakenly believe not being appreciated means they aren't good enough.

Many have observed that the challenges (liabilities) of their Top Card don't represent "who" they are. That is because you don't "play" your challenges when feeling secure. You play your Top Card when feeling insecure or challenged—when in "only if " thinking.

Strengths represent what you do when feeling secure. You probably have many of the strengths and challenges of every Top Card, (refer to the ratings you gave). The one you rated highest comes closest to representing what you do from your "only if" thinking. The one you rated second may come closest to representing what you do when feeling most secure.

We are at our best when we develop all of the strengths of all of the Top Cards.

The purpose of this activity is to understand—never to label. None of them represent who you are—only what you do; and **there are as many uniquenesses as there are similarities for each each Top Card.**

Top Card (Lifestyle Priorities)

Strengths
(Useful Side of Life)

Challenges
(Useless Side of Life)

Comfort

Strengths	Challenges
Easy going, Easy to please.	Avoids stress. (Leaves well enough alone.)
Easily satisfied. Flexible. Content.	Less interested in personal growth.
Loyal and supportive.	Comfort trumps the needs of the situation.
Dependable doing what you do well.	Predictable. Doesn't like change.
Happy to go along if minimum stress involved.	Withdraws from conflict when feeling cornered.
Diplomatic. Minds own business.	Unwittingly invites others to feel bored or annoyed.

Control

Strengths	Challenges
Willing to take charge.	Controlling.
Organized. Gets things done.	Too detail oriented.
Persistent. Doesn't give up.	Lacks flexibility and spontaneity.
Reliable. Faithful.	May not be aware of the needs of others.
Likes rules and follows them.	May create social and emotional distance.
Plans ahead.	Feels criticized when none intended.
Others feel taken care of.	Unwittingly invites rebellion.

Superiority

Strengths	Challenges
Loves learning and growing.	Over-extended and overwhelmed.
Idealistic. Altruistic.	Underestimates abilities of others.
Self confident. Generous.	Likes being the best. Needs recognition.
Highly motivated.	Likes to be right—or avoid being wrong.
Willing to work hard.	Critical (of self and others).
Open to new possibilities.	Unwittingly invites others to feel inadequate.

Pleasing

Strengths	Challenges
Loving and lovable.	Needs approval. Easily hurt.
Friendly and have many friends.	Oversensitive. Avoids dealing with conflict.
Considerate. Gives a lot.	Gives in and compromises too much, and then feels resentful.
Peacemaker, compromiser.	Feels rejected when none intended.
Avoids creating conflict.	Unwittingly invites annoyance when feeling unappreciated for so much giving.
Cooperative. Willing to volunteer.	

I can give up
CONTROL,
as long as
I can control what
I give up.

Don't bother to think.
I've done all the
THINKING for you.

with ORGANIZATION
and STRUCTURE.

Positive Discipline

Please cut in
front of me.

If you don't like
what you see

wait a minute, I´ll CHANGE

YOUR WAY -
NOT MY WAY

Let´s all be
MERRY

YOU SHOULD KNOW
WHAT I WANT. I
SHOULDN´T HAVE
TO TELL YOU

I HOPE you

APPRECIATE

all I DO for

YOU

EXCUSE ME!
I´M SORRY!

Help!!!

I can´t say NO

Positive Discipline

Just let
THEM do it

Nothing gonna change
—MY WORLD—

Don´t forget
to smell the
R O S E S

GO AHEAD AND CHANGE. BUT DON´T ASK ME TO

Positive Discipline

CAUTION

Driver is reviewing daily planner, checking voicemail, and applying mascara.

JUST DO IT! (right)

Never mind. I'll do it.

I intend to make a difference in the world.
IT'S IMPORTANT!

I was not born to be **MUNDANE**

A+ **OVERACHIEVER on board**

DON'T WORRY

I criticize myself too.

If you want to HELP, **DO IT MY WAY.**

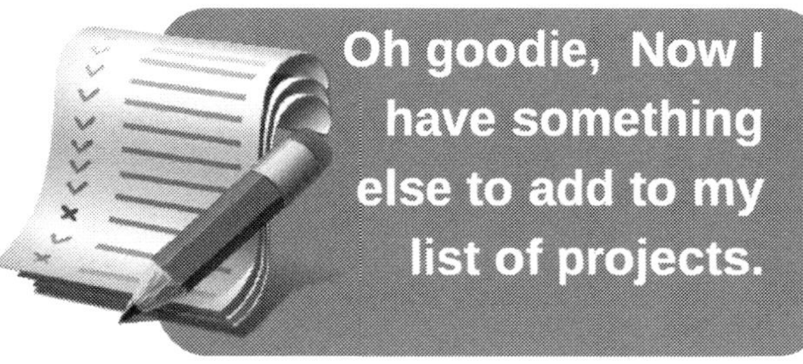

Positive Discipline

Top Card (Be Attitudes)

After participants have completed the Top Card Activity and are seated, share something like this: Now that you are more aware of your Top Card: the number one priority goal in your life, we will close with a reminder of the blessing of each of these—the BE ATTITUDES of how each can bless and contribute to Life.

Blessed are those who's Top Card/Number One Priority is ***Pleasing*** for

They are the ones who remind us to be curious/ to ask first to understand before being understood

They remind us to always look at the other side

They remind us the importance of cooperation and collaboration

They are the ones who model horizontal relationships

They are the ones who_____________________.

Blessed are those who's Top Card/Number One Priority is ***Comfort*** for

They are the ones who remind us not to sweat the small stuff

They are the ones who remind us to stop and smell the roses

They are the ones who remind us to take time to rest

They are the ones who remind us to slow down and breathe

They are the ones who_____________________.

Blessed are those who's Top Card/Number One Priority is ***Control*** for

They are the ones who remind us the importance of form and function in the world

They are the ones who help keep us structured so we can manifest into the world

They are the ones help break down huge tasks into manageable pieces.

They are the ones who bring order to chaos.

They are the ones who_____________________.

Blessed are those who's Top Card/Number One Priority is ***Superiority*** for

They are the ones who are the visionaries.

They are the ones who are never satisfied with the status quo.

They are the ones who encourage us to dig deeper/to go below the surface of appearances and see patterns and connections.

They are the ones who see beyond the surface and can encourage from a deep place.

They are the ones who_____________________.

Created by Deborah Owen-Sohocki

Wheel of Choice

Objective:

To get children involved in creating a Wheel of Choice that provides problem-solving ideas for them to use when faced with a challenge.

Materials:

Two lists from the Two Lists activity.

A white paper plate for each participant.

Enough colored markers for each participant to have at least two.

Large circle divided into 8 pie slices on a flip chart paper.

A deck of Positive Discipline Tool cards

Optional: some blown up examples of Wheels of Choice

Comment:

The more involvement children have in the process of creating their wheels of choice, the more likely they are to feel motivated to use them.

Directions

Part One:

1. Pass out the deck of Positive Discipline Tool Cards so that each participant has several.

2. Display the list of Challenges from the Two Lists activity and ask them to choose one challenge that children could be involved in focusing on solutions such as: not sharing, whining, tantrums, sibling fights, not doing homework, not doing chores, not getting dressed in the morning, etc.

3. Display the flipchart with the large circle divided into 8 pie slices.

4. Ask them to brainstorm solutions that might help solve the problem. Let them know it is okay to refer to their tool cards, or to brainstorm from their own wisdom/experience.

5. When each solution is suggested, ask the person who made the suggestion to come to the flip chart and write their suggestion in one of the pie slices along with a picture or symbol inside the slice to represent that solution.

6. We have just created a Wheel of Choice. How did you feel about being involved in the process? If you were a child, would you feel more motivated to use it because you helped create it? Even as adults, did you feel more capable because you were involved instead of just being presented with a completed Wheel of Choice?

Part Two:

7. Ask participants to pretend they are a 4 to 12-year-old child, and to choose a challenge they would like help with.

8. Pass out a paper plate and two markers to each participant.

9. Have them use a marker to draw a pie divided into 4 slices if they are roleplaying a child that is 4 to 6 years old, and 6 to 8 slices if they are roleplaying a child that is 7 years or older.

10. Ask them to form pairs (one to be the parent and one to be the child) and let them know they will take turns being in each role.

11. The parent and child will brainstorm solutions that might be helpful regarding the chosen challenge, and will write them down in one of their pie slices, along with a picture or symbol. **Be sure to let the child take the lead.**

12. Allow about 5 or 6 minutes—reminding them to brainstorm and draw quickly. Let them know they can switch roles as soon as they are finished with the first one.

13. When they have finished, ask if anyone would like to share their Wheel of Choice? Allow as much sharing as you have time for.

14. Ask them to look at the Characteristics and Life Skills list. As children, what characteristics and skills were they learning? Have them name them out loud

15. Invite participants to share what they learned from this activity.

16. Let them know that when they do this with their children, they might want to include yarn to thread through hole punches so the child can hang it up or hang it around their neck.

Comment:

The Wheel of Choice Program includes activities to teach 14 problem solving solutions: https://www.positivediscipline.com/catalog/download-products

---

Some sample Wheels of Choice. Notice that they have even more than 8 solutions.

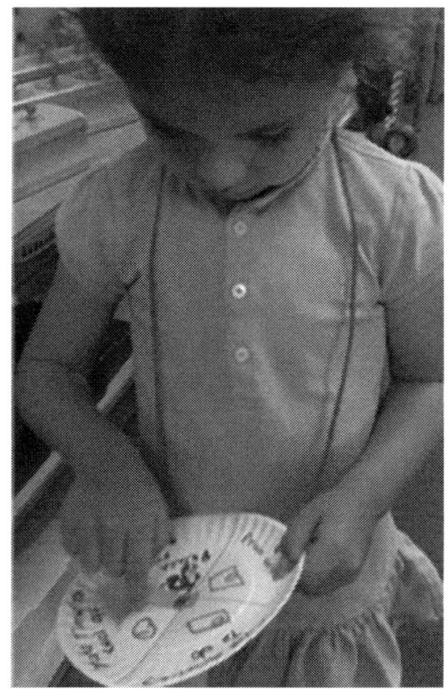

Students with special needs can participate in making their own Wheels of Choice. Courtesy of The Carrie Brazer Center for Autism in Miami, Florida.

Notes

The Two Lists: Where Are We and Where Do We Want to Go?

Objective:

To help parents think through what it is they really want for their children.

By listening to other parents' problems and other parents' dreams they realize they are not alone.

Introduce the Tool Cards.

Materials:

Flip chart

Label one chart paper with

"Challenges" and another with

"Characteristics and Life Skills"

Marking pens

Comment:

This exercise is very effective at the beginning of any introductory talk or class because it provides a "road map" for what they want. They can be assured that the parenting tools they will learn will help them achieve the long-term results they want for their children.

Directions

1. Let the participants know that together you will be creating two lists that will create guidelines (or a map) of where they want to go, and some challenges that will help them get there.

2. Ask for a volunteer to record on a flip chart while you invite others to brainstorm a list of challenges they have with their children. Typically, every group comes up with a list such as whining, talking back, not listening, fighting, biting, temper tantrums, lack of motivation, won't do homework, morning hassles, bedtime hassles, etc. Feel free to say, "What about __________ if some of your favorites are missing?"

3. Ask the group "What characteristics and life skills do you think children need to be happy, contributing members of society?" Ask for a volunteer to record while a group brainstorms a list that will include such things as self-esteem, responsibility, kindness, compassion, respect for self and others, problem solving skills, sense of humor, resilience, love, honesty, etc. Ask, "What about _______?" to any you want added.

4. Point out that all the challenges can be used to help children develop the characteristics and life skills that will help them become happy, contributing members of society—starting in their own homes. Use your sense of humor to inform participants, "Now you can get excited every time you are faced with a challenge because it offers an opportunity to teach skills such as problem solving, responsibility, and cooperation. You will see how all the Positive Discipline tools you will be learning to deal with the challenges, also help children develop the characteristics and life skills."

5. Save the two lists and post them every class as a constant reminder of what they want for their children and how they can use the challenges to get there. For example, during a role-play, you can ask a participant who is role-playing being punished and then being encouraged through one of the Positive Discipline Tools, to look at the list of Characteristics and Life Skills and ask which method is helping him or her develop them.

6. In the last week of your parenting class, go back to the two lists and ask how many feel they have some tools to deal with the challenges. Ask for a few people to choose a challenge they had and some tools they used to solve the challenge. Then have them look at the list of Characteristics and Life Skills and share how the Positive Discipline tools they used might have helped their children develop some of them.

Extension

In the last week of your parenting class, pass out the tool cards so that everyone has at least one. (They may have 3 or more if the group is small.) Have everyone choose one challenge from the list of Challenges. Then have them look at their tool card (or cards) to see if they have one that might help with their challenge. Have them share with a partner. Then ask if anyone would like to share with the whole group.

Winning Children Over vs. Winning Over Children

Adapted from a workshop by John Taylor. *Person to Person*, available at www.add-plus.com

Objective:

To show how cooperation is gained through mutual respect and cooperative efforts.

Materials:

None

Comment:

Many parents who successfully "win over children" have not asked the question, "If you are the winner, what does that make your child?" The loser. Is that what you want your child to be? Through mutual respect, you "win children over" to cooperation rather than winning over children.

Directions

1. Ask participants to form parent/child pairs. Encourage them to avoid being in a group with someone they came with. (That way when they go home, they have more experiences to share.) Let them know that one of them will be a parent and one will be a child about age four and you will invite them to role-play three "scenes from a day at the mall." Remind them that the idea with role-playing is to exaggerate and have fun.

2. **Scene 1.** The two of you have been at the mall for about two hours. The child has had enough. The parent is in a hurry and the child does what most healthy normal children do — rebel. It can be VERY helpful to role-play this as a demo. Ask for a volunteer to demonstrate this while you play the child. The volunteer's job is to be a parent in a hurry. During the role-play as the child, protest, then protest again and then have a "tantrum." If attire permits, sit on the floor, pound your fists and say something like, "You never listen to me; your shopping is more important than me; I hate you!" Then invite the pairs to do something along the same vein. Remind them it only took 30 seconds.

3. Process by asking the parents first, "What were you feeling? What were you thinking or deciding about yourself or your child?" Repeat for the "children." (Note: it isn't imperative that the parents be processed first, but once they've been "heard" they listen better to the "kids" and after the last scene, the kids really give the most powerful message, so it is nice to have them last.)

4. **Scene 2.** Invite the parent/child pairs to go to the mall again. This time the parents are ALMOST done and as they finish up their last errand/purchase they promise their children an ice cream cone if they can just wait 5 more minutes. Give them the hint that for a normal four-year-old, five minutes is about ten seconds and so the scene is likely to look like child pulling the parent. Process as above.

5. **Scene 3.** Invite the pairs to go to the mall one more time. This time they will give developmentally appropriate control to the child and still be self respectful. Explain that means, of course, that the trip won't be four hours, but maybe just long enough to do two errands. It is helpful to ask the role-playing "kids" to be moderately cooperative here. You can tell the group that this might seem far fetched, but that our experience is that when kids are treated this way, they really step up to the plate. Do a short demonstration with a volunteer who will play the child. This demo in itself teaches parents. While still in the car you have explained to the child that you will be doing two things at the mall today, returning one of your shirts and getting new shoes for the child. Then get out of the car holding the child's hand. Ask the child if it is safe to cross the parking lot (he will usually join the role-play and look both ways, but if he doesn't, invite him to check by looking both ways).Then offer a few other choices such as "How fast would you like to walk?""Which side of the fountain would you like to walk on?""Which store do you want to go to first, the shoe store or the shirt store?" If the "child" starts walking too fast, let the group know that you will be self respectful, and then tell the child that is too fast for you could he/she go a little slower. If the "child" starts resisting or asking for choices that don't exist, you can calmly say, "That isn't one of the choices," and also remind the role-player that, for this activity, it is helpful to be cooperative just so that we can get a sense of how it feels. After the demo invite the pairs to do this. Again, it only takes 30 -45 seconds. Process as above.

EXPANDED VERSION:

In addition to the above:

6. Divide the group into small groups. Give each group a typical situation where cooperation would be helpful regarding: morning routine, bedtime routine, dinner hour.

7. Have each group brainstorm ideas which encourage cooperation.

8. Have each group role-play their situations using the ideas they brainstormed.

9. Process as above.

Hints:

This is a great introduction or early activity and so it is common that parents aren't used to finding their feelings in the processing. They will often respond with thoughts first. It is helpful to ask them to notice it in their body and that it can usually be stated with one word. Use the feeling chart to help with feeling words.

Mistaken Goal Charts

Mistaken Goal Charts

1	2	3	4	5	6	7
The Child's goal is:	If the parent/ teacher feels:	And tends to react by:	And if the child's response is:	The belief behind the child's behavior is:	Coded messages	Parent/teacher proactive and **encouraging** responses include:
Undue Attention (to keep others busy or to get special service)	Annoyed Irritated Worried Guilty	Reminding. Coaxing. Doing things for the child he/she could do for him/ herself.	Stops temporarily, but later resumes same or another disturbing behavior.	I count (belong) only when I'm being noticed or getting special service. I'm important only when I'm keeping you busy with me.	**Notice Me.** **Involve Me Usefully.**	Redirect by involving child in a useful task to gain attention. Plan special time. Say what you will do. (Example: I love you and will spend time with you later.") Avoid special service. Have faith in child to deal with feelings (don't fix or rescue). Help child create routine charts. Engage child in problem solving. Use family/class meetings. Set up nonverbal signals. Ignore behavior with hand on shoulder.
Misguided Power (to be boss)	Challenged Threatened Defeated Angry	Fighting. Giving in. Thinking, *"You can't get away with it or I'll make you."* Wanting to be right.	Intensifies behavior. Complies with defiance. Feels he/she's won when parent/ teacher is upset even if he/she has to comply. Passive power (says yes but doesn't follow through).	I belong only when I'm boss, in control, or proving no one can boss me. You can't make me.	**Let Me Help.** **Give Me Choices.**	Redirect to positive power by asking for help. Offer limited choices. Don't fight and don't give in. Withdraw from conflict. Be firm and kind. Don't talk—act. Decide what you will do. Let routines be the boss. Leave and calm down. Develop mutual respect. Set a few reasonable limits. Practice kind and firm follow-through. Use family/class meetings.
Revenge (to get even)	Hurt Disappointed Disbelieving Disgusted	Hurting back. Shaming. Thinking, *"How could you do such a thing?"*	Retaliates. Intensifies. Escalates the same behavior or chooses another weapon.	I don't think I belong so I'll hurt others as I feel hurt. I can't be liked or loved.	**I'm Hurting.** **Validate My Feelings.**	Acknowledge hurt feelings. Avoid punishment and retaliation. Build trust. Use reflective listening. Share your feelings. Make amends. Show you care. Encourage strengths. Don't take sides. Use family/class meetings.
Assumed Inadequacy (to give up and be left alone)	Despair Hopeless Helpless Inadequate	Giving up. Doing things for the child that he/ she could do for him/herself. Over-helping.	Retreats further. Becomes passive. Shows no improvement. Is not responsive.	I can't belong because I'm not perfect, so I'll convince others not to expect any-thing of me. I am helpless and unable. It's no use trying because I won't do it right.	**Don't Give Up On Me.** **Show Me A Small Step.**	Break task down into small steps. Avoid labels. Encourage any positive attempt. Have faith in child's abilities. Focus on assets. Teach skills—show how, but don't do for. "Let me know when you are ready, and I'll show you how." Set up opportunities for success. Enjoy the child. Build on his/her interests. Use family/class meetings.

Mistaken Goal Chart (How Adults May Contribute)

1	2	3	4	5	6	7	8
The Child's goal is:	If the parent/ teacher feels:	And tends to react by:	And if the child's response is:	The belief behind child's behavior is:	Adults mistaken belief:	Coded messages:	Parent/teacher proactive and empowering responses include:
Undue Attention (to keep others busy or get special service)	Annoyed Irritated Worried Guilty	Reminding Coaxing Doing things for the child he/she could do for him/ herself	Stops temporarily, but later resumes same or another disturbing behavior. Stops when given one-on-one attention.	"I count (belong) only when I'm being noticed or getting special service." "I'm important only when I'm keeping you busy with me."	"I feel guilty if you aren't happy." "It's easier to do things for you than to watch you struggle." "I don't have faith in you to deal with disappointment."	**Notice Me. Involve Me Usefully.**	Redirect by involving child in a useful task to gain useful attention. Say what you will do, "I love you and _____." (Example: "I care about you and will spend time with you later.") Avoid special services. Say it only once and then act. Have faith in child to deal with feelings (don't fix or rescue). Plan special time. Involve child in creating routines. Touch without words. Set up nonverbal signals. Involve child in finding solutions during family and class meetings—and one to one.
Misguided Power (to be boss)	Angry Challenged Threatened Defeated	Fighting Giving in Thinking "You can't get away with it" or "I'll make you" Wanting to be right	Intensifies behavior Defiant compliance Feels he/ she's won when parent/ teacher is upset Passive Power	"I belong only when I'm boss, in control, or proving no one can boss me " " You can't make me."	"I'm in control and you must do what I say." "I believe that telling you what to do, and lecturing or punishing you when you don't, is the best way to motivate you to do better." "I don't practice the importance of teaching you contributing ways to use your power."	**Let Me Help. Give Me Choices.**	Acknowledge that you can't make him/her do something and redirect to positive power by asking for help. Offer a limited choice. Don't fight and don't give in. Withdraw from conflict and calm down. Be firm and kind. Act, don't talk. Decide what you will do. Let routines be the boss. Develop mutual respect. Get help from child to set reasonable and few limits. Practice follow-through. Involve child in finding solutions during family and class meetings—and one to one.
Revenge (to get even)	Hurt Disappointed Disbelieving Disgusted	Retaliating Getting even Thinking "How could your do this to me?" Taking behavior personally	Retaliates Hurt others Damages property Gets even Intensifies Escalates the same behavior or chooses another weapon	"I don't think I belong so I'll hurt others as I feel hurt." "I can't be liked or loved."	"I give advice (without listening to you) because I think I'm helping." "I worry more about what the neighbors think than what you need." "I have to hurt you to teach you not to hurt others."	**I'm Hurting. Validate My Feelings.**	Validate child's hurt feeling (you might have to guess what they are). Don't take behavior personally. Step out of revenge cyle by avoiding punishment and retaliation. Suggest Positive Time Out for both of you, then focus on solutions. Use reflective listening. Share your feelings using an "I" message. Apologize and make amends. Encourage strengths. Put kids in same boat. Involve child in finding solutions during family and class meetings—and one to one.
Assumed Inadequacy (to give up and be left alone)	Despair Hopeless Helpless Inadequate	Giving up Doing for Over helping Showing a lack of faith	Retreats further Passive No improvement No response Avoid trying	"I don't believe I can belong, so I'll convince others not to expect anything of me." "I am helpless and unable." "It's no use trying because I won't do it right."	"I expect you to live up to my high expectations." "I thought it was my job to do things for you." "It is too scary to have faith in you."	**Don't Give Up On Me. Show Me A Small Step.**	Break task down to small steps. Make task easier until child experiences success. Set up opportunities for success. Take time for training. Teach skills/show how, but don't do for. Stop all criticism. Encourage any positive attempt, no matter how small. Show faith in child's abilities. Focus on assets. Don't pity. Don't give up. Enjoy the child. Build on his/her interests. Involve child in finding solutions during family and class meetings—and one to one.

Parents Helping Parents
Problem Solving Steps

(Component No. 4)

Parents Helping Parents Problem-Solving Steps

1. Ask for a volunteer (with a real challenge that has not yet been solved) to sit next to you and explain that he or she is now a co-facilitator because everyone can learn from the demonstration. Ask for a scribe to write on a flip chart: the volunteer's name, spouse's name, the names and ages of all the children, and other household members.

2. Ask the volunteer to share a newspaper headline of the concern (just a few words). Ask the group for a show of hands of those who have had a similar concern or feelings. Point out how many people he/she will be helping. The scribe can now sit down until Step No. 9

3. Ask the volunteer to describe the last time the challenge happened, in enough detail, so the group can role-play. "What did you do and say? What did the child (or others) do and say? And then what happened?" Include others who may have been in the room or another room.

4. Ask, "How did you feel?" If he/she has trouble (or says, "frustrated"), show the "Feelings Column 2" on the "Mistaken Goal Chart" and ask him/her to choose the feeling that comes closest.

5. Ask the volunteer to read columns 3 and 4 after the chosen feeling, to verify if this is how he/she reacts, and how the child responds. If it doesn't fit, ask the volunteer to find the rows in columns 3 and 4 that do fit. Then read column 5 to identify the belief, and back to column 1 for the mistaken goal.

6. Let the group know that the Mistaken Goal is just a working hypothesis and that we learn about beliefs and how to encourage even if we aren't exactly "right".

7. Set up a role-play. Invite the volunteer to role-play the child. Include volunteers to play people who might have been in the same or another room. Ask for volunteers to play each part, starting with the lines they heard during the description of the problem. Advise that they "act" the part while being in the here and now to respond to what is happening now, not how they think the child usually responds—and to exaggerate and have fun.

8. Stop the role-play as soon as you think they have had time to experience feelings and decisions (usually two minutes or less). Ask the role-players (starting with the child) what they were thinking, feeling, and deciding (to do) as the people they were role-playing.

9. Put the volunteer in a "cone of silence" (to listen, but not respond). Ask the group to brainstorm solutions. Be sure they are addressed to the scribe at the flip chart, not to the volunteer. Invite the group to refer to the last two columns of the Mistaken Goal Chart, the Positive Discipline Tool Cards, or ideas from their personal wisdom.

10. Ask the volunteer to listen closely while the scribe reads all the suggestions, and then choose one to try. Bring back the volunteers to role-play with the volunteer playing him/herself (so he or she can practice) or to play the child if a punitive suggestion is chosen (so he/she can experience the child's reaction). At the end of the role-play, process the thoughts, feelings and decisions of each role player, starting with the child.

11. Ask for a verbal commitment from the volunteer to try the suggestion for one week and report back to the group.

12. Invite 3 or 4 people from the group to express their appreciation for the volunteer by asking, "What help did you get for yourself by watching this? What did you see that you appreciate about the volunteer? What ideas did you see that you could use?"

Parents Helping Parents Problem Solving Steps (PHP)

Many parenting classes fall apart and start losing participants because the parents aren't getting help with specific problems or some parents are monopolizing all the time with their problems. No matter how much information they have, many parents can't make the connection between what they are learning and how to apply it when their kids misbehave. The PHP process solves this problem as they role-play using the Positive Discipline tools for "real" challenges.

The PHP process also helps parents realize how much they know when they aren't emotionally involved. Have you noticed how easy it is to have ideas and perspective for other parents' problems, but when it's your own you feel lost, frustrated, and don't know what to do? A wonderful benefit of the PHP is that parents can be consultants to each other in a safe environment. During the brainstorming process for solutions, many ideas are suggested and the volunteer parent gets to choose one rather than feeling criticized and told what to do.

Without role-play practice, it is very common for parents to decide to try a new parenting tool and then get home and fall right back into their old habits. During the role-playing part of the PHP process, they can practice. For example, one woman chose the suggestion to ask her child curiosity questions. During the role-play she struggled and started telling instead of asking. The leader was able to say playfully, "Excuse me, what did you say you were going to do?" The volunteer laughed and said, "Oh, right," and started again, this time doing what she had decided she would do.

When first starting this process, some parents may feel shy about role-playing. Have faith. It won't be long before they will be "fighting" over who gets to be the volunteer and will be having fun role-playing while laughing and learning. This will become the favorite part of every parenting class.

Role-play reluctance

Avoid feeling hesitant about asking parents to role-play. They will pick up on your attitude. If you have faith in the process, it won't be long before they will catch your spirit. In the beginning, you may need to use several methods. (1) Just wait quietly for a volunteer. Eventually, someone will get uncomfortable with the silence and jump in. (2) Beg in a joking way, e.g., "I really need your help and I promise you'll love it eventually." (3) Share your story of how much you did not like role-playing in the beginning (if this is true for you), and how much you learned to enjoy it because you learned more this way than in any other process.

There is a tendency for some facilitators to skip this component, or to put it off until they are more comfortable. The following was shared by Jody McVittie, a Positive Discipline Lead Trainer.

Based on my years of teaching a variety of groups, I have learned that the PHP is one of THE MOST VALUABLE TOOLS in parenting classes. It doesn't address every problem, but it TEACHES HOW to address problems. Parents know this, and though it may take a little while, they REALLY appreciate the PHP by the end of the class. It does more too. I now believe that we can teach and discuss until we are blue or purple, but it has little long-term effect until parents actually get to DO things differently. Parents need to do more than discuss to shift perspective. Much of the shift for most folks (but not all) comes through role-play, through actual engagement with the material through application, and through listening to others' feelings and decisions.

Lectures make you the expert, which means that parents leave wishing they could take a mini you home with them. That isn't helpful. It isn't empowering.

Another Certified Positive Discipline Trainer (Eryn Rodger, Santa Cruz, CA) had this to say about PHP:

I used to put PHP at the end of the night's agenda, thinking that if we ran overtime with the experiential activities I had planned we could always scrap it (I lacked confidence with the steps anyway). However, in all my class evaluations, the participants would list PHP as one of the things they liked best about the class and that they wished we could have done more. Now, I make PHP a priority. Practice has definitely made it better; and now it's one of my favorite parts of the class too! It really drives home the point that we are all valuable members of the larger parenting community and we can be wonderful resources for one another in a culture that at times seems to promote isolation in child rearing.

The PHP Problem Solving Steps have been field tested for more than forty years and are effective and safe. Therefore, use the steps as they are written. We suggest giving all participants a copy. This way parents can follow along, seeing what comes next.

Keep a copy of the PHP in your lap so everyone can see that you are following the steps (as opposed to sounding like an expert). Ask a volunteer to to keep a finger on the steps and interrupt you if you miss a step.

You'll notice in steps 5 and 6 we refer to the Mistaken Goal Chart. This chart is an integral part of the PHP Problem Solving Steps. We suggest you make a handout of the chart for each parent to refer to during this process. Some parent educators make laminated copies of the PHP and the Mistaken Goal Chart back to back.

In the next section you'll find an expanded Version of the PHPPSS. This will help you understand more fully what can happen in each step. Become familiar with it, but do not use it as a guide during your classes.

Expanded Version of the Parents Helping Parents Problem solving Steps

The following information on the 14 steps is for expanded information only and is not to be used when doing the PHPPSS in classes and workshops.

1. Invite the volunteer sit next to you and explain that by volunteering he or she is now a co-teacher with you because everyone can learn and get help while observing and participating in this process. They will also be able to use some of the suggestions we create for your situation even when they have a different situation. Thank you for volunteering to be a co-facilitator with me in this process.

2. Ask for another volunteer to write, at the top of a flip chart paper, the volunteer's name, his or her spouse's name (if there is one) and names and ages of all children and other household members.

3. Ask for a brief statement—a one-word or one-sentence newspaper type headline of the problem. Sometimes the parent may give too much detail. Interrupt and say, "If you could describe the problem in one word or one sentence what would it be?" In this step, you are looking for a general idea of the problem, not the details. If the problem is something unusual, like "my son pees in soda cans," generalize the problem to the group saying, "How many of you have kids who do behaviors OR HABITS THAT SEEM CHALLENGING to you?" It's important to ask the group if they have a similar CHALLENGE because it is encouraging for the volunteer parent not to feel alone or inadequate by knowing others are or have been in the same boat.

4. Now is the time for details. Ask the volunteer parent to describe the last time the problem occurred in enough detail and dialogue (like a movie script) so that the group can get an idea of how to role-play the situation in about 60 seconds. If the volunteer needs help describing the situation, ask, "What did you do? What did the child or others do? Then what happened? What happened next?

    In this step, you are looking for a specific example of the problem. Unless you focus on one incident, you, the volunteer parent, and everyone involved will become overwhelmed and leave without satisfactory help. One episode represents a microcosm of what occurs between this parent and child. Focusing on and understanding the single incident makes the dynamics more manageable. This is called Holism in Adlerian Psychology. Solving a small part will change the "big" problem too.

    Specifics are important because what the parent did and the child's response to what the parent did provides more clues about the mistaken goal and thus the reason for the child's misbehavior. For example, if the child stops the behavior for a while in response to what the parent did but starts up again a few hours or days later, the mistaken goal is probably undue attention. If the child resists cooperation (actively or passively), the goal is probably power. If the behavior is hurtful to people or things, the mistaken goal is probably revenge.

    Asking for a description of the last time the problem occurred, that includes details and dialogue for role-players, helps the parent focus on the incident instead of telling stories about background and causes. Background details are a distraction to this process. Those details could be discussed forever without focusing on solutions. Sticking to the steps as outlined keeps the focus on finding a solution for a specific incident that brings clarity to the whole.

5. Ask the volunteer, "How did you feel?" If the volunteer has difficulty expressing a one-word feeling, refer him/her to the second column of the Mistaken Goal Chart and ask him/her to choose the group of feelings that is the closest. Do not use the feelings faces charts in this step because you want to focus on the feeling on the Mistaken Goal Chart that provides a clue to the purpose of the child's behavior. Ask the group, "How many of you have ever felt that way?" (Again, this is important so that the volunteer knows that he/she is not alone.)

    Most people are not used to identifying their feelings. Explain that it takes only one word to describe a feeling. If the parent is going on and on about what he/she thinks instead of what he/she feels, or if he/she comes up with a vague feeling such as "frustrated" (which could be used for all Mistaken Goals) use the Mistaken Goal Chart and ask the parent to find a feeling in the second column that comes closest to describing his/her own feeling. It is important for the parent to pick a feeling, because the feeling gives clues about the belief behind the child's behavior, which we call the child's mistaken goal. If appropriate, you can explain to the group, "What the parent feels gives us the clue to the child's mistaken goal. For example, if the parent feels annoyed this is a clue that the child's mistaken goal is Undue Attention and the mistaken belief is that the child doesn't count unless others are paying attention to him or giving her special service." Some people get this confused and think you have to know what the child feels in order to understand his/ her goal. We're looking for the parent's feeling as a barometer of what is going on.

6. Based on the feeling the parent chooses, ask the group to guess the child's mistaken goal using the Mistaken Goal Chart. Don't spend a lot of time trying to figure out the goal, especially if the conversation turns to analysis. Say "Let's see what further information we get from the role-play." Even if you never know for sure what the mistaken goal is, people will get help from role-playing and brainstorming.

7. Ask "Would you be willing to try something new?" This question is important to clarify a commitment to trying something else. Once in awhile a parent might say something like, "I have already tried everything." You might say, "Are you willing to choose one to see if you gain more understanding of why it isn't working?" It is extremely rare, but if a parent does not show a willingness to try something else do not proceed. Thank him/her for sharing this much and stop the process, saying, "Let's move to the appreciations step so we can let our helping parent know what we've learned from his/her sharing."

8. Set up and perform a role-play of the scene that was described. Remember that the role-play need not take longer than one or two minutes to give all the information needed. Use your intuition to determine which role the parent should play in order to learn the most. As a general rule it's helpful for the parent to role-play the child to "get into the child's world." Sometimes a parent might be feeling vulnerable and it might be best for the parent to watch the role-play instead. Later, when role-playing the suggested solution, it's usually best to have the parent play him/herself to practice implementing the new suggestion. Again you might feel it best for the parent to watch or to play the child to experience the child's reaction to the suggestion.

    Assign someone to play each part. Have the appropriate number of people represent members of the household (even if they are in a different room—they still know what is going on and have feelings and are making decisions about it). Tell them to start with the dialogue they heard during the description of the problem.

    Some facilitators are afraid that people will object to role-playing, and some people do. But a facilitator who is confident about the value of role-playing won't be discouraged by the resistance. Proceed to set up the role-play with confidence. When you ask for volunteers to play roles, be quiet and wait. Someone will fill the void of silence and volunteer. You might joke with them in your own way, or say, "I feel resistance. It reminds me of my resistance before I found out how valuable this is and how much fun it can be. Okay, who are the brave souls who are going to jump in and help me show how much fun this is?"

To get the role-play started, remind someone of their opening line or ask the volunteer parent to remind someone of an opening line.

9. Process the role-play by asking players to share, one at a time, what they were thinking, feeling, and what they were deciding as the people they were playing. This information sheds more light on the problem, and the processing serves as a debriefing for role-players who may be left with a lot of stirred up feelings they need to express. Asking the "children" what they were deciding (to do) helps parents see the long-term results of their actions instead of just the immediate result. Remember, feelings can usually be expressed in one word. (See the second column of the Mistaken Goal Chart)

10. Ask the group to brainstorm for possible solutions the volunteer parent could try. Ask a volunteer to write down every suggestion on the flip chart. Ask everyone in the group to refer to the last column of the Mistaken Goal Chart for ideas, to the Positive Discipline Tool Cards (if you have divided them out to the group in advance) or to make suggestions from their personal experience. Brainstorming allows each person to participate. It helps people accept and value how easy it can be to solve other people's problems. When it's someone else's problem we are not emotionally involved, so we have objectivity and perspective. Once we accept this we can appreciate the value of being consultants to each other instead of thinking we should be able to solve all our own problems or that we are failures if we even admit we have a problem.

    Encourage the group to think of as many alternatives as possible. Make it safe for them to make suggestions by respecting and writing down each suggestion on the flip chart. This is not a time for discussion or asking questions of the volunteer parent nor is it time to analyze any of the suggestions with the volunteer parent. Interrupt anyone who tried to get off the steps and remind them how important it is to stick to the steps to help the volunteer—and everyone else.

    Suggestions will improve as participants learn more of the tools recommended in the Positive Discipline books. Do not censor negative suggestions. If a negative suggestion is chosen be sure the parent role-plays the child so that he/she can experience what the child might feel and decide in response to punitive suggestion.

11. Have the scribe read all the suggestions aloud and then ask the volunteer to choose one he/she would be willing to try. Once in awhile a parent will say, "I've already tried all of them." Say something like, "Sounds like you really care and are trying everything you can think of. Would you be willing to pick one you have already tried and we'll see what we can learn from the role-play about why it isn't working?"

12. Role-play the chosen suggestion so the volunteer can practice. In most cases it is best to have the parent play him/herself. Many times we'll have a good idea, but when we try to apply it, we incorporate some of our old habits such as lecturing, controlling, throwing in a little humiliation and then wonder why it didn't work. All this will come out in the role-play, and those watching will also gain some insight about why some of the things they do may not be working. Rarely, a parent may prefer just to watch, while some prefer to play the child to get that perspective.

    If the person role-playing does start lecturing or doing something other than the chosen suggestion, it is okay to interrupt and say, "Excuse me. What did you say you were going to do?" This almost always causes laughter as everyone recognizes how easy it is to sleep into old habits.

If the chosen suggestion is a punitive one, the role-play will demonstrate why it doesn't work when you process the child's thoughts, feelings and decisions. It is important to ask all role-players what they were thinking, feeling, and deciding in order to learn how a situation affects everyone. **Finding out that a chosen suggestion didn't work doesn't mean the time has been wasted. Everyone will learn many valuable things during the process.** Do not try another suggestion. Trust the process and accept that we learn as much from what doesn't "seem" to work, as what does. Also, accept that this is a process that keeps "cooking". Often parents come back the next week and share what they tried that did work based on what they learned.

13. Ask for the volunteer's commitment to try the suggestion for one week and report back to the group at the following meeting. Let the parent know how important it is for the group to hear the results of his/ her efforts so everyone can know how the suggestion works in the real world.

If the suggestion did not produce positive results in the role-play, ask the volunteer what he/she learned from it. Ask if he/she would be willing to see what happens based on what was learned and ask him/her to report back to the group next week. Let everyone know that part of the process is the learning that takes place at a subconscious level.

Many parents find that they do something from their own creativity the next time they encounter the problem because of what they learned during the Parents Helping Parents Problem Solving Steps.

14. Ask the group for appreciations for the volunteer—what help did they get for themselves by watching the demonstration. What did they see that they appreciated about the volunteer? What ideas did they see that they could use? This is the time to give back to the volunteer by telling him/her what this experience gave to the group members. Appreciations may sound like this: "I learned ______.""I felt ______.""I have the same problem, so now I can try ______.""I know how hard it is to share ______.""Thank you for ______."

Practicing the Steps

If you are feeling nervous about using the PHP steps in a parenting class, the following activity will help you practice with friends or colleagues. The purpose of this activity is to give you confidence and experience, NOT to replace the PHP steps in your parenting classes.

This is done by threesomes taking turns being the facilitator, the volunteer, and the observer. You could set up your practice sessions by asking 2 other friends or colleagues to follow the instructions with you. We are confident that you will succeed by simply following the steps to the letter. During your parenting classes you will follow the "Parents Helping Parents Problem Solving Steps" short version. However, be sure you have read the Expanded Version of the steps and that you have practiced several times in small groups.

ACTIVITY: ABC Groups for Parents Helping Parents Problem Solving Steps

Materials:

Parents Helping Parents Problem Solving
Steps (short version)

Mistaken Goal Chart

ABC Groups Job Descriptions

ABC Groups Typical Problems

Flip Chart (or paper and pencil)

Directions

Comment:

It is very important to have faith in the process. Even if the last role-play seems more like a failure than a magical solution, point out that the process still worked. The volunteer will still experience some encouragement just from learning he or she is not alone. It is just as important to learn what doesn't work as what does. And most important, the whole process works in many subconscious ways. We don't know what insights the volunteer may have gained from the role-plays. Often volunteers will report during a follow-up meeting that they felt inspired to do something from their own creativity because of what they learned during the process. Sometimes they learned to be more gentle with themselves because they felt the empathy from the group members.

A. Instructions for the person who is the Volunteer

1. Present a real first-party problem. In other words, what is a real problem you have had recently? It doesn't have to be a parenting problem to work. This process is effective with any relationship concern.

2. Relax and allow the facilitator to lead you through the 14 steps.

3. Participate in the role-play both times. When there are only three people, you do not have the luxury of watching.

4. Join in the brainstorming for suggestions. In larger groups, the volunteer usually just listens while others brainstorm.

B. Instructions for the person who is the Facilitator

5. Lead the volunteer through the steps. Keep the handout of the steps in your lap and follow them. DON'T improvise!

6. Participate in the role-play if needed.

7. Join in the brainstorming for suggestions. In larger groups, the facilitator may or may not join in the brain-storming.

C. Instructions for the person who is the Observer

8. Record names as required in Step 2 of the 14 steps, and the brainstorm ideas.

9. Participate in the role-play.

10. Join in the brainstorming for suggestions.

11. With the PHP steps handout in your lap, keep your fingers on the steps so you can interrupt if the facilitator gets off track. The job of interrupting is an important one since sticking to the steps is essential in this process. Interrupting can be done with dignity and respect: "Excuse me I think we are off track." "Excuse me I think you skipped a step." "Whoops! You forgot to ask others if they have ever felt the same."

ABC Group Job Descriptions Handout

Each person in the group will take a turn in each of the roles (jobs) required for practicing the Parents Helping Parents Problem Solving Steps.

A. Instructions for the person who is the Volunteer

1. Present a real first-party problem. In other words, what is a real problem you have had recently? It doesn't have to be a parenting problem to work. This process is effective with any relationship concern.

2. Relax and allow the facilitator to lead you through the 14 steps.

3. Participate in the role-play both times. When there are only three people, you do not have the luxury of watching.

4. Join in the brainstorming for suggestions. In larger groups, the volunteer usually just listens while others brainstorm.

B. Instructions for the person who is the Facilitator

1. Lead the volunteer through the steps. Keep the handout of the steps in your lap and follow them. DON'T improvise!

2. Participate in the role-play if needed.

3. Join in the brainstorming for suggestions. In larger groups, the facilitator may or may not join in the brainstorming.

C. Instructions for the person who is the Observer

1. Record names as required in Step 2 of the 14 steps, and the brainstorm ideas.

2. Participate in the role-play.

3. Join in the brainstorming for suggestions.

4. With the PHP steps handout in your lap, keep your fingers on the steps so you can interrupt if the facilitator gets off track. The job of interrupting is an important one since sticking to the steps is essential in this process. Interrupting can be done with dignity and respect: "Excuse me I think we are off track." "Excuse me I think you skipped a step." "Whoops! You forgot to ask others if they have ever felt the same."

ABC Groups Typical Problems

As we teach the problem solving steps to the ABC groups in our workshops, we have discovered several problems that occur over and over. It may help if we emphasize these again, and if the Observer makes a special point to interrupt when they happen.

1. Facilitators don't follow the outline and stick to the steps.

2. People get caught up in the story. It is important to stick to explaining about "one time" when the problem occurred. Background information is not necessary for this process.

3. The group members analyze, question and evaluate information.

4. The group forgets to suggest some of the tools presented in the book or from the last column of the Mistaken Goal Chart. Each person in this group should have a copy of the Mistaken Goal Chart and Positive Discipline Tool Cards to help generate brainstorming ideas. Of course once the brainstorm energy kicks in, there will be other creative ideas from the group.

5. The group skips steps, such as the role-playing or appreciations. Every step is important in small groups or large.

Group Dynamic Posters

poster 1

poster 2

The Monopolizer

poster 3

The Quiet Member

poster 4

The Debator

poster 5

poster 6

What if . . . ?
Yes, But . . .!

poster 7

If Only My Spouse Would . . .

Final Thoughts and Resources

Final Thoughts from Lynn and Jane

From Lynn Lott

In 1969 I took my first parenting class and in 1970 I taught my first parenting class. My instructor wasn't very good, which was a great thing, because I realized I could do better. It was my start into the world of teaching parenting. Over the years I soaked up information from the Canadians who had some lovely manuals, and from John Taylor who loved to teach information through experiential activities. I taught classes so regularly that if I wasn't teaching one, my kids would suggest that I do because I was getting "cranky" as a parent. For me, teaching parenting classes gave me the core knowledge that has helped me be the mother, wife, friend, person, and therapist that I am today. Don't underestimate what you can learn from teaching parenting.

I'm worried that you will stop yourself from the wonderful experience of teaching parenting by being a perfectionist instead of a learner. If you are one chapter or one activity ahead of the folks in your classes, you'll be fine. You're out there spreading the word, not trying to look like a big shot! Really! I know the tendency is to over-study, over-plan, and over-prepare. If my magic wand could bop you on the head, I'd wish for you to have the courage to be imperfect and the desire to use this manual to help you help others—and make it easy on yourself. You'll have so much fun that you'll want to teach parenting classes often, and every time you do, you'll reach another level of understanding about the human condition.

Teaching parenting classes was the jumping-off spot for me that catapulted me into the world of lecturing, writing, and working as a therapist in private practice. I've supported my family for more than 30 years as a result of teaching parenting. The very basic ideas you'll find in this manual have applications in every part of your life if you will let them. Don't be fooled by ads on TV trying to convince you that every man, woman, child, and dog has a disease and needs some kind of pill to get better. Hang on to the paradigm that thoughts create feelings, feelings create behaviors, and behaviors are creatively learned and decided by each and every human. Remember that when belonging and significance are threatened, discouragement prevails…not disease.

Keep in mind that mistaken thinking about belonging and significance can lead to some pretty dysfunctional behaviors and that it is through encouragement that things can get better. It's an art form and not a quick fix. Allow yourself to be creative instead of fear-driven and you'll be out there making the world a better place, person by person.

From Jane Nelsen

I first learned about Adlerian parenting when I attended a class at Brigham Young University where the professor said, "I'm not going to teach you a bunch of theories, but one theory that really works to help children learn self-discipline, responsibility, cooperation, and problem solving skills." That was intriguing to me. I really wanted to be a good mother, but really didn't know how. Now I know why. I would be too controlling until I couldn't stand myself and then too permissive until I couldn't stand my kids.

Learning to be kind and firm at the same time (and to have the courage to be imperfect) has taken many years. I didn't become perfect (still haven't), but I learned to implement Adlerian strategies (from the book "Children the Challenge" by Rudolf Dreikurs) well enough to see such great improvement in me and my children that I wanted to start sharing what I had learned with everyone.

To make a long story short, I started teaching a parenting class to my friends, got my MS degree doing a project on a parenting class with parents of educationally, physically, and emotionally challenged children, became a school counselor in the Elk Grove, CA School District, and Director of Project ACCEPT (Adlerian Counseling Concepts for Encouraging Parents and Teachers) where I worked with teachers and six para-professionals taught parenting classes. We attended the same workshop with John Taylor and learned to add the experiential component to our classes.

Our project obtained great statistics, we received more funding to disseminate Project ACCEPT in California, and I HAD to develop a two-day workshop that began with a two-hour lecture, which I learned to do kicking and screaming all the way. Then I got good at it and loved giving lectures. Out of this experience, I wrote Positive Discipline.

It was only after working with Lynn that I learned to eliminate almost all lectures from parenting classes and experienced the increased value of learning from doing. After having problems with one of my teenagers (told you I wasn't perfect), I went to a workshop with Lynn and loved it so much I talked her into writing Positive Discipline for Teenagers with me. She taught me how to do her two-day workshop, then called Teaching Parenting. It was hard for me to give up all lectures. I felt in control when I was lecturing. Never mind if people didn't learn as much. Now it is more and more difficult for me to give lectures—well, not difficult. I just don't like it as much. Lynn and I added a bunch of activities to go along with our new book, revised the Teaching Parenting Manual and re-named it Teaching Parenting the Positive Discipline Way.

I too have found that the processes in this manual have helped me be a better therapist (I too went on to get my license in marriage and family therapy), a better writer, and has given me a much great understanding of human nature and the value of creating respect in all relationships.

Websites

There is a wealth of materials available to enhance your learning about Positive Discipline and to help you deal with your class or workshop preparation. We hope you will take the time to explore these websites.

www.lynnlott.com

Many new parent educators struggle to understand the top card activity which can be so valuable to both leaders and participants. On this website, click on "Try This" to discover your top card in a fun and interactive way. You'll want everyone you know to try this to discover information about themselves, as well as how to be encouraging to themselves and others. This website also includes long excerpts from many of the Positive Discipline books for people who would like a taste before they buy.

If you are looking for a therapist who can work with you either in person or by phone, this website gives information about how to contact Lynn Lott, M.A., M.F.T.

www.positivediscipline.org

The Positive Discipline Association is a non-profit membership organization for people who have received Positive Discipline training and would like additional support and advanced training. Joining the Positive Discipline Association will provide you with a connection to a group of like-minded individuals who are creating respectful relationships in homes and schools.

www.positivediscipline.com

This is the official website for Positive Discipline. You will find many resources for your parenting classes as well as support materials that will help you in your Positive Discipline journey.

Notes